About the

Elaine joined the Army in 1982, aged 21, as a student nurse. After qualifying as a staff nurse, she obtained a commission, becoming a junior sister in the rank of lieutenant. Her ordeal began in 1987, after rumours about her sexuality reached the military police. After being forced to resign, she met Robert Ely, who had been discharged from the Parachute Regiment after nearly 20 years' service, and they founded Rank Outsiders, a campaign and support group, in 1991.

Since leaving the Army, Elaine initially struggled to find work that could rival the prospects and camaraderie of her Army career – she has had nearly 20 different jobs, mostly in nursing but also including stints at Eurostar, as a security guard at the Tower of London and briefly as a tree climbing instructor. She is now working as a medical administrator for a GP practice, following a momentous decision to take her name off the nursing register after her parents suffered serious ill health. She lives in the Isle of Wight.

Praise for *This Queer Angel*

'The inside story of the long, heroic battle to overturn homophobia in the British Armed Forces. Inspiring!'
– Peter Tatchell

'*This Queer Angel* is a richly textured and deeply human tour de force. Chambers is a deft storyteller who movingly chronicles her battle to live authentically. Unputdownable.'
– Dr Emma Vickers, Senior Lecturer in History, Liverpool John Moores University

'Stereotypically "Angels" are assumed to be straight or sexless – and natural other halves for alpha male soldier heroes. Elaine offers something path-breaking: the first ever book about a lesbian nurse in the armed services. Even better, it's the record of a rare woman at the forefront of Rank Outsiders' revolutionary battle to change institutional homophobia. *This Queer Angel* is a vital addition to nursing history and to the queer-aware new historiography of the army, navy and air force. It's honest and funny too.'
– Dr Jo Stanley, FRSA, FRHistS, author of *Women in the Royal Navy* and co-author of *Hello Sailor: The Hidden History of Gay Life at Sea*

'It may have started out as a history book, but as you turn the pages, it turns into a compelling, evocative, moving, funny story of the life and times of an extraordinary woman. The writing is sharp and the thinking richly informed and highly observational, and the deft use of contemporary cultural references brings the stories of life in the 80s and 90s flying off the page. It also has an unusual quality in contemporary history books of also being extremely accurate. Read it before someone turns it into a film.'
– Ed Hall, Founder of the Armed Forces Legal Challenge Group, author of *We Can't Even March Straight*

'There are people serving in today's Armed Forces who owe this queer angel a massive debt of gratitude, and I hope they read Elaine Chambers's powerful story, which she tells with scorching honesty and better humour than her persecutors deserve.'
– Simon Edge, author of *The Hurtle of Hell*

This Queer Angel

This Queer Angel

Elaine Chambers

To Jo,

I hope you'll enjoy the
fuller version!

Elaine Chambers

Unbound Digital

This edition first published in 2019

Unbound

6th Floor Mutual House, 70 Conduit Street, London W1S 2GF

www.unbound.com

ISBN (eBook): 978-1-91261-839-2

ISBN (Paperback): 978-1-91261-838-5

Cover design by Mecob

Printed and bound in Great Britain by Clays Ltd, Elcograf S.p.A.

This book is dedicated to those veterans whose lives were affected by the ban.

Contents

Dear Reader,

The book you are holding came about in a rather different way to most others. It was funded directly by readers through a new website: Unbound.

Unbound is the creation of three writers. We started the company because we believed there had to be a better deal for both writers and readers. On the Unbound website, authors share the ideas for the books they want to write directly with readers. If enough of you support the book by pledging for it in advance, we produce a beautifully bound special subscribers' edition and distribute a regular edition and e-book wherever books are sold, in shops and online.

This new way of publishing is actually a very old idea (Samuel Johnson funded his dictionary this way). We're just using the internet to build each writer a network of patrons. Here, at the back of this book, you'll find the names of all the people who made it happen.

Publishing in this way means readers are no longer just passive consumers of the books they buy, and authors are free to write the books they really want. They get a much fairer return too – half the profits their books generate, rather than a tiny percentage of the cover price.

If you're not yet a subscriber, we hope that you'll want to join our publishing revolution and have your name listed in one of our books in the future. To get you started, here is a £5 discount on your first pledge. Just visit unbound.com, make your pledge and type CHAMBERS19 in the promo code box when you check out.

Thank you for your support,

Dan, Justin and John
Founders, Unbound

Super Patrons

Mark Abrahams
Steve Acres
Jocelyne Ah-Yave
Gill Aldridge
Kelly Allen
Mandy Allen
Shirley Allison
Helen Almond
Susan Ashby
Karen Attwood
Michelle Ayling
Sue Battison
Natalie Bavister
Cari Beard
Christine Beckett
Val Bell
Zoe Berryman
Joan Beveridge
Sally Bibb
Ali Black
Fiona Blair
Bert Boer
Nacera Boukezzoula
Gail Bowley Bentley
Mark Bowsher
Adam Bretherton
Chris Brickell
Debbie Briody
Joseph Brown
Steve Brown
Angela Burgoyne
Catherine Burton
Sharon Cabassi
Bill Callaghan
Katie Callaghan

Carol Cape
Jamie Carrahar
Rhona & Poppy Carse
Andrea Susan Causer
Jackie Chambers
Roland 'Roly' Chambers
Jo & Kara Chambers-Grant
Karen Chapman
Cat Charles
Katie Cherry
Charmaine Chugg
Penny Claxton
Tracy Cole
Susan Coleman
Val Coleman
Jenny Collier
David Cooke
Janet Coombs
Sonya Cooper
Tremaine Cornish
Mara Cortesi Fraser
Maureen Coshall
Sarah Cotman
Sue Coulcher
Charles Coull
Stephanie Cowan Howard
Jonny Cox
Margaret Cox
Robert Cox
Trudi Coyne
Stuart Crabb Brooks
Graham Critchley
Yvonne Croke
Paula Cunliffe
Debra Curtis

Julia Darbyshire
Caitlin Davies
Melissa Davies
Linda Dawkins
Zöe Dawson
Mo de Gruchy
Jacqui de la Maziere
Connor Deacon
Anna-Louise Dearden
Willow Digweed
Les Dodd
Stuart Dover
Steven duKamp
Ros Earwicker
Susan Edwards
Carolyn Ellis
Robert Ely
Amy England
Keith Evans
Melissa Eveleigh
Sarah Everitt
Joseph Fahy
Salma Faraji
Sian Ferguson
Brandy Fields
Marlies Findlay Alsem
Gemma Fowler-Robinson
Joy Frye
Gwyneth Garbutt
Ricky Gellissen
Georgie
Vanessa Gilding
Silver Girl
Constance Glazier
Anne Gleed
Peter Gracey
Elaine Graham
John Grant
Kate Green
Kay Green
Christine Greene
Nicki Greenwood
Allan Gregory
James Gregory-Monk
Helen Hadebe
Ed Hall
Kate Harbottle-Joyce
Sue Harratt
Martine Hartley
Karen Hawver
Pam Henderson

Thomas Hescott
Emma Hey
Wendy Hill
Cindy Hilliar
Ayla Holdom
Linda Holmes
Neil Holmes
Sue Hunt
Dee Inott
Lorraine Isaac
Damian Jenkins
Ian Johnson
Michael Johnson
Shelagh Johnson
Alison Jones
Carmen Jones
Claire Jones
Craig Jones
Heather Jones
Sarah Jones
Joseph Kelly
Matthew Keyes
Gaynor Kirk
Eleni Kyriacou
Simon Langley
Corey Lonergan
Julie Long
Paula Longuehaye
Guy Lowe-Barrow
Debs Luraschi
Duncan Lustig-Prean
Patrick Lyster-Todd
Jean Macdonald
Hannah MacKenzie
Tracy MacSephney
Caroline Mann
Bernadette Martin
Jessica Martin
Lucy Martin
Audrey Maughan
Lucy May Maxwell
Su Mayfield
Sherry McBain
Caroline McEwan-Smith
Marc McKenna-Coles
Simone Mckeon
Sally Mckeown
Paul McMahon
Karen Mercer
Heather Miller
Ann Miller-McCaffrey

Sally Mitchell
Des Mohan
Remus Monk
Stephen Moody
Tony Moody
Marcos Morley
Sally Moules
Alison Muir
Johanne Mundie
Cathy Munro Mbe
Jo-Anne Munt
Anwen Muston
Mark Nelkin
Lynne O'Connell
Karen O'shaugnessy
Jean Owen
Sarah Oxley
Matt Paget
Caroline Paige
Annette Parry
Stu Pearce
Theresa Peters
Gwen Pettigrew
Hazel Phillips
Jane Pizii
Janet Pope
Amy Pritchard
Tim Pritchard
Jayne Prosser
Bex Prys Jones
Sebastian Richter
Sue Riddle
Rob Ridley
Emma Riley
Carolyn Rivett
Jacque Routley
Kris Rudyk
Emma Saccomani
Donna Salisbury
Mike Sansom
Phil Sayer
Vicky Scovell

Lynsey Searle
Mandy Sellars
Ashley Semadeni
Michele Serre-Mackenzie
Yvonne Simpson
Jeff Smart
Beverley Smith
Alastair Smith-Weston
Rosemary Smyth
Patrizia Sorgiovanni
Trudie Stables
Gina Starnes
Kirsty Stevenson
Sarah Strong
Karen Styles
Jonathan Swan
Fiona Thompson
Jillian Timbrell
Barbara Timms
Xanthe Toll
Christine Tollet
Sophie Tournier
Caroline Vaine
K G Valente
Pip Varley
Ram Venkatesan
Emma Vickers
Rebecca Vincent
Rina Rai & Russ Waller
Debbie Walsh
Julie Warren
Katie and Emily Watson
Ruth Wells
Hannah Whales
Helen Wilkinson
Hayley Williams
Pauline Williamson
Eileen Witham
Louise Wolstenholme
Sarah Wright
Christine Young
Trudie Zegners

Introduction

Until very recently, I hadn't really given much consideration to the question, 'But, why do you even feel the need to tell this story?' After all, the events that I am writing about happened over 30 years ago. What purpose is there in raking over the past? Initially, publication wasn't my main motivation. Through the intervening years I had so often found myself at a loss whenever anyone enquired, 'But what actually *happened*?' It was impossible to easily and briefly recount the bizarre sequence of events that led to a fateful day in August 1987 – one that would change my life irrevocably. So, although I'd often assume a jokey tone when replying, 'God! I'd have to write a book to explain it!', an idea took hold. A book, telling the whole story, warts and all, might actually not be such a daft idea. It would act as a sort of journal, a way to order my thoughts and try to make some sense of it all. This was when the key thing was simply to get it written down. Whilst I may have harboured secret daydreams of an instant bestseller, masses of publicity, film rights, sudden riches, retiring to a little French hamlet – deep down I understood that what I was doing was basically therapy on the cheap.

It was also a way for me to finally try to exorcise a very painful and difficult period of my life. I felt that by getting it out of my head and onto paper, I would somehow be able to leave the past behind; compartmentalise it into a convenient box that I'd decided to label 'This Queer Angel'.

As the words emerged and memories revived, I came to realise that my cathartic experience might not only be of benefit to me.

I have no delusions of grandeur – my story is neither the worst nor most shocking example of how 'the ban', as it was known, that prevented openly lesbian, gay, bisexual and transgender personnel from serving in Her Majesty's Armed Forces, ripped apart lives with such devastating effect. As far as the Ministry of Defence (MOD) – which you may read as 'UK government' – was concerned, my case was but one of hundreds, or possibly thousands, over many decades. Just one routine matter, an inconvenient issue to be dealt with then forgotten.

I think the game-changer for me was the realisation that my own experience, and therefore multitudes of others' similarly terrible, painful, embarrassing, humiliating, devastating, intrusive, excruciating, life-altering, cataclysmic expulsions were as *nothing* to those agents simply enforcing successive governments' policies. They really were 'just doing their job'. As far as the military was concerned, regardless of the minutiae of each individual case, no matter how simple or how complex, homosexuality (the umbrella term then used to describe any sexual persuasion other than heteronormative) was enough to ensure that, effectively merely by existing, *an offence had been committed*. And even if, as was often the case, a choice had been made to follow a path of celibacy or to enter into heterosexual relationships, discovery of any homosexual tendencies would still automatically lead to dismissal. Just writing a letter, confiding in a diary or journal; having a 'suspect' book, film or magazine in your possession; even confiding in a padre or MO (medical officer/doctor) could potentially jeopardise everything.

No matter how flawlessly brilliant a career had been, how consistently superb a work record, how long the list of achievements and attainments, how many years of unblemished service – just one revelation could end it all at a stroke. This was the day-to-day reality of living with this secret.

Discovery of this perceived anomaly in your character ensured termination of your chosen career. A sort of military equivalent of *Logan's Run* or *Gattaca* – 'imperfection' must be removed before it can taint those fortunate enough to fit the 'normal', desirable ideal. Those responsible for my departure were merely carrying out their daily duties. In much the same way that I would be called upon to run the ward in the absence of the senior sister; or would have to attend Mobile Army Surgical Hospital (MASH) exercises to prepare for nursing in wartime conditions in tented hospitals; or, when I was appointed unit sports officer, running umpteen basic fitness tests to get everyone through their six-monthly trial – it was just a case of following protocol. Everything I went through, all the unbearable losses: it was simply the sad fallout of enacting a policy that had to be adhered to, no matter what. No exceptions, no excuses, it was to be followed to the letter. Though I did subsequently discover that those supposedly rigid rules were sometimes bent even more than I was. More of that later.

As if discovery wasn't bad enough, the worst aspect of the ban's effect was the fact that there was a clear impetus for the Royal Military Police to actively seek out any potential 'offenders'. Anyone unfortunate enough to come to their attention could unwittingly initiate a domino-effect, McCarthyist witch hunt of epic proportion.

Having initially started writing the story many years ago, I was never able to get further than the opening chapter. I would set the scene of when the Special Investigation Branch of the Royal Military Police – the military equivalent of the CID – were first called to a British military hospital in West Germany to investigate very serious allegations that had been made against me. I tried various ways of writing – first person, third person, factual, fictional – but none struck the right chord, and I couldn't quite figure out why. So the words lay in the notebook, in a frantic scrawl.

Then, a few years ago, I discovered Charlie Haynes' Urban Writers' Retreat and decided to take the plunge. I booked a day-long workshop in London's Spitalfields, an area I'd meant to explore years earlier. Some friends were sceptical – 'Why pay to sit somewhere and write? Why can't you do it at home, for free?' – and I found myself justifying something that just instinctively felt right. Libraries these days seem to be incredibly noisy, having morphed beyond recognition from those of my childhood, now offering computers, CDs and DVDs to borrow, café and exhibition spaces. Anyway, the nearest library was a fair distance away in Wealdstone, with no parking. Home wasn't an option either, as by the end of 2012 I had returned to Harrow Weald in Middlesex (north-west London) to share the home of my birth with my widowed dad. His love of loud country and western and jazz music, especially after a Sunday afternoon session 'on the sherbet' at his local club or at The Horns pub in Watford, meant peace and quiet were a rarity. Charlie offered a quiet space, gorgeous food (her culinary skills are legendary) and an ambience that encouraged productivity. No sharing of work or set writing exercises – participants come along simply to write. Sitting at a desk, surrounded by the gentle tap tap tap of laptop keyboards and the rustle of notebooks, discreetly watching others' creative processes at work had an amazing effect upon me. I wrote more in one day than I had in ten years. I went home feeling inspired and excited at the possibility that I could finally get this thing finished.

Then, having pretty much recorded all of the key events that make up the bulk of this madcap story, in something of a stream-of-consciousness rambling, fate led to my deciding it was time to show some real courage. I'd been given the details of two different publishers. Although the format was nowhere near finished, the content was almost complete. I emailed my offering to them both on the same day. I cannot lie, having heard and read so many stories of the commonplace experience, of aspiring writers being able to wallpaper a room with their dozens of rejection slips, I was beyond shocked and elated to hear back from them both within 24 hours, and neither of them saying, 'Thanks, but no thanks.' It was staggering and of course gave me a huge fillip to think that maybe what I had to say might merit further investigation.

I had been wary of the inherent sensitivity of writing about others whose parts in the story were essential to include, yet whose permission I could not obtain. I initially thought I should try to write it as if it were a semi-fictional story. Draw upon the experience, yet change identities and locations enough that, should it fall into the hands of a key player, they might not recognise themselves. As will become apparent, some of us who were caught up in the investigation behaved less than honourably at times.

However, despite the benefits of fictionalising all or part of the story, I knew in my heart that I had to tell it completely truthfully. This was, after all, *my* story to tell. Over the years, many others have told parts of it, tasters of what I'd experienced – Kate Muir in *Arms and the Woman* (1992); Edmund Hall in *We Can't Even March Straight* (1995); Peter Tatchell in *We Don't Want to March Straight: Masculinity, Queers and the Military* (1995); Joan Bakewell in the BBC2 documentary *Heart of the Matter* – 'Falling Out' (first broadcast in 1991), and many other newspaper and magazine articles, TV and radio programmes. No one had ever written about queer nurses, nor had any woman involved in LGBT activism in the military told her story. It was time for my voice to be heard.

Therefore, what follows is the true story, unembellished and as accurate as my memory allows. Some protagonists' real names are used when I have been given their express permission. Otherwise, I have used pseudonyms.

As might be expected, I am acutely aware of the very sensitive nature of this book. Part of the reason it has taken me so long to be able to write objectively and without rancour is because I have needed time to recover. Not only from the pain and humiliation of the experience, but also to allow the simmering rage to diminish. The passage of time truly is a great healer, although I don't think you can ever fully recover from such an assault. But the strength and intensity of feeling eases. As I get older my spiritual growth – yes, cheesy at that sounds, I *am* on a 'journey' – enables a clarity and forgiveness that has freed me from the anger and negativity that wrought such devastation for far too many years.

There are many abbreviations in use in the military and medical/nursing worlds, so, for the benefit of any civilian readers, full descriptions are used. Throughout much of what follows, I refer to the Army, but of course all branches of the Forces applied the ban equally assiduously, so this story could just as easily be about any LGBT member of the Royal Navy, Royal Air Force or Merchant Navy. In one rare example of completely equal treatment, homophobia, discrimination, ignorance, bigotry and prejudice were applied across the board, no exceptions made.

There is a myth that it was Queen Victoria's apparent refusal to believe that women could be lesbian that led to the exclusion of lesbianism from the appalling legislation that criminalised homosexuality until the 20th century in some parts of the UK.[1] Whatever the truth of this, it is certainly the case that our Armed Forces were the only institutions to ensure that we girls were treated as abominably as the boys as far as the 'unnatural acts' of any form of homosexuality were concerned.

I've probably written a lot less than might be expected about the day-to-day realities of nursing within a military hospital. Or even of being based in Germany during the Cold War in the 1980s, when the threat of attack felt very real. Nor have I attempted any research into the historic reasons behind successive governments' continued support of, belief in and brutally inflexible enforcement of this heinous policy. I think that's a book that needs to be written by an academic.

Instead, this story is as much an exploration of what it was like to grow up gay in the wider world, not just an institutional one like the Army. This was a time of much less tolerance than today (in some parts of the world at least). It is therefore a very personal, sometimes intimate and revealing story, focusing particularly upon the investigation and subsequent fallout from those five months in 1987. The decision to expose my most private and intimate thoughts, feelings and experiences in this way was not an easy one. Talking about sex isn't something that, if you'll forgive the pun, comes naturally! Most of the protagonists in this story, whether straight, gay or indifferent, were nearly all in their twenties – fit, young, healthy, well-paid, often away from home for the first time, discovering life. Surrounded by many others just like themselves, they were people who, through the very nature of the environment in which they were living and working, would develop deep friendships – the famous life-long camaraderie for which the military is very well known. It was a vibrant, exciting and wonderful time. I thought it was imperative to illustrate the very human and personal cost of this

---

1. Indeed, discrimination went on into the 21st century, until the 2004 Civil Partnership Act, the 2006 and 2007 Equality Acts and the Marriage (Same Sex Couples) Act 2013 were passed into legislation.

hateful piece of legislation. I felt that it was necessary to fully evoke the emotional impact of a life lived mostly in the shadows.

One other impetus for taking the scary step towards publication is the fact that, whether I care to admit it or not, this story is a very important part of the increasing canon of work that records, commemorates and celebrates key moments in LGBT history. (I chose to use the word 'queer' in the book's title because it is very divisive, a real 'Marmite' descriptor – to me it sums up the essence of being different from heteronormative society.) I have been reminded that there are very few records written from a female perspective, particularly in relation to queer military history. I hope that this effort will help redress the male-dominated imbalance and give some much needed insight into a time when one of our oldest, most revered and respected institutions espoused the wholesale persecution of many of its own personnel.

As I finished writing the first draft of this book, in November 2017, the horrific anti-gay purge in Chechnya had come to light and Donald Trump tweeted his intention to ban transgender troops from serving their country. With the resurgence of right-wing ideologies threatening hard-fought victories for freedom, equality, and acceptance of diversity, I believe my experiences are but one small reminder of why we must never return to such unenlightened times. To quote the 20th-century pragmatist philosopher George Santayana: 'Those who do not remember the past are condemned to repeat it.'

The Beginning of the End

A fair-sized bedroom, situated on the first floor of the officers' mess. The whole building is solid, well-built and typically 'Army' in its outward appearance. Standard issue, uniformly hideous soft furnishings, magnolia paint on every wall, identically styled wardrobes, chairs, beds and dressing tables, all made of wood, functional, built to last. In the far left-hand corner is a large porcelain sink with the original taps, probably dating back to immediately after the war, when the Luftwaffe incumbents were supplanted by British military hospital personnel.

A young-looking sergeant is glancing out of the only window. She seems to be deeply embarrassed and cannot return my gaze. When she notices me observing her, we both redden slightly and avert our eyes. I sense a mutual understanding, a recognition.

I look down at my hands, devoid of any adornment as I'm still in uniform – no varnish, wristwatch or jewellery allowed. Nails neatly clipped almost down to the quick, my skin dry from the constant washing and use of paper towels, my cuticles ragged and untended. I find myself idly wondering if I'll get arthritis in old age as my knuckles are already quite big. An inner smile plays at the corner of my mouth as I recall Sadie's lewd remark about my fingers.

My reverie is interrupted by a gruff cough as WO2 (Warrant Officer, Class 2) Lentman clears his throat. He starts reading from a printed sheet, MOD Form 811A, explaining to me that this is a 'Notice to Suspect at Interviews with Service Police'. Once more, my train of thought careers wildly down a very different track –

Suspect?! Bloody hell! My crazed imagination immediately lurches into yet another scene – I'm a latter-day Atticus Finch, mounting an impassioned plea to a jury of my peers, my eloquent defence causing deeply ingrained, long-held prejudices to crumble.

'We'll start now, ma'am.' I look up at him from my subjugated position, sitting on a chair by the dressing table. Although my rank is superior, I am obliged to cede to his authority over me. His being a Red Cap instantly makes my Queen's commission worthless.

'Yes, of course.' I feel like Alice, getting smaller and smaller, my voice not seeming to belong to me.

'Are you happy for Matron to stay as witness, or would you like someone else?'

What a ridiculous question! My heart is pounding like crazy, racing as if about to burst; I don't want *anyone* to witness what's happening, let alone that woman. She cannot even bring herself to look at me, her tight-lipped, stern, humourless face is deeply pained. It feels as though she has already made up her mind as to my guilt.

The sergeant is now trying to put on a pair of latex gloves. It may be the stultifying tension or the heat – the window is shut on this hot summer's evening – but she is clearly struggling. I'm instantly taken back to my earliest days as a 'baby' student nurse, convinced there was no way I could ever qualify. Three *years* of training when even the simplest of tasks seemed so impossible! Trying to feel a radial pulse through the thick wrist of some overweight Territorial Army squaddie, admitted whilst on exercise, playing at Rambo, suspected of having had a minor heart attack whilst trying to run for cover, or perhaps just constipated because he can't digest 'Compo' food rations. Reading the seemingly invisible line of mercury in a glass thermometer. Taking blood pressures, trying to hold a stethoscope against the crook of the elbow and squeeze the sphygmomanometer bulb at the same time, even *hearing* the subtle 'lub dub' sounds of blood pushing against vessels, let alone interpreting their meaning...

A sharp snap jolts me back to the present: the cuff of the glove twanging against her wrist, two of the fingers flailing loosely. They'd brought a box of 'large' to suit Mr Lentman's needs, but he is already busy, working his way through several packets of photographs he'd found. The fact they felt they needed to wear latex gloves just to search my room makes the whole thing seem even more sinister – and also absurd.

I sit there, outwardly silent, calm and orderly, knees pressed tightly together, ankles crossed, my dress smooth over my lap, beautifully pressed, medal and shoes gleaming – a perfect example of military training, ready for anything. Inside I am laughing hysterically at the madness of it all.

As they continue their very methodical search of my small room, I begin to weigh up my options, limited as they are. Ultimately, as I know there is no escape, I try to buy myself a little thinking time. I decide not to let them know that all the 'evidence' they need is right there on my single bed, nicely bagged up for them by yours truly. No, I sit very still throughout the three hours they take to ransack my life. It feels as if I am having a minor emotional breakdown. My thoughts are chaotic and rambling as they look at every single one of the thousands of photographs I own; pull each of the hundreds of LPs and singles from their covers; root through all the drawers, both wardrobes and the cupboards, checking pockets in clothes; even emptying my laundry bin – talk about airing your dirty linen in public! They flick through the pages of dozens of paperbacks; pull letters and cards from envelopes; open the box containing many years' worth of diaries going back to my early teens, long before I'd even thought of joining up.

Then Lentman empties out the two carrier bags I'd frantically filled with letters, books and cards earlier that afternoon. He is speed-reading his way through my life, searching for the words that are relevant to the case against me. Every now and then, he emits a little 'hmm' as he reads something that hits an investigative chord.

I don't know how I refrain from laughing out loud when he holds up three unlabelled VHS tapes: 'Can you tell me what's on these, ma'am?'

My slightly raised eyebrow, à la Roger Moore, gives him no clue, but I SO want to assume a breathy, pseudo-sexy voice and say, 'Lesbian biker nuns on acid.' Instead I hear myself reply in a slightly bewildered and amused tone, 'I think it's a James Dean film and

Victoria Wood's *As Seen on TV*. Do you want me to play them for you?'

'That won't be necessary,' is the reply, but his facial expression is utterly readable, his disappointment tangible – I am clearly telling the truth, and I imagine how annoying it must be not to find some salacious, perverted filth to bag up with the rest of the gathered 'evidence' of my depravity.

Behind my bemused expression, reality hits home. Deep down, I know this is the beginning of the end for me.

Girl Calls

So, what on earth had happened for me to find myself in such a terrifying situation? Maybe as you read this you are wondering: why on earth would anyone identifying as lesbian *choose* to enlist in such an archaic institution as the Army in the first place? You may well have bought into the widely-held notion that people like me deserve no sympathy – even if for no other reason than the fact that I knew before I joined up that homosexuality was not permitted in the Forces, right? Well, you'd be wrong. I'd been led to believe that an Army career might well be ideal for anyone not fully on the straight and narrow side of life. Before I explain the very tangled web of events that culminated in the Special Investigation Branch crashing into my life on that fateful day, Friday 21 August 1987, I want to set the backdrop to help clarify the events that led to a shy, insecure, Mittyesque, sexually befuddled bookworm deciding to enlist.

I first vocalised an interest in serving Queen and country back in 1979, but the seed was firmly planted on 25 February 1974 when BBC2 broadcast an extraordinarily brave, yet controversial drama. I'll never know why I was allowed to stay up late to watch it, especially as it was preceded, unusually, by an announcement warning of the adult content. Aged only 13 and raging with hormonal confusion, I experienced the first profoundly disturbing and erotic introduction to my Sapphic leanings. With Mum and Nain (pronounced 'nine', the Welsh word for 'grandmother'), I watched a short play in a series called 'Second City Firsts'. One of the actors was a very young Alison Steadman, in an early role.

The play, written by James Robson, was called *Girl* and centred around a Women's Royal Army Corps barracks. As the story unfolded, I was totally unprepared for the flashback scene that greeted me – two women in bed, clearly naked. Although our front room wasn't very well-lit (this being the era of filament light bulbs, thank goodness) I was convinced that my beetroot blushes were not only visible but palpable. I was burning up, scanning Mum and Nain's faces for any sign that they knew how I was feeling. The strength of my response made me feel certain they must have known. The tightening of the muscles in my pelvic floor, along with a wave of 'butterflies' in my stomach was overwhelming.

This was the first time I'd ever been sexually aroused by intentionally Sapphic stimulus. Prior to this, my first physical sexual awareness had been apparently fairly commonplace and innocuous, if rarely acknowledged – climbing the ropes in PE lessons at junior school. Clinging to the top, pretending to be suddenly and unexpectedly afraid of heights and thus needing to keep still, knees raised, whilst secretly thinking how wonderful this delicious sensation was, pulsating between my legs. Yet also somehow innately aware, even at such a tender age, that I shouldn't mention this new-found pleasure to my friends. Once I came down to reality, landing on the grubby mats upon which we had to practise our forward rolls, I instinctively felt it wouldn't be wise to ask if anyone else felt the same way.

So, as the play continued, in an open way, with two of the four characters being clearly and, perhaps more surprisingly, unashamedly lesbian, I was acutely aware of tension in the front room. But in fairness to Mum and Nain, they didn't make too much fuss, just tutted and sighed when the 'fruitier' moments occurred. Although ultimately quite a sad story, there was some humour and quite near-the-knuckle language, that was probably beyond my innocent ken. But the scene that literally blew my world wide open came towards the end of the story. Myra Frances (playing serially seducing Corporal Chrissie Harvey) and Alison Steadman, the raw recruit Jackie Smithers, had been dancing closely together to Dionne Warwick's 'This Girl's in Love'. It had never occurred to me that

14

dancing like this could ever apply to anyone other than the standard boy/girl, man/woman configuration! They even referred to the song being the 'top of the gay girls' hit parade' and stating that, as such, it would soon be on company orders that it had been banned from all NAAFI[1] jukeboxes.

Another word was used that was new to me. When asking Jackie what had made her join the Army, Chrissie's much more savvy and cynical character reacts to her having said 'I dunno – adverts I suppose, mainly,' by laughing and quoting from the telly ad – 'Really?! "You're *someone* in today's women's army", all that? A photo of a dyke's dream, an Amazon in green lovat, supervising the rescue of a truck from a Kraut bog, baking your fanny on the beach in Cyprus, sitting near the swimming pool in Singapore with six hairy Grenadiers gazing up your box!' After holding one another tightly, Jackie asks Chrissie if she'll miss her when she's gone back to civvy street. After telling her 'Yes', they kiss passionately, not once, but twice. *This*, not Anna Friel's oft-cited, but comparatively tame effort, in the Channel 4 soap *Brookside*, was the first lesbian kiss *ever* to be broadcast on British TV and *I* had witnessed it! I didn't realise it at the time, but the setting of a training depot had subliminally crept into my subconscious...

This was revelatory for me, utterly mind-blowing – in just 30 minutes my pre-existing schoolgirl 'crush' had morphed into something infinitely more painful. Seeing the physical, passionate relationship possible between two *women* had awoken something in me that I'd previously never even considered.

My feelings towards friends before that very instant had been totally innocent and naïve; almost akin to the Victorian notion of 'companions'. I was still such a child; a gangly, tall, rather boring soul. My best friend Viv was, to my eyes at least, glamorous, intriguing, worldly-wise. Her parents had divorced and her mother remarried. Every summer, during the school holidays, she would visit her father in Italy, sending me postcards signed off 'Ciao'. I often asked myself

---

1. Navy, Army and Air Force Institutes, the official trading organisation of HM Forces, providing retail and leisure services to the British Armed Forces, such as bars, clubs, canteens, shops, etc.

why she had chosen me as a friend. Latterly, I thought that my very drabness might have made her feel even more fabulous than I already believed her to be.

Viv was forever trying to goad me into doing 'rebellious' things or to simply 'loosen up a bit, Elaine!' She would put Consulate cigarettes into the pocket of my blazer at home time, telling me to smoke them later, or try to get my spectacles off me – 'Come on, let me do you a makeover!' She would try to persuade me to bunk off school or see X-certificate films at the Harrow Granada with another great friend, Janet. We were nearly caught out once when we noticed our art and form teacher, Mrs Spring, across the aisle as we watched the very disappointing Jack Nicholson film, *The King of Marvin Gardens*. 'An X-certificate for a flash of tit and some fake blood?!' was our considered critical review. That was also the night that I nearly set fire to the place, hastily trying to stub out the ciggie I was attempting to smoke in a Dietrich-style pose. As I coughed and spluttered, I missed the tiny iron ashtray on the back of the chair. The butt fell between the folded-up seat in front, nearly igniting the coarse red velvet fabric. A dribble of Kia-Ora prevented a sequel to *The Towering Inferno*, before we made an early exit to the bus station.

But it wasn't Viv who had been the secret object of my affection – much as I adored being part of her coterie of girls whose lives seemed so much better than my own, living in their massive detached houses in Stanmore, Hatch End and Pinner. No, it was Heather, a beautiful girl in the same year as me but in a different form, who became the focus of my burgeoning Sapphic leanings.

Heather's maths lessons took place in our form room and she'd chosen my desk as her regular place to sit. One day I saw she'd written a note to me on the wooden lid of said desk. What vandalism, what exquisite joy! I couldn't believe that *she* would even notice me. I wrote a little note in reply and thus began a correspondence that made me so unbelievably happy, even though much of what she wrote was about her then boyfriend, Kevin. I was simply elated that she considered me worthy of desecrating Harrow Education Authority property.

Walking along the corridors between lessons, when dozens of

girls were changing classrooms, I could spot her instantly, even at 50 or 60 yards away. My hands would become clammy, my heart pound, the hairs on the back of my neck stand on end and my guts would tighten and tense. Despite the powerful physical response her presence elicited in me, my fantasies never went beyond idly daydreaming about kissing her. I really was very sexually innocent. I became utterly obsessed and enraptured by her, but solely in a romantic, admiring way. If she sat next to me on the 114 bus on the way home, I was deliriously happy for the rest of the evening.

As the end of our final term approached, I spent a great deal of time after school painstakingly copying an accurate reproduction of our lengthy correspondence, complete with exact copies of goggle-eyed cartoons of hated teachers and the like, into an exercise book. I wanted to ensure I never lost this link to her.

Ill-Fitting Boyfriends

Despite my early Sapphic leanings, I did my very best to conform. Every relationship I've had with men was, with the clarity and wisdom of hindsight, a ridiculous, doomed attempt to convince my friends, family, work colleagues and the wider world that I was a completely 'normal' member of society. And perhaps, above all, trying to convince myself that this was what I really wanted.

I'm sure to many younger people today, such a situation would be unthinkable and probably a cause for derision. I honestly always knew, deep within the very essence of my being, that I was 100 per cent lesbian from the moment I reached puberty. Yet still I fought it – all I had known was the laughter, mocking, disgust and hatred towards queers, lezzers, poofs, dykes, gay boys, ho-mo-sexuals – this last descriptor always said in that clipped, RP voice of a 1950s BBC presenter. So, I persisted in my ultimately vain efforts to cure myself of this unwanted predilection. I never understood why there was such intense vitriol reserved for anyone unlucky enough not to be heterosexual – *why* were lesbians such a threat? But I also knew I didn't want to have such loathing directed at me personally. The desire to fit in, to be liked and respected, was at times overwhelming.

My first serious boyfriend was Jon. He was about four or five years older than me and a friend of my schoolfriend Viv's long-term fella, Alfie. I think we must have been set up by those two, as I don't honestly think we would have had enough in common otherwise, but I thought he was quite nice looking and he was earning a wage, and being taken out for meals and having drinks bought for me seemed quite grown up. We started seeing one another while I was at sixth form college. Here, there were no female temptations distracting me, so I determined that my crush on Heather was exactly that – a fleeting phase that Jon would put an end to, once and for all.

After a couple of months, with my 17th birthday approaching, it was decided that we would go to a nightclub, a plan necessitating either fake ID or borrowing a friend's older sibling's driver's licence and carefully memorising the date of birth in case the Neanderthal bouncers decided to quiz us.

A very sophisticated night ensued, with Viv and my friends bopping all night beneath the disco mirrorball, drinking exotically-named cocktails while the boys talked cars and football at the bar, only gracing the dance floor with their presence when the obligatory last dance slowies were played. How smug I felt, having my loaded 21-year-old man with me!

When we got back to my house (he even treated us to a black cab rather than a smoky minicab) my family had all gone to bed, so we went into the front room where I put my present from him on Dad's music centre turntable – David Bowie's latest album, *Heroes*. We dropped the volume right down and settled in for a kiss and a cuddle. As we had been 'going steady' for a while now, I'd made up my mind it was time to let him 'go all the way', if that was what he wanted, in anticipation of things getting more 'serious' between us. Maybe it was the fact that every creak or noise from upstairs had us fretting about whether Nain or my parents would come downstairs, or perhaps because lying on a scratchy carpet wasn't too comfortable, but the romantic glow of the Princess Raeburn coal fire wasn't really sufficing to make me suitably wet… Jon didn't seem to mind though, and the so-called foreplay was *very* cursory before he started easing down my knickers from under my pinstripe pencil skirt (no mean feat!) – a Wembley Market special, boy I was a classy bird. Then he pulled his jeans down – his erection really shocked me – and as I got hold of him and made what I thought was to be my first attempt at 'tossing him off' (what romantic descriptions we used in those days) he said he wanted to 'make love' to me. I remember worrying that I maybe hadn't been on the pill for long enough. But, having had a lovely birthday and being under the impression that Viv and a fair few other school and college pals were regularly doing it and seemed to think it was wonderful, it seemed churlish not to let him. I'd had my present, now it was his turn.

Well, as someone who'd found tampons a total nightmare to get used to, I took one look at the girth of his decently sized prick and just knew there was no way on God's green earth that I'd ever get that thing inside me, let alone pumping up and down! We did try, but he managed ooh, about an inch before he had to give up and let me continue to plan B, which was not really a masterclass in great technique. Many years later, I saw a 'Wicked Willie' cartoon that could have been drawn from poor Jon's very frustrating experiences that night! Needless to say, he didn't manage to deflower his virgin girlfriend, so we called it a day just a few weeks later. I briefly went out with another guy from their crowd, Martin – who in my view was better looking and kinder than Jon, who could be quite cutting at times. But this too was doomed to failure. Every attempt at any sexual interaction felt more like I was trying to do the right thing and impress the so-called boyfriend. I never felt any form of arousal or desire.

Everything changed for the better in 1978. Art was a 17-year-old squaddie and we met on one of our regular Saturday night jaunts to the Bandwagon disco, based in a pub at Kingsbury Circle. This, along with Baileys nightclub in Watford, was a favourite with me, Viv, and our closest mates. Our weekend wasn't complete without getting off with someone whilst dancing the slowies at the end of the evening.

It was almost a contest and it felt like a terrible failure if you didn't get asked by some long-haired, spotty oik to dance. This consisted of going around in a very small circle whilst in the grip of an arse squeezer reeking of lager and fags. True success would involve being snogged by said lummox or better still, getting a love bite as a souvenir – urgh!

On this particular night, something sensational happened, for which John Travolta, Robert Stigwood and the Bee Gees can be thanked or cursed, dependent upon your viewpoint. A small group of nice looking, slim lads with short hair actually spent a great deal of the night on the dance floor, by themselves, throwing some very impressive shapes, causing the hairy lummoxes to glower and fume even more heavily than their Benson & Hedges allowed. Occasional not so *sotto voce* comments could be heard between discs – 'Bunch of poofs!' 'Load of benders!' – but we girls were enthralled! This was just around the time that *Saturday Night Fever* was released, causing a disco-fuelled explosion.

These 'new men' as they'd maybe be called today, were in fact young soldiers on leave. Based with an infantry regiment, they were soon to be setting off to the then very tough and dangerous posting of Belfast, so they were out to have a great time before they went.

I'd had my eye on him throughout the evening. He was slim, not very tall, with light brown, slightly wavy hair and an open, smiley, cheeky face. But the thing I liked most of all was the way he danced – a really neat little mover, confident but not so cocky that he looked as if he were a narcissistic ponce.

The slowies came on and – bingo! – over he came, grinning that cheeky grin. 'Would you like to dance?' Would I?! You bet your sweet life I would. We danced round for all of the smoochy songs, telling one another a potted history of what the other wanted to know, before exchanging a fairly chaste kiss and finding a scrap of paper towel upon which to swap our respective telephone numbers.

He rang me the very next day, much to my surprise and delight, and we arranged to meet up again. He came from Barnet, not too many miles north of my home in Harrow Weald.

Two weekends later his family were holding a party for him to say farewell and to celebrate his 18th birthday. He'd been a boy soldier but was still very young to be facing a really tough posting at such a tender age, as part of the British peacekeeping force. He'd admitted to me that he was pretty scared about going – a lot of the patrols he'd be doing would be either on foot or in small armoured personnel carriers. This was when the Troubles were at their height and he knew he'd be facing daily barrages of abuse from Republican families. Bombings were commonplace: the Provisional IRA detonated over 50 bombs between 14 and 19 November that year. He felt the odds were stacked fully against them. You had to maintain a dignified professionalism whilst being verbally abused in the vilest way imaginable; spat at, having rocks and worse thrown at you and knowing a sniper or car bomb could be just around the corner. In the wake of Bloody Sunday in January 1972, when British soldiers shot 28 unarmed civilians during a protest march against internment, the guidelines they had to follow seemed to suggest that you virtually had to have the bullet winging its way to your heart before you could even think of lifting your weapon, let alone discharging it.

In the less than three weeks before he left, our families met up, getting along very well indeed. Funnily enough, Dad actually knew one of Art's uncles through golf, a guy known as 'Jaws' because he could talk for England, so it seemed fate had brought us together.

Although we didn't have much time together, I really believed I was falling in love with him. He was just such a lovely, genuinely nice guy. His folks were good fun, real 'salt of the earth' types and they seemed to like me and my family.

We all went to the party and had a great time, apart from at the end of the night when we were dancing to the slowies again. Although all our folks were there, we just held one another so tightly, eyes closed because we were both trying so hard not to cry. Although it was a plane he was getting on the next day, Rod Stewart's lyrics to 'Sailing' seemed to have been written specifically for us: 'Far away across the sea – to be near you, to be free…' It was unbearable! After everyone had gone to bed, I snuck along the landing from my room to his and cuddled up in his single bed. I'd have happily let him fuck me, but he knew I wasn't on the pill and he didn't have any condoms, so I tried to give him a 'hand job'. He was so patient and understanding with me, even though I was totally mortified, convinced that my ineptitude would cost me this wonderful new boyfriend. I'd try to sneak another look at one of Mum and Dad's hidden dirty magazines sometime and see if I could learn how to do things the 'right' way for him. My own needs really weren't foremost in my mind at that time.

After he left for Belfast, we had to content ourselves with a once-weekly phone call from a box, the very irritating 'bip bip bip bip' signalling yet another 10p piece was needed at far too frequent intervals. This was long before mobile phones and the like, so texting, emails or even Facebook messaging were unheard of. No, the mainstay of our communication was by writing to one another. How thrilled I was every time another aftershave-scented epistle dropped onto the hall mat. My collection of photos to show my friends was increasing every time. He would sometimes request that I write 'dirty' to him, so I of course obliged with a little soft porn; wet dream fantasies to keep him wanting me...

Mum seemed delighted with events, causing me huge embarrassment one day when she brazenly said, with a knowing smile, 'I think we should get you down the doctor's and sort out going on the pill – Art'll be back for your eighteenth...'

I turned puce, looked away and just said, 'Mu-um!'

She was laughing but there was a serious side too – she didn't want me to follow her own path. She'd had me illegitimately in 1960, aged only 19, at a time when such things mattered, unlike today. I've never known my genetic father. Dad adopted me after marrying Mum in 1965, when I was four years old.

The very beginning

Towards the end of July, Art and I had talked, during one of our regular phone calls, about getting engaged. I was all for it, but we decided to wait and see if we were still as determined when we saw one another again when he came home on leave, in October. This was going to tie in nicely with my 18th birthday, so we thought we'd throw a party, then make the announcement that evening with all our family and friends present – I was *so* excited!

To celebrate, he told me that my birthday present would arrive soon, along with one for my younger half-brother Ian, whose 13th birthday was just three days before mine. He said he'd wanted to send them early so we could enjoy them now. We were all stunned when they turned up – a top of the range game for Ian – it had to be linked to the TV set, which was tuned into the VHS channel, and then, wow! – the slowest-moving game of 'tennis', conducted with luminous green lines that had to be manipulated to bounce a little square green ball to and fro, accompanied with irritating 'blip' noises whenever contact was made.

My present was a brand new, black and white portable TV. I couldn't believe it, my own telly – no more having to fight about whose programme would take priority. Art must really *love* me to be spending his wages in this way, I thought. He was only a private, not earning a great deal, and these were expensive gifts.

Only a short while later, early in August, I had the shock of my life. Unusually, he phoned in the daytime. He normally rang in the evenings, after 6pm when the cheaper rate applied. His voice was strained and I immediately knew something terrible had happened. 'What's wrong, Art?'

Both my parents were in; Mum's ears pricked up and she came to the hallway from the kitchen, potato peeler in hand, looking at me with a quizzically raised eyebrow and silently mouthing 'Is he all right?'

I ignored her, focusing intently on what my 'fiancé' was telling me. He started very hesitantly, seemingly unable to get to the point. He wasn't going to be able to make it to my 18th. At first, I assumed he'd been unable to get the leave dates he wanted, so I started assuring him that it didn't matter, we could set another date. No, he finally managed to spit it out, it wasn't the Army causing the problems, in fact he wouldn't be coming back at all. He'd met someone out there, another woman. He didn't sound elated though; his voice was quavery, uncertain. It was hardly the voice of someone relishing having to dump me. I asked, 'Who? How? Where?' Mum was still right by me, now looking angry, wondering what was going on.

He told me she was ex-WRAC, quite a bit older than he was. He tried to start excusing the betrayal as being due to his hating the posting, loving and missing me and his family *so* much that he got involved almost without really *meaning* to! He'd been pretty drunk… At this point I handed the receiver to Mum – '*You* speak to him!' – and I hurtled upstairs and threw myself onto my bed, burying my face into the pillow and sobbing massive convulsive tears of anguish, choking on raw, bewildered, enraged and humiliated emotions.

A few moments later I heard Mum's livid voice – 'You fucking *wanker!*' – as she slammed down the receiver. Amidst my snot-nosed wailing, I smiled limply – good on yer Mum, he *is* a wanker!

After calming down and being comforted by Mum and Dad, I collected the huge pile of letters, tore them into tiny pieces, then threw them into the grate of the Princess Raeburn and put a match to them. I then put all his photos into an envelope and returned them to him with a note saying his new girlfriend could have them as I certainly didn't want or need them anymore. The serious degree to which I was upset was never in question – Dad even opened his best brandy and insisted I drink it to help calm me down. Unheard of!

We did later speak with his family and they were as annoyed as we were and couldn't apologise enough for how much he had hurt me. They thought he was a complete fool and that he'd live to regret losing me. It was of some consolation, but at the time I was totally broken-hearted. For many years afterwards, the opening notes of 'Sailing' could make me cry.

London Calling

After leaving school and then sixth form college in the summer of 1979, I became infatuated with a young woman a couple of years older than me. I had started my first job, working at a hotel in London's Bloomsbury. I was a receptionist/telephonist/cashier, earning the princely sum of £32 a week, but with accommodation and meals (when on duty) thrown in. My first home away from my family was in Tavistock Place. I had a small room on the third floor of a building shared with several other hotel employees, provided by the hotel chain. We shared a bathroom, kitchen and toilet, but there were no bills to pay, and linen and towels were provided, complete with very attractive company logo in red. It really was the life of Riley, living in 'digs'.

Three of the team I worked with also lived there. One was Rose, a fabulous character, quite a bit older than me and a wonderful guide to living in the heart of London. She was very funny and kind. When we went for walks she would suddenly put a hand over my eyes and say, 'Don't look! Which road are we in?' in an effort to orientate me and show that I didn't need to spend a small fortune on the Tube to get around. She was hugely popular with the male guests and she often had dates, enjoying being wined, dined and showered with gifts. I really loved her company.

Another team member, who then seemed much older and wiser than the rest of us, but who I think was probably only in her forties, was Pat, a New Zealander who was working as a switchboard operator, but whose first love was music. She had a great singing voice but had been thwarted in her teens when her parents refused to let her join a jazz band as their lead vocalist to go on tour in Europe. She had therefore abandoned any thought of ever singing again publicly, until she met a pianist at Dingwalls in Camden Lock. He was the bandleader, with the fabulous moniker of Ignatius, but we all knew him as Iggy. They were utterly besotted with one another and Pat found herself taking to the stage again for the first time in years.

Also in the team were two women who had a significant impact upon me. The first was Helena, a 27-year-old Geordie with copper-coloured hair, green eyes and a wealth of experience of life's adventures. It was she who introduced me to the exotic world of wine: the curve of the green bottle swathed in wicker… aaah, Mateus Rosé, what class! By contrast I was so insecure, ignorant of the world, inexperienced in all aspects of life and the living of it. Helena regaled me with tales of when she had lived and worked in Paris, sharing an apartment with her French boyfriend… and the tragedy of the night they dined out, only for him to have the mother of all asthma attacks, leading to a frantic taxi ride to the nearest hospital where he died in her arms! These stories, shared in my room, made me feel alive, appreciated. She inspired me to believe there must be more out there and I truly felt I loved her, but it wasn't in a physically-attracted way like I had felt at school. This was more a case of idolising her warmth, strength of character and humour.

One of the earliest memories I have of feeling *truly* connected to another person occurred one evening when we were talking about all sorts of things. She said something the likes of which I had never heard before: 'If a gunman charged in here right now and said, "One of you has to die, who's it going to be?", I'd say, "Me – I'm so happy right now, it wouldn't be scary."'

At first, I railed against this – what on earth was she saying? How ridiculous that such a lovely, intelligent, articulate person should suggest this, even as part of a wine-fuelled hypothesis. I protested vociferously that it should be me, not her – I had nothing interesting to offer her or the world. I had totally screwed up at school and college, despite having had the potential to have made it to university. I had been nowhere, done nothing, hadn't even the vaguest notion of what career I might pursue. At just 18 years old I was already coasting through a life that had barely begun – my brother's punk refrains of 'no future' seemed wholly apt.

Helena then explained what she meant. She was decades ahead of her time. Nowadays we'd call her philosophy mindfulness or living in the moment. Then she just clarified what I'd obviously completely misunderstood. She wasn't expressing suicidal tendencies nor an overblown romanticised death wish to join her late boyfriend. She was simply saying that she was extremely happy right *now*, here in my tiny, sloping-floored room, drinking Mateus. Exchanging ideas with a young woman who was so desperate to make something of her world, life and being. I was overwhelmed to feel that she valued my thoughts and opinions in this way.

Helena has the dubious 'honour' of being the first person to whom I dared offer a dedicated poem. Some months later, she left London for a more senior position in a hotel in Bowness-on-Windermere. I felt utterly bereft, but she was true to her word and regularly sent me very lovely, informative, beautifully handwritten and entertaining letters. She also said she'd be more than happy to show me around if I ever came up to the Lake District. So of course I saved up for my National Express ticket and eventually got to see her. I stayed in a small B&B a mile or so from where she lived and worked. We went out for a lovely meal one evening and I very nervously tried to explain to her what her friendship meant to me, and why I was so upset that she had left London. I was struggling so hard to make it plain that, although I did indeed feel as if I was in love with her, it really and truly wasn't in a sexualised way. It was *very* painful and uncomfortable because I couldn't easily convey this to her. The tension was so powerful because I think she knew I might be gay and may have worried that she had inadvertently and unintentionally given me what I might have thought were 'signals'.

The next evening, my last, we had another excellent meal in a wonderful restaurant. I eventually plucked up the courage to tell her I had written a poem to try to explain how I felt. That I didn't ever want her to worry or feel uncomfortable around me. I wanted her to read it after I had gone, but she took the paper from me and said she wanted to look at it now.

I was absolutely terrified as I sat watching her very attentively as she slowly read my words. After what felt like an age, she turned her face towards me and her green eyes were wet with tears. She told me that no one had ever written anything for her before and that she was speechless. She said she had to go outside to get some air. I was terrified that I had lost her friendship by being too insistent upon trying to explain my feelings. But when she returned, she just said that she had been overwhelmed and very touched.

Acceptance

Caught off guard by your awareness,
I reflect upon the short time I have known
You share the invincibility of nature.
Her qualities are yours – not for the asking –
Just yours.
I must strive to clear my mind,
Free it from restrictions you no longer feel.
My questioning futility is consort to the mesh
That stifles me from within.
Your receptive mind and flexibility give you
Strength, beauty, pride and immortality –
Facets of nature I shall never truly know

There's nothing to match the angst of an introspective teenager!

We did stay in touch for a year or two longer, but she eventually returned to Newcastle, where I think she got married. And I joined the Army, so we lost touch. She will always hold such a special place in my heart. She really was one of life's rare souls – a warm, loving and gentle human being.

Alongside my 'intellectual' growth through my blossoming friendship with Helena, a more visceral liaison had been developing. This was Gemma (Gem), three years my senior – she lived on the first floor and also worked as a receptionist. She too had what seemed to be vast amounts of life experience, but this was much simpler and more violent. She came from a small, close-knit Yorkshire village.

She was fairly recently divorced, having come to work in London to escape her ex-husband. He had been her childhood sweetheart, a good-looking lad, short, with dark hair. Sadly, his temper was equally short and dark – he'd physically abused her for some years. She eventually made her escape after he broke her nose, leading to hospitalisation.

We hit it off almost immediately, once I'd managed to get the hang of her accent and dialect – using 'while' to mean 'since' threw me for a bit, but I soon rose to the challenge! We quickly became inseparable; socialising in local pubs and restaurants, holding impromptu parties back at our rooms, often inviting total strangers to join us. The Marquis Cornwallis pub was a good place to start, just around the corner from us. As we staggered the short distance back along Marchmont Street, I would furtively cast what I hoped were discreet glances at the Gay's the Word bookshop, but I never dared stop or look closely at the wares on display in the window. This iconic, nay, legendary independent LGBT bookshop was founded in 1979, just one year before I'd started work. It was used as a community and information resource for lesbians and gay men, with a large free noticeboard detailing various gay organisations and events. As well as being a book store, it was used after hours as a meeting place for various groups such as Icebreakers, the Lesbian Discussion Group, Gay Black Group, Gay Disabled Group and TransLondon. I yearned to take a closer look, but simply didn't dare.

My new best friend, Gem, was resolutely heterosexual, as was Helena, so I quashed any thought of being able to realise my woman-kissing daydreams and tried really hard to convince myself that I was going through a somewhat prolonged 'phase'. I needed to find a nice bloke, see what all the fuss was about, discover the joys of being 'screwed'.

The time came soon enough – I would lose my virginity in June 1980, aged 19. It was a truly awful experience, mainly because I was drunk and the man who deflowered me was an insensitive opportunist.

Near our accommodation was a police hostel. We had been invited to attend a summer ball there, how could we resist? Policemen, cheap booze, spitting distance from home – what's not to like? We all put on our glad rags and wandered over. Edward was slim and good-looking. He seemed attentive and had an interesting story to tell, having trained as a nurse (quite unusual for a man in those days) before deciding to change direction from one uniformed life to another. He kept the drinks coming too, so my meagre pay packet would last longer than usual this week. Gem, Rose, Mary, Bev and Sue had all copped off too, so it seemed safe enough to accept the invitation to go to his room for a nightcap and to look at the 'great views' from his window.

Funnily enough, the polluted night skies over London weren't really conducive to seeing the stars that night, despite his having switched off the light. Small talk over, he made his move. The kissing was fine, a darn sight better than the very first time I'd ever been French kissed, by a 16-year-old lad I'd met at a friend's party, whose 'technique' left more slimy saliva over my face than in my mouth. Being licked by a bulldog with a bad cold would've left me drier and may even have been marginally more enjoyable!

As Edward got bolder, unbuttoning my blouse and groping my breasts through my bra, I tried to relax and enjoy what was happening. After all, nearly everyone I'd ever known seemed to aspire to this. Certain classmates were forever trying to outdo one another when recounting how far they'd gone with their respective acne-ridden, bum-fluff whiskered boyfriends. Whispered talk of 'first base' and being 'fingered' had left me bewildered and vaguely disturbed as I'd listened on the peripheries of others' blossoming sexuality.

As he squeezed my nipple I felt a vague sense of arousal, not in direct response to his touch as such, more because I was imagining Gem in his place. I began to protest as he pushed me down onto his single bed; despite his slender frame, he was very strong and my pleas for him to stop were initially rebuffed with, 'Don't worry, I'll go easy – it'll be fine.' I could feel his erection straining against his flies as he deftly pushed up my skirt and pulled my underwear down below my knees; I was regretting having opted for stockings rather than tights, knowing his ardour might not have diminished as such, but that I might have been able to buy a little time to try to sober up enough to figure out how to get him off me.

My head was swimming and a sense of panic was making me feel nauseated. Any vicarious pleasure I might have had from my fantasies was completely destroyed as he forced himself into me, without using any protection, lubrication or even a cursory attempt at foreplay. The amount of alcohol I'd had meant I just couldn't seem to muster enough strength to force him off me. I'd been sitting on the end of his bed before it all began, so my knees were bent over the edge and I couldn't get my feet onto the floor to get enough purchase to really push up. I started crying and saying, 'Please stop, you're hurting me!' but he held me down by gripping me round my biceps. The only saving grace was the fact that it didn't last long and, once he'd finished, it seemed as if he hadn't realised it was my first time, my silent tears seeming a surprise to him. He tried to kiss me, but I turned my face away, wiping my sodden eyes with my hand. He became contrite, but in an odd way – sounding as if he'd quite like us to see one another again and start dating. He even began by saying that he hadn't been able to help himself, because I was 'so lovely'. I almost found myself thinking that maybe this was normal and that I shouldn't feel this way.

He tried to lie next to me, as if wanting to cuddle me, but I said I needed to get back as I was working the next day. When I got in, I went straight to Gem's room. She was keen to hear how my evening had gone. I was totally stunned and found myself saying something utterly ridiculous: 'I think I've been raped!'

She didn't respond as I might have expected. She seemed momentarily quizzical, then started laughing – 'You THINK you've been raped? Don't you know?!'

I started laughing too – how bloody stupid did that sound? Christ! I didn't have a leg to stand on. I'd allowed him to buy me drinks all evening, gone willingly up to his room and he was a policeman, so would know all the legal loopholes. The wait for my period seemed hellishly long.

Recalling that night, I can only reel in shock at my muted reaction to what had happened. Gem's amused response had served to further reinforce that I was completely out of step with all the girls and women I had ever loved, respected, admired, sought to emulate. She'd even asked me if he'd been any good! How on earth would I know, having been a virgin? All I knew was that it had bloody well hurt like hell!

School friends, aunts, my beloved mum, Gem – they all *loved* men, *wanted* to have sex with them, apparently really *enjoyed* having sex with them. What was wrong with me? Why did I feel like this? I *so* wanted to be normal – to feel as they did. I was ashamed and deeply troubled about the intensity of my 'crushes'. I can hardly believe this, but looking back, I genuinely felt a sense of it having somehow been partly my fault, believing I must have been in some way responsible for what *he did to me* as I begged him to stop.

Gem

Although Gem almost certainly grew to understand the nature of my deepening affection for her, we never broached the subject. I just contented myself with idly fantasising, as had been my way since childhood – my family always referred to me as a real daydreamer, away with the fairies.

A big turning point, for me at least, had come in the late summer of 1980, when Gem and I went away for a long weekend in Paris. It had taken quite a bit of planning and saving up, but eventually the time came to board the train, then the hovercraft, then another train – and finally, we were there! My lifelong fascination with France had begun with our first family holiday back in the early '70s. We went camping every year, always visiting a new region. Something inside me just totally identified with France and I felt so at home. Paris was wonderful and I wanted our stay to last forever.

When we returned, I began some serious research into the possibility of doing a lengthy working holiday, such as grape picking, with food, accommodation and a small amount of spending money thrown in. Initially Gem seemed to be completely engaged with the project, but it was soon apparent that I was the one investing the time and effort into trying to make it a reality. This was pre-internet, don't forget, so visits to the library, SNCF (French Railway) offices and the French Embassy were all part of the groundwork. I didn't care though, I was inspired, energised and raring to go; I wanted this so badly.

My family were less than thrilled, thinking I was completely mad to give up a 'good' job, but I was determined. Mum even challenged me about my reasons, causing me to blush crimson when she angrily asked, 'What *is* it with her? You're acting like a lovesick schoolboy! She's got some sort of weird hold over you!' I feigned complete disgust and bluffed my way out by insisting it was my Francophilia that was behind the idea. Funnily enough, it'd probably be called a 'gap year' now.

My dreams were shattered when Gem returned from a visit to her older brother, Jim, a squaddie based out in Germany. I'd gone to Heathrow airport to meet her and her younger brother, Pete, when they got back. It was meant to be a surprise and she did seem genuinely pleased to see me, if a little shocked. Because Pete was there, we didn't talk properly until later that evening. I'd managed to get even more brochures and advice about working abroad and couldn't wait to show her. She was a bit sheepish, but eventually she told me she'd decided she couldn't come with me after all. She said she'd worried that I'd be fine because I could speak some French but she was afraid she wouldn't take to it as well as I was likely to. I tried to make her forget her anxieties, but she then got to the real reason: she'd met someone, a friend of Jim's.

She showed me a photo – I couldn't believe what I was seeing and hearing. He was called Jeff – a rather stout, not even good-looking to my biased mind, squaddie. And a 'tankie' to boot, so any physical shortcomings weren't likely to be compensated for by a keen intellect or scintillating conversation! (Meow!) My inner rage was bubbling over, but, really, she wanted to give up on *our* dream for *this* pathetic specimen? I was seething inside yet somehow managed to do what I had done all my life: stifle my true emotion and display a calm, kind, understanding and annoyingly sweet exterior. The brainwashing since earliest school days was deeply ingrained. You must suppress signs of any emotions that may make the person towards whom they are directed feel uncomfortable. No matter what the cost to yourself, do not impose your feelings upon another who would neither welcome nor understand them.

In a nanosecond I contemplated screaming, declaring my love, passionately kissing her, slapping her, laughing in her face, storming out. Instead, I feigned delight at her wonderful news and asked when she was seeing him again. Maybe acting would have been a better career choice for me?

Her rejection of our plans and, therefore, of *me*, led to my recognising the enormous differences between us. Not only in terms of sexuality. It helped me to accept her inevitable fate – doomed to marry for a second time, have kids, return to the very village she had so desperately sought to escape. This spurred me into action. I didn't want to go to France alone – that was *our* baby, born from walks in the Jardin des Tuileries; extortionately priced, supposedly *bien cuit* steaks in the Tour Eiffel restaurant, converting me to eating my meat rare thereafter; wandering through the *marchés aux puces*, agog at cast iron spiral staircases for sale; our *bateau mouche* trip on the Seine, wide-eyed at such stunning architecture and beautiful bridges.

No, I knew I had to do something different – not least to get away from her ghastly new boyfriend. I met him once at King's Cross station. Gem was taking him to meet her parents, so, having fallen for my phoney display of happiness at her new-found love, she had invited me to join them for a coffee before they left. Despite my antipathy and, yes, I hate to admit it, jealousy, my curiosity was piqued. I think she really wanted him to meet with my approval. She even seemed sincere in her wish that I might also be lucky enough to find a lovely fella myself, perhaps one of his 'great' friends! I just couldn't bear the thought of his freedom to touch her with those vile hands, with their short, podgy fingers, or knowing we would never again share a bed, as we had on many occasions when visiting her family home. I used to lie awake for hours, listening to her shallow breath, enduring an exquisite torture of being so close to her yet knowing we'd probably never actually kiss or touch… a masochistic delight.

We'd shared so many memories that bound us together, including one particularly bizarre episode (which became known as the hammer incident) that saw an earlier boyfriend become the first person to call me a dyke in a deliberately insulting and aggressive manner.

Gem had been seeing another hotel worker, called Phil. He was very possessive, jealous and insecure, disliking anyone who seemed too close to her. His behaviour, being reminiscent of her ex-husband's, led to her chucking him, but he then became a thorough nuisance, forever turning up at our place, incessantly ringing the communal doorbell and standing in the street beneath her window, yelling up to her.

On this particular evening we were in my room, drinking and listening to records. My room was on the third floor at the top of the building, overlooking the street. Gem's room was two floors down, on the first floor. We heard Phil yelling up at her empty room, his once-charming Irish lilt now menacingly slurred from a skinful of lager – 'Come on Gemma! I *love* you! You can't do this to me!'

As these episodes had been going on fairly frequently for a few weeks, Gem was beside herself. She was worried that the others in the house would lose patience and report it to management. She was also afraid that he might get physically nasty too. She began to cry and said how scared and fed up she was.

Then we heard the doorbell ringing – the little bastard wasn't giving up tonight! Gem was looking pale and scared by now, visibly shaking. We heard the front door open and realised that he'd barged his way in and had rushed to her room. The banging on her door was accompanied by increasingly frantic yelling: '*Come on!* You've got to talk to me – I love you!'

Gem was panic-stricken. 'Christ! What the fuck can I do?! He'll come up here, I know he will!'

I grabbed her round the shoulders and told her not to worry, we'd switch the light off and just sit it out until he left, but we both knew he'd have seen that my light had been on… Then the footsteps came crashing up the stairs. We both looked at my single wardrobe at the same time – 'Quick! Get in there!' Her face was a crazy mix of genuine terror and bewildered amusement at the stupidity of it all. It was like a Brian Rix farce but minus the giant lampshades and loose trousers!

As she squeezed herself into a cramped seated position in the bottom of the wardrobe, Phil arrived on the landing. Gem looked absolutely shit-scared by now, but I whispered to her that she'd be fine and I wouldn't let him get to her. I locked her in, pocketed the key then grabbed a hammer I'd been using for putting up picture hooks.

Phil started pounding on my door. 'Gem, Gemma, just talk to me, *please*! I know you're in there, come on now, *please*!'

I was a foot or two from the door so I started quietly saying to him, 'Phil, she's not here – please, just go home!' For a moment, as silence fell, I dared to hope that he might be listening.

'You fucking lying bitch! I know she's in there! Come out Gem, come on!'

I tried again, but after two or three similar exchanges, I decided to try another tack. 'Right – she's bloody well *not* here, but if I open the door and show you, will you please go home and sleep it off?'

By now he'd started kicking my door as well as thumping on it – the building was old and the door wasn't going to hold out that long. There was just a Yale lock and the wood at the bottom of the door didn't even meet the frame. My heart was pounding as I put the hammer behind my back into my right hand, then opened the door. He hurtled past me into the middle of my tiny room, head darting frantically from side to side, corner to corner, then rushed to the crooked sash window, nearly pulling the curtains off the pole to check she wasn't dangling by her fingernails over the pavement three floors down! Bloody idiot! As he turned back to face me, his red-faced, bloodshot gaze fell upon my wardrobe. He glanced back at me, but I was lightning fast and positioned myself in front of the locked doors, now revealing my weapon of choice.

'Get out of my way you fucking DYKE!' he shouted, virtually spitting the word at me.

I could feel my face flush: this was the first time I'd heard the word since seeing *Girl* all those years earlier. I think part of my profound embarrassment whenever I heard the word stemmed from the fact that, deep down, I knew it was true. How had he known?

It was also the catalyst that flicked an inner switch in me that I rarely use. I brandished the hammer in front of me, directly level with his weasel-like, contemptible little face, and, in a voice I hardly recognised as my own, said through visibly clenched teeth, 'Listen to me, you little shit! I want you to get out of my room right now or I'm going to smash your fucking skull in, d'you understand? She's *not* here and it's about time you got it into that fucking stupid head of yours – it's *over*! Now get out or I'll be calling the police.'

My nerve held out and although I had been genuinely scared as to how he might have reacted, my vehement fury had been completely real – no element of performance or blagging. I really would have been ready to fight to protect the woman I thought I loved. Despite his state of inebriation, he had the sense to know I wasn't kidding, so he turned and left, effing and blinding all the way. Once I was certain he'd left not only the building but the street, I unlocked the wardrobe and Gem literally fell out into my arms. Just feeling I'd protected her made me feel incredible. I was struck at how 'wrong' it was to not want to break away from the tight hug. I wanted to hold her like this forever. We sat on the floor, convulsed with the weirdest mix of tears, post-tension trembling and hysterical laughter. She'd been terrified listening to the showdown, unable to do anything but await the outcome.

From that day on, we adopted the eponymous Jilted John song as our own and would often be heard singing 'Phil-ip is a moron; Phil-ip is a moron'. There was just one bizarre postscript after this particularly eventful evening – a day or two later, I came home from work to find a tampon hanging from my door. The blue string was pushed into the keyhole, and a crude effort had been made to make it look as if it had been used – ketchup I think. I really couldn't figure out what message he was trying to impart, he just seemed such a pitiful little tosser.

However, our shared memories now counted for nothing. Gem announced she was marrying Jeff, and I had no place in her future. It was time to move on.

We Recruit!

It was almost a whim that led to my visiting the Central London Recruiting Depot one day in the late summer of 1980. I was 19 years old.

As well as needing to get away from Gem, the deep and meaningful discussions I'd had with Helena were making me long to get out in the wider world. Much as London is an incredible city, our hours at the hotel were long and unsocial, our salaries poor and prospects non-existent. Promotion would come slowly and haphazardly, basically only when there were 'dead men's shoes' to fill. There was no real union presence. This was especially true of the more menial roles behind the scenes, such as porters, kitchen workers and chambermaids. Many were from the Philippines, working all hours to send their paltry earnings to families back home. It wasn't long before I was looking for an escape route.

However, my first visit to the recruiting depot served only to confuse me. I'd decided to see if it was possible to enlist into the Women's Royal Army Corps as a driver. I had no long-term thought as to exactly *what* I might drive or how one earned promotion based on a fabulous in-depth knowledge of the Highway Code. No, I really just wanted to learn to drive. When I'd been living at home, my family hadn't been able to afford to pay for me to have driving lessons and my Saturday job at Cedars Pharmacy paid the princely sum of £2 per day – 50p extra if you mopped the floor on rainy days! Whilst I was at school, Harrow Driving Centre offered a course for £9 that included a theory lesson to gain a basic understanding of how a car worked, two lessons on the simulator, then five shared lessons, where three pupils would take turns to drive over the course of an hour. It was an excellent 'off road' facility in Alexandra Avenue, between Rayner's Lane and Northolt, so 16-year-olds could get a taster without endangering other drivers. I have never forgotten the total exhilaration I felt when I first drove – it is something that I love beyond belief, even to this day. But at that time, I had never managed to have any more lessons, so the Army offered me an opportunity to not only gain this skill, but to get away from the hotel and out into the wider world. My only skills were languages and my only experience was in the hospitality industry, yet I yearned to escape the stultifying tedium of my life. A flashback to Myra Frances, so smart and sassy in her uniform, set the dream in motion. I had no other, better ideas... why not give it a try?

The recruiting sergeant ran through my details and sighed. '*Everyone* who applies to join the WRAC wants to be a driver and there's a two-year waiting list,' he said. 'You've got A levels, so why don't you join the QAs instead?'

Two years? A lifetime! Having never heard of the QAs, I was duly sent away clutching a set of glossy brochures and printed lists of current pay rates to peruse. It turned out that 'QAs' stood for Queen Alexandra's Royal Army Nursing Corps. Apparently I was destined to become a nurse, not a driver.

My family thought I'd gone mad. The Army? Nursing? Getting up early! Tidying your room! However, I liked the uniform; the possibility of travel; gaining a skill that was transferable back to 'civvy street' if it didn't work out, yet a secure, long-term career if it did; good salary; free board and lodgings; free dental and healthcare; sports facilities; pension plan.

Towards the end of my two years at sixth form college, I had met a lovely man called Stuart at a friend's party. He was about to enlist as a soldier in 3 Para. We briefly dated and I remember him warning me that there were lots of 'dodgy' women in the Army, especially in the WRAC. He said that if I ever did decide to join up, I might find myself being hit upon and that I should just tell them where to get off. I remember thanking him for his advice whilst thinking,

'Ooh, if only!' An image of Corporal Chrissie Harvey in *Girl* would instantly pop into my mind and cause a not unpleasant sensation 'down below'.

The only *slight* downside seemed to be the fact that you had to initially sign up for 22 years, they owned your arse and could send you anywhere they chose, and you might get killed… hmmmm. On the other hand, it's supposedly full of lascivious women intent upon seducing raw recruits… where do I sign?!

Before enlisting, there was a series of rigorous interviews, tests and assessments. At the time I applied to join up, I was advised that there was an 18-month to two-year waiting list. During this time, one is given a legal document, a 'rules of engagement' contract which is very detailed and explicit. Four sides of A4, very small font. Nowhere does it state that homosexuality (the blanket term to describe what is now referred to as LGBT) is a bar to service. Nor does it inform recruits that pregnancy will lead to dismissal (as was the case until August 1990).

When I joined up, women had only two options as far as the Army was concerned – the WRAC or the QAs. Basically, career options in the QAs consisted of becoming either trainee student or pupil nurses, ward clerks or ward stewardesses. Students did three years, leading to qualification as a Registered General Nurse; pupils did the two-year course to become an Enrolled Nurse (General). Male nurses were enlisted into the Royal Army Medical Corps along with doctors, operating theatre and laboratory technicians, radiographers, physiotherapists, etc., though they completed their training with the QAs. (Nowadays, both male and female student nurses become QAs.) The remaining medical corps was the Royal Army Dental Corps. Nursing sisters were officers, mostly direct entrant, NHS-trained and serving a two-year Short Service Commission (SSC).

The WRAC covered all the non-medical roles for women, who would be attached to specific corps or regiments once trained for their particular role. Nowadays, women are simply enlisted to whichever unit suits their needs career-wise. In 2016, it was announced by David Cameron that the ban on women in close ground fighting roles would be ended. Female soldiers can now join armoured units and have been able to apply for all close ground combat jobs since the end of 2018. The last bastion of male dominance has finally fallen. In those days, though, my options were more limited. So I found myself signing up to join the waiting list for the QAs to train as an Army nurse, despite the fact I had never felt remotely interested in nursing.

This wasn't the first time in my life I had drifted into something rather aimlessly. I often fretted at my complete lack of direction whilst at grammar school. In the second year, we were all asked to give very careful consideration to our O level subject choices, as they would have such an impact upon our future prospects of employment. Oddly enough, considering many of my friends and family believe me to be quite bright intellectually, university never came into the equation. I didn't even consider trying to make the effort required to stay in higher education. This was partly because at the end of our fourth year, the Department for Education decided in their wisdom to change our status from grammar to high school. This devastating move blighted many pupils' lives, even if we didn't fully recognise to what extent at that time. Our sixth form was to be abolished, necessitating moves to sixth forms or junior colleges elsewhere in the London Borough of Harrow. Apart from the trauma of leaving a school that I loved, friends were having to go their separate ways, dependent upon location and available syllabus subjects.

My strengths had been languages, history, geography and art. My Achilles' heel was maths and the sciences, so I opted to go to Lowlands in Harrow-on-the-Hill. I had hoped to do A level French and Spanish, along with Italian and Human Biology O levels. Annoyingly, this combination was not possible, so I made the mistake of opting for Spanish and English Literature instead.

Miss Maureen Thomas, my O level Spanish teacher at Heriots Wood Grammar School for Girls, ranks in my top five teachers/ educators. She was so passionate not only about the language of Spain, but its people, history, culture, architecture, food – everything. She was one of the first people who made me see things not as flat and two dimensional, but as vibrant, evolving and full of all the possibilities inherent in a life well lived. In comparison, my A level Spanish teacher at Lowlands, Mr Wilberforce, seemed to me as heavy as lead. He was physically very solid and turgid, but he also seemed to lack enthusiasm for the subject. I instantly detested his lessons and soon began to fall behind the rest of the class.

I didn't fare much better in my newly attempted O level language, Italian. At the start of the two-year course there were maybe seven or eight students, but by the end just two of us remained, myself and Ben Rickman, both of us deserving medals for having survived the incredible character of Mr Zadka. He was an ancient Pole, prone to irrational outbursts, erratic behaviour and a tendency to drool if he dozed off behind his desk at the front of his very small class. On one memorable occasion, Ben and I sat very quietly, stifling laughter as the eyelids began to droop, the lower lip drop and twitch, the head loll forward. After about two minutes he was well away, soft snores drowning out our whispers. It was impossible to look away as the saliva began to accumulate in a pool behind the fat bottom lip, gradually rising to a perilously close tipping point. We held our breath, transfixed... ewww – down it poured, a glistening pool began spreading out on the scratched wooden surface. Then his head jerked up, he schlurped up the spit, glared right at me and yelled, 'Vell? Vot is ze answer?!'

During those two years, I came close to being suspended because my reports all concurred I had the *ability* to do well, but seemed to lack focus, intent, motivation – call it what you will. Any 'wrong' thoughts were put to one side as I attempted to fit in with the status quo.

As my time at Lowlands approached its end, we were offered some very half-hearted, wholly uninspired careers advice. I was told my linguistic ability could enable me to travel, so why not become an air hostess? With no better suggestion, I duly sent a letter to British Airways. The reply was polite and succinct, thanking me for my interest but informing me that I was too young and should contact them again after my 21st birthday. It was then mooted that I might get the chance to speak these languages, whilst awaiting my coming of age, if I worked in hotels. So that's how I found myself leaving home, albeit only moving 12 miles deeper into the metropolis, to join Imperial London Hotels Limited. I'd felt very grown up in my black linen suit (collarless jacket, pencil skirt), white blouse, pearl grey tights and low court shoes as I got on the train to Euston. But in truth I had drifted into the hotel trade by chance, just as I was now apparently drifting into nursing.

Unsquandered Promise

I left Bloomsbury in November 1980 and returned home to my family. I managed to get what I'd originally hoped would be a fill-in job until the time I'd enlist in the QAs, working at a hotel in north London. I left after about five months as one of the middle-aged, married managers one day felt he had the right to put his hand up my skirt when I was up a ladder, hanging curtains in a soon-to-be-opened new suite. When I challenged him, he tried to defend his behaviour by saying that I needed to lighten up and asking, 'Why are you so tense, Elaine? You're such a serious young woman!' Harvey Weinstein isn't a new phenomenon, alas.

The next job was much better: postal officer at Stanmore branch office. I took to the job like the proverbial duck to water and was even told that, once I'd completed the year-long probationary period, I could be a serious contender for my own office and the title of Post Mistress! As far as a working life was concerned, it was actually a very good prospect, being managed along the same lines as the civil service, with decent pay, a regulated promotion structure, excellent pension prospects and some perks. The hours were regular, apart from Wednesday evenings. These were the late finishing 'balance' days, when the entire week's takings had to be balanced to within a few pounds. No mean feat considering the dozens of different transactions that were possible in any busy branch office. Each of us averaged around £21,000 worth of business every week and it was incredibly satisfying to balance to the penny, despite complex transactions and an enormously demanding public!

Stanmore was quite a small office but was extremely busy, and the customers were real characters. Another bonus was the other members of staff I got to know. We were a really close-knit team – very supportive of one another and often socialising together after work. I soon became close to a lovely young man called Steve. He was eight months older than me and had been really patient in helping me to complete my weekly balance sheets. We began dating and he was great fun, but in all honesty, the relationship felt more like that of brother and sister than potential lovers. We got on very well though and had such a laugh at work. One of my favourite photographs of the two of us was taken at the party held for his 22nd birthday in February 1982, less than a week before I finally enlisted.

I had really grown to love the job and considered jacking in the whole Army thing, because I honestly felt I might have found my calling; I gave serious consideration to giving up my QA dreams and really making a go of it at the Post Office. It had always been in the back of my mind that my ego had been somewhat stroked by the recruiting sergeant. His assertion that having A levels afforded me the apparently superior choice of becoming a Registered General Nurse, rather than a driver, had influenced me into taking a step that had never been in my orbit before. The oft-cited theory is that nursing is truly vocational, and it's true that the very best nurses I have ever had the privilege of working with certainly fit that description. I, on the other hand, have always felt as if I've been something of a fraud.

Right up to the time that I got on the train to Aldershot, I had doubts as to whether or not I had made the right decision. I honestly can't give a definitive reason as to why I decided to take the plunge and enlist, but something just felt right. I suppose, looking back, it was a mix of things. Although the Post Office was so much better than I could have hoped, I knew my relationship with Steve didn't seem likely to go much further than it had – he was a lovely man and I felt so close to him, but I also knew I had to see if Army life would suit me. I think, too, I'm often inspired when faced with a challenge. My parents' shock at the thought of my adapting to such a rigid, regimented lifestyle just made me feel all the more determined to prove their fears wrong. It was certainly true that I'd never been a morning person, nor had I been excellent at sports, so damn it, I'd show them!

I joined up in 1982, and I had the great fortune to be trained in what was called a modular style, with small classes and brilliant support. This was the era shortly before a much-lauded new method, Project 2000, was being launched nationwide throughout the NHS.

I really loved learning the skills necessary to become a good Army nurse. Although all military nurses, not just Army, ended up taking the same three-hour written examination as NHS-trained nurses in order to qualify as a Registered General Nurse and earn the title Staff Nurse, the three-year training that led up to it was quite different to the training methodology in use today.

We were under the aegis of the Army Medical Services (AMS) Schools of Nursing. These departments were situated within military hospitals, purpose built, often very grand, Grade I listed buildings of the late Victorian/Edwardian era. Within the UK, there were military hospitals at Aldershot, Woolwich, Catterick, Glasgow, Colchester, Haslar, Netley, Chelsea, Devonport, Tidworth, Millbank, Wheatley, Wroughton and Belfast. Overseas in Germany there were British military hospitals (BMHs) in Rinteln, Münster, Hannover, Berlin, Wegberg, Iserlohn, Hostert and Wuppertal. Cyprus had RAF Akrotiri, BMHs Dhekelia and Nicosia. Other well-known locations of military hospitals included Hong Kong, Singapore, Nepal, Belize, Gibraltar and Malta. Sadly, most of these wonderful establishments are long gone.

We completed our initial basic training at the QA Training Centre, known as the Royal Pavilion, in Aldershot, where we were taught the essential military duties – marching on the drill square, lots of physical training and running to pass the dreaded basic fitness test, ironing uniforms, shaping our grey felt berets, 'bulling' our black leather shoes to a mirror-like glossy shine, putting itchy khaki puttees on round our ankles, wrapping our disruptive pattern material (DPM) camouflage trousers and uncomfortable black leather boots up tightly, learning how to use gas masks and put them on within the required nine seconds of hearing the alarm and carrying out gas attack drills in a tent filled with the dreaded CS (tear) gas. The worst exercise was during these drills, when we had to take a massive breath in, hold our noses and close our eyes tightly, then lift our masks off our faces, shove a dried biscuit in our mouth, put the mask back on with said biccy still in gob, blow out hard and fast to expel any trapped CS gas, then state our name rank and number without pebble-dashing the inside of the mask with biscuit crumbs! All to illustrate how one would have to eat whilst under attack. We all agreed that crumbly biscuit was hardly the most practical foodstuff to eat whilst under siege – I suspect the choice really was just so our trainers could have a good laugh at our expense! Such fun!

After this, we were sent to Woolwich to do our six-week introductory nursing course, which would set us up for what was to come over the next three years. We were taught the basic foundations of anatomy and physiology, how to take temperatures, record blood pressures, do dressings aseptically, make beds, blanket bathe immobile patients and record notes accurately in the 'Kardex' documentation system, which were A5-sized records with very narrow faint lines, requiring succinct summaries of care given and relevant incidents.

It was during this period that we were finally told where we would be posted. The entire three years of our training was mapped out from there. There would be no surprises at all – we knew exactly when and where we would be working and when we would have our annual leave. At the age of 21, three years seemed like an eternity and seeing it all written down for the first time was quite daunting. I'd got Rinteln in Germany for the first 18 months, then back to the Cambridge Military Hospital, Aldershot, for the second 18 months up to qualifying, in July 1985. Nearly every ward allocation had been decided too – Surgical, Medical, Paediatrics, Maternity, Theatres, A&E, Gynaecology, Intensive Care, Cardiology, 'Families' (female surgical, orthopaedics, dental), Outpatients. The only placements away from the military environment were 'Community' (mine was spent at a large GP health centre in Aldershot and out with their district nurses), Psychiatry (Park Prewett, Basingstoke) and Geriatrics (Hydestile, Godalming).

Also marked out on our three-year timetable were the school blocks. They would take place over one or two weeks before placements, with another one or two weeks of 'consolidation' at the end. Most placements were around eight weeks long, although a few were shorter (three to four weeks), with the longest I did being 13 weeks. The time in school was spent preparing us for the types of patients we were likely to meet and care for, along with more detailed anatomy and physiology. Whilst on the wards we would usually have a nurse assigned to show us the ropes and the ward sisters would write reports on us. We would have to write a detailed 'care study', outlining a patient's admission, condition, treatment, outcomes etc. This being pre-computers, everything had to be handwritten, with any illustrative images hand-drawn, laboriously copied from the School of Nursing library books.

There were also four practical elements to be completed during the three years. A nurse tutor would come to the ward and observe very closely, sometimes chipping in with questions. The first was something like carrying out a bed bath or perhaps feeding a visually-impaired patient; the second was usually doing an aseptic dressing; the third was carrying out a drug round and the fourth was managing the ward for either a morning or afternoon.

Apart from the relative sizes of the student intake, the only other main difference from NHS training was the Mobile Army Surgical Hospital (MASH) exercises we would occasionally do. These were when we would practise nursing in a tented hospital in a wartime situation. Soldiers would be made up to look like the type of casualties we would be likely to encounter and encouraged to yell and shout in an attempt to make it more realistic. I can honestly say the only thing about these that made a big impression was the fact that it is very hard to try to sleep whilst wearing a gas mask. The few exercises in which I participated didn't feel realistic to me, but they did make me reflect upon the reality of working in an actual theatre of war. It was a sobering thought.

There were two 'in house' Army written exams to do. One, called Class Twos, was at the halfway stage, just before leaving the first posting, and passing this gained the first outward sign of progression away from the status of 'baby' nurse – a pair of grey felt epaulettes with a thin red stripe down the middle. The next was shortly before the State Final examinations were taken. They were a bit like a mock or practice exam and were known as Class Ones. Passing this upgraded the epaulettes to solid red.

Then, at the end, passing your Finals led to the folded white paper nurse's cap being replaced by the charmingly nicknamed 'frilly knickers' – a starched white linen cap with a ruched edge. The epaulettes disappeared but were replaced by a red Petersham belt with a heavy buckle displaying the QARANC insignia of Queen Alexandra's white cross of Denmark, topped with a crown, bordered with laurel leaves and the corps' motto '*Sub cruce candida*' (meaning 'Beneath the white cross', and nothing to do with a bad case of thrush, as some wags would joke!). The finishing touch was a one-inch circular badge with a blue enamelled background (green for State Enrolled Nurses) behind the Army symbol of a lion rampant in front of crossed swords, with the words 'Army Medical Services – Schools of Nursing' around the outer edge. Our Senior Nurse Tutor, the late, sorely missed Major Hilary Jones, had each badge engraved with our name, rank and number. An incredibly generous personal gesture that was so touching.

The thought of making it through three years of training to become a QA was just phenomenal. The corps can trace its heritage back to Florence Nightingale, who was instrumental in lobbying for the support of female military nurses. An Army Nursing Service had been established in 1881, but 27 March 1902 became the present QA Corps Day when Queen Alexandra's Imperial Military Nursing

Service was established by Royal Warrant. In 1949, the QAIMNS became a corps and was renamed Queen Alexandra's Royal Army Nursing Corps.

As a student nurse, I was neither brilliant nor awful – I loved the practical side of things and really enjoyed learning new skills, such as different dressing techniques, how to give injections, take bloods, pass nasogastric tubes, catheterise and the like, but it wasn't until we did our three weeks on Maternity that I began to be genuinely excited at the possibility that I may have found the specialism for me.

I had been totally unprepared for the incredibly powerful wave of emotion I felt when I first witnessed a birth. It was utterly beautiful and overwhelming. I was shocked to find tears pricking at my eyes as the young, first-time dad started crying as he put his huge hand so tenderly on his daughter's head and kissed his exhausted but beaming wife. I'd been very cavalier about 'Maty' in school, but in reality, I adored teaching the mums how to correctly and safely hold their slippery babies as they bathed them. I couldn't stop enthusing about the madness of two cells from two completely different people uniting, then creating a whole new human being – simultaneously both theirs yet wholly unique and their own person! And it also got me to thinking about how and why children develop in the way they do. I know now that my own parents had often wondered if they were in some way to 'blame' for having raised a lesbian daughter and an alcoholic son. As I grow older, it is strangely comforting for me to see that physically at least, I look so much like my maternal grandmother and sometimes sound very like Mum!

Had I stayed in the Army, midwifery would have been my intended specialism, but sadly it wasn't to be.

Steve had a day off from the Post Office and came to my passing out parade at the end of April 1982, along with Mum and Nain, after I completed my basic training. Dad hadn't been allowed any time off work, sadly. Steve and I posed rather chastely for pictures afterwards – a tender kiss for the camera. I was in number two uniform, he in a lovely powder blue, striped three-piece suit, shirt and tie – very smart. My posting to British Military Hospital Rinteln in West

Germany, after the next six-week phase of training at Woolwich, would effectively end the relationship. We did keep in touch initially, sending very funny letters to one another (he often covered the entire envelope with halfpenny stamps), but things gradually tailed off. As I was to discover some years later, Steve was about to embark on a very interesting parallel journey of self-discovery about his own sexuality after we broke up. Meanwhile, I had already begun to embark on my own epiphany...

Tapestry

Sadie and I had joined up at the same time. She wasn't really like Heather or Gem, being taller and of heavier build, but there was something very attractive about her. She had lovely pale blue eyes, rather foxy and naughty, and her voice was quite deep. I liked her sense of humour and found myself trying to amuse her and impress her generally. I seemed to be able to make her laugh a lot. After we'd completed our six weeks' basic training, we were all posted to the Queen Elizabeth Military Hospital at Woolwich for our six-week Introductory Nursing course. We were billeted in four-bedded rooms and I was sharing with Sadie, Ali and another woman, Tiff.

One of the things we had to do during this time was to get into small groups and work on a project to create an informative presentation about one of Nancy Roper or Virginia Henderson's 'activities of daily living', or ADLs. These women were important pioneers in approaching patient care in a much more holistic way, rather than thinking of patients only in terms of their illness, disease or condition. Their approach was viewed as revolutionary at the time and went a long way towards challenging traditionally held views of nurses as 'handmaidens to the doctors'. ADLs evolved to cover relevant aspects of patient care such as maintaining a safe environment, communication, breathing, eating and drinking, elimination (urine, defecation, etc.), washing and dressing, controlling temperature, mobilisation, working and playing, and sleeping. It is important that nurses consider all these elements in creating effective, individualised care plans for each of their patients.

We decided to be brave and went for 'expressing sexuality', which was invariably ignored by just about everybody when admitting patients – the entire care plan in this category would sometimes consist of one or two words such as 'married' or 'has children'. How terribly British to not want to talk openly about sexual feelings!

As the weeks passed, I found myself feeling more attracted to Sadie. Things came to a glorious head one evening when the two of us were alone in the communal kitchen area next door to our room in the billets.

We were sitting facing one another across a fairly small table, ostensibly revising for our end of course assessments. By this time, she had started seeing a massive guy who was a physiotherapist, very much a muscle-bound hunk. I asked her how things were going and she was smiley and evasive at first, then alluded to the fact that he was tasty but a bit thick. We started skirting around what attracted us to 'people', not men. While this verbal game progressed, we were knocking back cans of Woodpecker cider and had cassettes playing in the background. I truly do not know how I was privy to a piece of information about her but, somehow, I was. No one had told me anything or even gossiped – I just instinctively *knew* that there had been something going on with another QA, not a fellow recruit, while we were doing basic training at Aldershot. I started telling her that I thought I knew why she wasn't so happy with the hulk, she had other 'interests'. The to-ing and fro-ing continued for what seemed like hours but eventually I told her that I thought I knew who she'd been seeing and why she didn't want anyone to know. She was clearly very interested to know what I thought, but I kept telling her I couldn't say so in case I was completely wrong – she would be really mad with me and I would feel like a right plank! By this time, amidst much smiling and giggling, partly due to the cider, I decided to take the plunge and told her I knew about her mystery *woman*! She was utterly gobsmacked and kept asking me how I knew – who had told me? Had I seen them together? They'd been SO careful!

Once she decided she was probably safe to confide in me, she admitted I was right, but that it had just been a bit of a 'fling', nothing really serious. She then of course asked if I had ever been with a woman. I told her truthfully that I hadn't but that I was confused as to how I felt. She told me she wasn't gay but that her first experience with another woman had been before she'd joined the Army, with someone older, a definite 'out' lesbian. This woman had seduced her but, although initially terrified, she had ended up really enjoying it. She said she thought she was probably bi rather than gay, but was also at great pains to remind me that, although the Army was full of lesbians, you had to be careful as it was frowned upon!

Somehow, having broached this interesting topic, we found ourselves talking about first kisses. She told me how it had been so incredible for her when this woman had made her move. As we talked, I was getting more and more turned on, merely by thinking about the possibility of kissing her. We were looking very closely at one another, but I was very shy and kept looking away. I could feel myself blushing and just knew that my neck and throat were bound to be covered in the unattractive red blotches that always appear when I'm stressed, nervous or excited.

Sadie asked how I could know if I might be gay unless I actually tried it? I said I'd desperately wanted to kiss Heather and Gem, but it was never really on the cards, so what could I do? She then said, 'You could kiss me if you like.'

I was on fire in the depths of my groin, utterly aroused, throbbing like crazy and just desperate to find out once and for all. We were still at either side of the table and the curtains were open with the light on – what were we thinking?! I wrote a little note on a piece of buttermilk-coloured writing paper and pushed it across the middle of the table to her. It said: *I'm too scared to stand up!* I was afraid to break the tension by getting up, scraping the chair legs and walking round to her. I was convinced my legs would buckle under, or I'd stumble and crash into the table in my haste to get to her before she changed her mind or worse, said, 'Hah! Had you there for a minute!'

Carole King's *Tapestry* was playing softly in the background. She took her biro, wrote a few words and pushed it back to me. I was sitting right on the edge of my chair, pulsing with excitement, leaning forward with both hands under my chin, elbows on the table, somehow holding it together through pure tension, the adrenaline coursing through my veins. I glanced down at the note: *Move your elbows six inches towards me* – Christ! I did as I was told and she did the same, smiling slightly as she leaned in, her face close to mine, breath warm on my skin. My eyes stayed open as her mouth met mine – it was overwhelming. We took our time, slowly puckering and pressing against one another's soft lips, very gently exploring the feel and sensation. It wasn't a wild, wet, open-mouthed, clashing teeth and tongues type kiss, it was altogether more sensual and almost old-style Hollywood, but it changed my life irrevocably, in that instant. When we finally pulled apart, after what felt like forever, I was grinning like a Cheshire cat, overwhelmed with a sense of coming home!

Nothing happened for another day or two after, because we simply never had the chance to be alone together. I was desperate to take things further as she had my heart by then; I was a totally besotted, lovesick fool!

One day we went into London with Ali and Mac, one of only two male student nurses in our intake, enjoying the excitement of buying drinks in pubs on the Charing Cross Road. An affable drunk came along and Mac got into a crazy discussion with the old sot, something along the lines that he (Mac) and Ali were secret lovers, planning to elope and get married! We toyed with the idea and wondered if it was possible to just turn up at a Register Office and get hitched? What would happen when we got back to Woolwich? In those days, you had to leave if you got married, so we joked that it'd be one way to get out if we decided we didn't really like Army life. Sadie and I didn't get our chance to be their witnesses, but as we went up a long flight of stairs to the ladies' loo, she 'goosed' me, putting her hand between my legs as I went up ahead of her – I couldn't believe how brazen she was! We got into the cubicle and finally had a really passionate French kiss. We were in a clinch, running our hands over the backs of each other's necks and buttocks – I was so turned on I just knew I had to be alone with her where we could be uninterrupted.

The opportunity finally arose when she came to Harrow with me to visit my family. Everyone was home, so it was hardly ideal, but under the pretext of going to listen to records in my old bedroom (shared with Nain!) we managed to take things further. Trying to make love without getting totally naked, knowing that any one of four family members could bound upstairs at any moment, may or may not heighten tension and excitement, but I was just going crazy with desire. I had been really nervous about the possibility that when it came down to it, I might not find boobs and fannies a turn on – what if I didn't respond or what I was doing didn't make her wet and receptive?

Well, I needn't have worried – although I felt like a lovelorn, pubescent schoolboy faced with his first bra, I was delighted to be able to deftly unhook it with one hand behind her arching back, freeing her gorgeous, full breasts. Feeling her nipple instantly harden in my mouth made me feel hornier than ever. I was doing all I could to find what I hoped might work for her: licking, kissing, flicking, sucking and nibbling. Her gentle moans were giving me encouragement, so by the time she'd got my shirt open I was as wet as hell. We were on my very cramped single bed and knew we didn't have a lot of time, so we got each other's trousers and undies down to our knees, not the best position for my first Sapphic fuck, but I didn't care – any anxieties I'd had in the many years leading up to this moment simply vanished forever! I wanted her inside me so badly I felt myself tighten and pulse around her fingers as she pushed inside. There was no resistance or discomfort like with Jon, I was completely open to her. She was in the same state and I was just beginning to find a pace and rhythm that she clearly appreciated when Mum's dulcet tones bellowed up from the hall – 'Dinner's ready, come on down!'

After that, we only had one other chance to spend time alone before I was posted to Germany, in June 1982, and that was when we went to stay at her mum's house. By then, I was becoming inwardly borderline obsessional about her, desperate to spend time with her and get to know her even more. Even though we had spent barely any time alone together, I had been completely, irrevocably aware that, yes, I was indeed whatever name could be used to describe a woman who loved women. Being with her, touching her and being touched by her just felt so innately *right*, true, authentic – call it what you will. Even the most hateful, derisory insult would have had me yelling from the rooftops – 'Yes! You're right, I am!' I knew I'd discovered what made me tick, sexually – I had never known this degree of arousal was even possible! I was literally *aching* with longing and desire, simply desperate to be with her. It was an exquisite pain.

I knew the day was fast approaching when we would have to go our separate ways and I was absolutely dreading it. Having finally found that my long-held fantasies were a blindingly wonderful reality, I was dreading going to Rinteln, leaving her to be posted elsewhere in the UK. At the 18-month changeover point, I would return to the UK and would miss her again. I was so miserable. I was blown away by what had happened, even toying with the thought of asking if I could swap with someone and let them take my place in Germany.

Sadie was far more sanguine about it all, mainly because it was much more a bit of fun for her, I think. I think she liked me well enough, but no more than that. She did once make me feel as if it had mattered to her. One evening, when Carole King's 'So Far Away' came on, she told me to be quiet and really listen to the words. As the last notes faded, she looked genuinely sad and said that she'd always think of me whenever she heard it. We wrote to one another a few times, but deep down I knew it would probably never amount to anything more.

When I got to Germany, I had the torn-off piece of paper folded in my purse – it stayed with me for nearly two years. *Move your elbows six inches towards me.* I would occasionally take it out, unfold it and be instantly taken back to that incredible feeling, my sex pulsing, responsive...

Even though I had been overawed by what had happened with Sadie, *still* I tried to conform. This was partly due to an innate understanding of the danger of pursuing a lesbian relationship in such an environment, but also because of my heartbreak after meeting Sadie briefly at Euston station during a visit home. I had been so excited about seeing her again but she had news for me – she'd fallen madly in love with another nurse at the hospital where she was training! I was SO jealous, but when I finally met my nemesis it was impossible to be too mad with her as she was utterly charming and very funny. Although not classically beautiful, she was completely confident in her sexuality. Sadie was besotted by her new lover in the same way that I had been with her, so it was utterly heartbreaking for me.

When I went back to Germany I was asked out by a nice young man at a dance. He was Andy, known as 'Bruce' due to his obsession with martial arts and in particular the late, great Bruce Lee. He seemed very sweet and wasn't unattractive, but his kisses just left me cold. He once came over to the hospital and turned up outside Children's Ward when I was at work on my first ever night shift! He nearly got me into terrible trouble by doing that, so I had to call it a day.

My only other relationship during my time at Rinteln did ostensibly become quite serious. We were in a very fortunate position as QAs, because squaddies out in Germany were always on the lookout for women to come to their dances and balls. Most of them didn't speak German, so locals weren't often an option. Many of the WRAC were obviously butch dykes – which is ironic, I know, but unless it came to light in an official capacity you were more or less 'safe'.

It is hard for me to hypothesise as to why there *seemed* to be more gay servicewomen in the WRAC. I suppose it could be that it was simply more noticeable when there was a greater concentration of women together. Due to working with fairly significant numbers of men in the hospitals, such as male nurses, doctors, laboratory technicians, operating theatre technicians, clerks, chefs, quartermasters etc., we QAs would be much more likely to have many friends and colleagues who were openly heterosexual. They would be free to advertise any relationships they had with men. Taking a boyfriend or male lover to a night out at any NAAFI bar, rugby club, sergeants' mess, local pub or disco was commonplace, and a normal reflection of accepted social practice in civvy street.

So, QAs, being viewed by many of the lads as the 'better', more feminine corps, were always being invited to functions and we were therefore able to be very picky. Certain corps and regiments held more attraction than others – for example, the more technical regiments such as Royal Electrical and Mechanical Engineers and the Royal Engineers would get more female attendees at their events than, say, an infantry regiment or the Royal Pioneer Corps – reputedly full of squaddies too thick to ask questions, but very happy to follow orders to dig holes and build things. I am not in any way suggesting that any of these reputations were true, by the way, merely telling you what was believed at the time by a load of shallow young women looking for a good time!

When an invitation would go up on the billet notice boards, competition could be fierce if there was a restricted number of invites available. On one occasion, there was an opportunity to be picked up and taken by coach to Sennelager, a town with a military base about an hour's drive away, for a Royal Scots Dragoon Guards Ball. Everything was free – transport there and back, all drinks, a full regimental dinner, raffle tickets, the works! Unusually, the dinner was a semi-formal occasion with officers and ORs (other or ordinary ranks, i.e., anyone in the lower ranks such as private, trooper, rating, etc.) attending together. Mixed functions like these were fairly rare. I put down my name at the top of the list, closely followed by those of all my friends. This was one do we weren't going to miss!

When we arrived, we were 'piped in' to the huge hall by a very handsome young soldier in full kilted regalia, all very exciting. I was seated between two officers, so made a very conscious effort to be on my best behaviour. The chap to my right had a very Scottish sounding name but spoke with the plummiest of BBC accents, which was a little disconcerting. Angus was an unmitigated prat; totally pretentious, arrogant and generally 'up himself'! Once he'd got through the introductions and realised I was only a mere private and student nurse, he set about trying to show off and make me feel intimidated – well, he'd picked the wrong oik for that! Having always been an avid reader, I took great delight in being more than a match for him in every topic he broached, from literature to films and politics. He was such an arrogant moron; it was deeply enjoyable showing him up to be a first-rate wanker!

By the end of the delicious meal and the excellent demonstration of Highland dancing, Angus seemed quite smitten and intrigued by me. As he stood up to pull my chair back, I saw him trying to surreptitiously glance at my cleavage. He was about to ask me onto the dance floor when a skinny young lad with dark brown hair and pale blue eyes suddenly stepped between us.

'Er, would ye like ter have a wee dance? Aw, gaw on, yer know yer want tae!' His lilting Scottish accent, cheeky grin and the fact that he seemed a teensy bit pissed made him so much more appealing and real than that stuffed-shirt prig.

I was about to reply when Angus interjected, glowering at his rival with undisguised loathing, 'Is he bothering you?'

I answered him with my eyes fixed firmly on my 'wee Jock'. 'No, not at all!' I said, then took the lad's hand and walked to the dance floor, saying 'I'd love to, thanks!'

Joe was celebrating his 21st birthday and was fairly well oiled at this comparatively early stage of the evening, so we shared a number of bops and a couple of 'slowies' but didn't even kiss, mainly due to his pals constantly coming over and plying him with more and more bevvies. We exchanged phone numbers, but I wasn't really expecting to hear from him again.

But I did, and we began dating, although this was fairly difficult due to the distance between Rinteln and Sennelager. He didn't have a car and there wasn't a direct rail link. Luckily for us, my good friend Amy (Ames) had started seeing a friend of Joe's who happened to own a car. Thus began a series of double dates with her and Charlie.

Although Joe was nice looking and great fun, we really had absolutely nothing in common. He was from Stirling and I understood his accent fairly well, but he had a disconcerting habit of also using Cockney rhyming slang! He took to calling me 'Gregory' as I wore spectacles then: Gregory Pecks = specs! Totally ridiculous and annoying, but it was hard to be cross with him as he was simply very sweet and likeable. He would say things that left me baffled – 'Ach Gregory, ma clathes are killin' me!' I'd have to work out what he was saying, then translate the rhyming slang – 'Oh Elaine, my clothes pegs are killing me!' – Clothes pegs = legs – 'Oh, are your legs aching, Joe?' 'Aye, they are, hen! Ah've bin playin' footie all weekend!'

After a couple of months of seeing one another most weeks, it seemed only fair to take things a stage further. I didn't dislike our necking sessions – he was a good kisser, but whenever he groped at my breasts I'd find myself imagining Sadie in his place. Trying to find somewhere with some privacy was nigh on impossible, due to sharing rooms. We even took an enormous risk on one ridiculous occasion, trying to fit a 'quickie' in, lying along the hideous nylon-covered armchairs in the communal sitting room. Not a great choice, due to the resultant static electricity and the chairs moving apart. We gave it up as a bad job, amidst much hysterical laughter!

Still, one night he'd come down in Eddie's (another friend) car, and we were parked outside in the bays beneath Surgical Ward. We couldn't go to my room because my roommate was in, so when we'd got back from a meal in town we found ourselves trying to 'go all the way' in a very uncomfortable position with the passenger seat back down, me sitting astride him but with my left thigh catching on the window winder and the right knocking against the handbrake and gear stick console! Far from ideal, but he'd somehow managed to get inside me and it wasn't an unpleasant sensation until I noticed something move and happened to glance up at the first floor – a staff nurse was leaning out of one of the toilet windows, smoking a sneaky fag! I realised that if I could see her, then she could probably see me! I flung myself down onto his chest, my head hidden from view behind his left ear – 'This is no good – we *have* to find a way to get a bed!'

When Mum and Aunty Dora came to visit me in Rinteln, they of course met Joe and were immediately smitten. Mum was a dreadful flirt, or do I mean a very good one? She had the time of her life every evening in the NAAFI, drinking cheap spirits and loving being surrounded by young, happy people.

Outwardly, the relationship was going really well. Although we rarely had the opportunity to fuck, when it happened it was enjoyable enough, despite my never reaching orgasm. I faked it for Joe's sake because he genuinely wanted to make me come and wasn't an inconsiderate lover.

Despite my 'straight' credentials being in good shape due to having Joe with me at the usual round of NAAFI discos and other soirées, rumours began. One particular episode that left me seething with rage also resulted in physical pain. Another student, Wendy, was sitting up talking with me one night. The conversation came round to same-sex attraction. I was very surprised at where this seemed to be leading as I thought she was looking to confide in me about her own Sapphic leanings. I was initially very wary as I hadn't for a moment seen it coming and was not remotely attracted to her. She always struck me as rather childlike and twee, albeit quite a funny character and not unlikeable. I gradually felt as if I could trust her, and having told her a bit about my own experiences I felt oddly relieved. My deceitful behaviour with poor Joe was perhaps bothering me more than I cared to admit...

Only a few days later I was out drinking in Hubies bar, a German-owned pub right opposite the main entrance to the hospital, with Nessa, one of my best friends, and Tasha, who knew Wendy. Tasha told me that Wendy had been telling anyone who would listen that they should be careful never to find themselves stuck in a lift with me! I was absolutely apoplectic with rage – what an utter bitch! I couldn't believe how stupid and trusting I'd been – would I ever learn? I went into the loo and smashed my clenched right fist through the small, opaque window – the pain seared through as the cuts began to bleed. I rinsed the hand beneath the cold tap then wrapped it very clumsily in a wad of paper towels – 'Shit!' Luckily the noise of the other drinkers and the music from the jukebox had covered the sound of my destructive outburst, but I left quickly to go and decide what to do.

In the end, I opted for ignoring the evil little madam, but she managed to get one further nasty dig in after. She sent a letter to Ness, Ames and me – we were best friends and known as the three musketeers because we were so close, despite being very different characters. After a few pages of general chit chat she ended with a very odd PS: 'By the way, what do you think of my new catchphrase? "Tufty is a homosexual kleptomaniac." Catchy, eh?!' Ames and Ness were completely baffled, so I explained. I'd briefly been nicknamed 'Tufty' whilst at Woolwich because I'd tried to save money and cut my own hair, which luckily grows incredibly fast and thickly. I'd ended up with a weird little tuft sticking up at right angles through my long fringe. I'd also told a story about a so-called friend at school sticking a note to my back that I'd carried around nearly all day without knowing. It said, 'Beware – I am a kleptomaniac!' At 13, I didn't even know what that meant, but I do remember feeling very hurt at such a cruel trick. Wendy knew these stories and for some reason was revealing them to my friends. Cruelty heaped on cruelty.

As I had already confided in Ames and Ness about my 'confusion', they felt I should just ignore the jibe and try to concentrate on making it work with Joe. They were my best friends and I utterly trusted and respected their opinions. So I would listen to their advice and try hard to fit in with the status quo. The fact that Ames' relationship with Charlie was becoming serious helped me too, because we often went out on double dates.

Ladder Climbing

After Rinteln came the second 18 months of training. This saw a return to Aldershot, where I'd done my basic training. The Cambridge Military Hospital, known as CMH, was where I would spend the next two and a half years. This wonderful place pretty much served as the area's main general hospital, with 70 per cent of our patients being civilians with no military connections. We were immensely proud to hear rumours that ambulance crews were often begged to come to us rather than the nearest NHS hospital. Our wards were incredibly well staffed and our standards of care extremely high. With the benefit of hindsight, I can honestly say this was amongst the happiest times of my life. The incredible people I was working with, the friendships that were being forged and the wonderful social life all led to the most incredible feeling of belonging and personal satisfaction at having decided to follow this profession. I had a real sense of purpose and the possibility of a long, stable and developing career ahead of me.

When I eventually decided to apply to become an officer, I opted for a three-year Short Service Commission (SSC). I had now been a private in the ranks for over four years, and although I was pretty certain that I was suitable officer material, I knew that there would be a bit of an adjustment to make, so didn't want to make the bigger commitment of five years. At that time, five years sounded like a lifetime – I know now that it passes in the blink of an eye.

There was an interesting anomaly. If a nurse from the ranks was commissioned after her 26th birthday, she had to commit to a minimum of a five-year SSC. If an NHS-trained nurse came in as a direct entrant, she could opt for a two- or three-year SSC.

As my 26th birthday was coming up in October 1986, and I knew the application process was quite lengthy, I had explained to Matron at CMH why I would like to apply for a commission comparatively early. Luckily for me, she agreed.

In the months that followed, I felt as if I was perhaps being 'tested' to assess my suitability. Having only very recently qualified as a staff nurse, in July 1985 I was seconded to Ophthalmic Outpatients under the tutelage of a fantastically knowledgeable and charming consultant, Lieutenant Colonel Peter Brown. Any fears I had (and there were many) due to squeamishness were soon quashed. His absolute love of his specialty was infectious. Some senior consultants could be very dismissive of lower-ranked personnel, but he seemed to take great delight in sharing his expertise and explaining everything so well that it became utterly fascinating rather than repellent. To this day, I take great delight in showing people the best way to self-administer eye drops and knowing how to safely cut off eyelashes.

After a brief return to Ward 14 ('Families' Ward, basically everything bar gynae) I was then told by my pal 'Speirsy' that I was rumoured to be in the frame for the next posting to Welbeck Abbey. I think my response was probably along the lines of 'Yeah right! Fuck off, you wind-up merchant!' as Speirsy was very good at keeping a straight face whilst spinning yarns. Sadly, this time she wasn't joking, nor were the rumours untrue: I *was* to be sent to the wilderness of Welbeck Abbey for an unspecified length of time. This was deemed to be a bit of a nightmare because it was pretty much in the middle of nowhere and you were the only QA there. The role was to act as 'Matron' (read 'school nurse') to the 16- to 18-year-old boys boarding there. It was equivalent to a sixth form college for boys preparing to join the more technical regiments and corps as junior officers – a sort of pre-Sandhurst training ground.

The abbey itself was rather impressive, a Gothically-styled pile located in acres of grounds. The nearest town is Worksop and it's close to Sherwood Forest in Nottinghamshire. As Matron, I was expected to live in the so-called 'hospital' in a small flat situated on the ground floor. Any patients were upstairs in one of two six-bedded wards. There was a kitchen between them in which one of the house masters' wives would prepare their meals twice a day (lunch and dinner); breakfast was cereals and toast. The rest of the ground floor was given over to the doctor's office (a local GP came twice a week) and a waiting room and lounge area.

My duties included assisting the GP with general health assessments and running twice-daily surgeries in Matron's Office in the Abbey itself. This was a half-mile walk away, along a single-track road through mainly wooded land. There were two lodge houses along the route, both of which wouldn't have looked out of place in a Brontë story. It felt gothic and faintly sinister, especially as the posting started immediately after Christmas, during the coldest, most miserable time of the year.

When I arrived, I was picked up from the station by one of the house masters, a pleasant man called Mr Pring. I was to have a couple of days' handover from my predecessor to explain what I had to do, then that was it.

I was very unhappy to be there in the middle of winter. There was only one day off a week, and without a car it was pretty much impossible to get to Worksop and back other than by spending a small fortune on a minicab. Even then, you had to carry a bleeper in case one of the boys needed nursing care. I think I went in once, looked around WH Smith, ate a roast lunch in a cafe, sat alone and very bored, then went back to the hospital.

Another thing I struggled with was the fact that, as a lifelong townie, I was frankly scared shitless whenever I made the journey to my surgery! It was very dark when I had to do the evening stint, so I had to take a torch with me. The trees, bushes and undergrowth were forever rustling and creaking, causing me endless torments: imagining mad locals, bent on rape and murder, or wild Baskervillian hounds, ready to tear open my jugular and feast on my blood as I lay dying, my gurgling shouts unheard, carried off on the bitter north wind! Although I am making light of it, I really was genuinely terrified and absolutely *hated* those walks.

Mrs Pring one day suggested I use the old bicycle instead, as it would be much quicker and hopefully less scary to be whizzing along the road instead of yomping as fast as I could. I was delighted at the prospect until I actually gave it a go. The bike was ancient, huge and rusty. I managed to get to my surgery with great effort, the pedals heavy as hell, sticking and clicking on the chain – no gears at all. On the way back, in a raging storm, being absolutely lashed with rain and the north wind howling in my frozen ears, the pedals stuck and stopped suddenly, throwing me off at reasonably high speed onto the road. My tights were ripped to shreds and my knees and hands were bleeding and very sore. I was crying in rage and pain as I picked the bloody thing up, cursing as I hobbled the rest of the way back, dumping it where it had been before. The following day my left knee was massively swollen, so I had to leave 30 minutes earlier to get to surgery on time. The small room was of course situated up four very long flights of stairs, right near the top of the building. Rochester's wife in *Jane Eyre* was constantly in my mind; where was Grace Poole to help me up?

The next day, the GP kindly saw me after he'd finished with his queue of sickly boys. He diagnosed bursitis and recommended two to three days of rest and keeping the leg elevated. How the hell was I supposed to do that with a total of two miles' walk and what felt like 800 steps four times daily?! I really felt like I was being punished, but somehow managed to keep going.

The so-called surgeries were frankly hilarious. The main complaint was what the boys charmingly referred to as 'scrot rot' – a sweat-induced rash or fungal infection around their testes which they always seemed *very* keen to show me! They would come into the surgery and when asked 'What can I do for you?' would eagerly stand up, thumbs in the waistband of their tracksuit bottoms, ready to whip them down and say 'I think I've got scrot rot, ma'am! Would you like a look?!' Luckily, my predecessor had pre-warned me that, as there were very few younger women at Welbeck, many of the boys would try to get their nether regions handled by Matron in an attempt at embarrassing her – so my stock response was always the same. As I handed them a tube of Canesten cream I would say, 'No thank you, Fortescue-Smythe [insert name here]. Use this and if it's no better in a week, come and see the doctor!' Oddly enough, as the GP was a bearded, middle-aged man, the number of scrot rot cases quickly diminished after they got wind of this.

The only time I had any 'patients' at the hospital was when there was an outbreak of flu. I think the most we had was perhaps eight boys, but again there wasn't really a great deal for me to do for them, other than dishing out medicines and checking temperatures.

The only interesting case was a lad who had complained of an unusual, tender and painful rash on his lower abdomen. It was decided to admit him, on the pretext of my needing to do daily dressings, in order to try to discreetly observe his behaviour. This was because, after many weeks of not really getting to the bottom of what was causing the rash, it was thought he might be behind the problem himself. The small areas had initially looked a bit like the blisters of shingles, but upon closer inspection it seems he might have been deliberately burning himself with cigarettes.

Apparently, he was at Welbeck very much under duress. His parents were from a long line of career soldiers and he was expected to continue the tradition. He absolutely hated the discipline of Forces life and was trying to fake a condition that might exempt him on medical grounds. It was all very sad and desperate really. Because I was cleaning and redressing the 'rash' every day and he had no way of accessing cigarettes, of course it began to heal.

Less than a year later, during my Student Officer course, I attended a dance at the Royal Military Academy at Sandhurst and he was there. He remembered me, and we chatted briefly. I'm pleased to say that he certainly *seemed* happy.

I was somehow surviving Welbeck, helped by a couple of visits from friends. Mac, the male nurse in our student intake, came up for a day or two and so did a student nurse called Morag. It was during her visit that I enjoyed the highlight of my time there. A master's daughter invited Morag and me to join her and her boyfriend in an illicit walk in the abbey's strangest secret: a network of tunnels that had been constructed by a previous owner back in the 19th century, the rather eccentric Fifth Duke of Portland. Allegedly he had done so because he wanted to be able to survey every corner of his estate without getting wet in inclement weather!

I had noticed what looked like a narrow roadway sloping down into an entrance opposite the hospital, but had made the erroneous assumption that it led to some sort of storage facility. Now I was to see what really lay behind the huge doors.

We met near the abbey and she took us a little way into the grounds nearby. We soon happened upon the rusting cast iron shell of what had once been quite a large hot house, modelled upon the Kew Gardens style. Most of the glass had gone and nature had taken over, with brambles and bushes wrapped around the once ornate frames. We carefully made our way through what had been the door and went to the far end. There were steps down into a huge area – a large room around 30 to 40 feet long and 20 to 30 feet wide. Off to one side there was a doorway, behind which there was a tunnel that led to what had once been an underground stable, where a coach and two horses could be made ready to take his Lordship around his estate. We had an amazing tour round many of the now disused tunnels. There were points where tracks had been laid to move goods and supplies around on flatbed wagon trucks. Sometimes we were just below the surface of the ground – along the length of the sports pitches above us were windows to look out, literally level with players' feet – and at other points in the grounds there were strange, mushroom-shaped objects, nearly two feet across, which were sited above air holes, presumably to prevent rainwater from pouring in. It was absolutely incredible and I am so pleased I got to see it.

One day I was visited by the deputy matron of CMH. Again, I'm fairly certain I was being assessed as to my suitability to become an officer. I've never understood why it was sometimes felt that taking a commission from the ranks might be risky. I couldn't see why a direct entrant nurse from the NHS would be any more or less suitable than an Army-trained nurse. I don't know how prevalent that attitude was, but there was at least one officer who made it quite clear that she felt that way.

I was on my best behaviour with Lieutenant Colonel McManus, offering tea and biscuits, making sure I put the milk in after the tea, hoping and praying that was the preferred way. She seemed content enough with my small talk and went on her way. I hoped I'd made a good impression on her.

I eventually escaped Welbeck, despite having a dreadful fright when the bursar told me they were very happy with me and had been hoping to keep me on for the next couple of terms! I needed to be commissioned before my next birthday, so was incredibly nervous until I was finally assured I was going back to Aldershot.

Soon after my return, it was time for the assessment weekend at the QA Training Centre. This was not dissimilar to the process I'd undergone to join up in 1982. We stayed at the Royal Pavilion and attended a variety of talks and films advising us of the pros and cons of Army life. 'We' were a variety of candidates hoping to be selected to become commissioned officers. I was the only QA-trained candidate; everyone else was an NHS-trained nurse, a direct entrant candidate. There was a taster of the basic fitness test (which I of course knew about) then we each had to give a 10-minute talk or 'lecturette' to everyone in the group. We were given free reign – a topic of our choice. This was actually very hard, so I talked about the difficulty of choosing the perfect topic. We were asked if anyone would volunteer to go first, so I immediately stuck my hand up. My thinking was a) get it over with and b) if mine's the worst, I'd hate to go last after having heard all the brilliant ones. Luckily, my strategy paid off and it seemed to go down well.

There was a small interview, then back to the billets for me.

The final ordeal, and last stage of the process, having got through the assessment, was the commissioning board itself. I had done my best to prepare for it, having been warned that it was pretty intense. One was expected to be well-informed on current political and cultural topics, yet there was an unspoken understanding that overtly personal or political views should not be expressed. The nursing element wasn't really the strongest focus, oddly enough, and I certainly don't recall being too worried about whether or not my knowledge and skills were up to date. Still, I had been preparing in the weeks leading up to it by reading a wide variety of newspapers and making the effort to watch current affairs programmes such as

Question Time. It caused me to become a bit of a fan: I still try to catch it whenever I can.

The actual board consisted of five people sitting behind an enormous desk in a very grand, oak-panelled room. One was taking notes and the others took it in turns to ask the questions. They were all very senior officers and as I was sitting on a chair right in the middle of a huge room, at a distance of about 6 feet from the desk, I was very careful to ensure my skirt was sitting smoothly over my knees, with my legs crossed at the ankles – all very ladylike and Eliza Doolittle. I remembered to maintain eye contact and look at each of them, also to speak clearly and take my time. I was fairly happy with my performance and didn't try to blag it if they asked something about which I was unsure. I just told them so and it seemed to go down well.

When I'd finished, I made my way to Euston to meet Mum and Aunty Wendy. Because we'd known I'd be in London, we'd booked tickets for a matinee performance of *Cabaret*, with Wayne Sleep as the Emcee. In my hurry to get to the station on time I tripped over a paving stone and went flying, causing my tights to be ripped to shreds and my knees to be badly grazed. A passing commuter very kindly helped me up. I was really shaken by it as I had absolutely crashed down. When I found Mum and Wendy we noticed that my skirt had split up the back seam – I looked like I was about to audition for a role as an Apache dancer! Luckily I had a change of clothes with me, because the final part of a very packed day was to be a journey to Maidstone to stay with some student nurse friends of mine who were on their psychiatric placement there. My black ski pants might have been the height of fashion, but they were so tight against my sore knee – what a price we pay for looking good!

We had a great time at the show, then went our separate ways. I'd been told that the board's decision usually took a number of days or even weeks to come through, so set off to Maidstone intent on having a great time. Not long after getting there, someone knocked at my friend Claire's door, asking if an Elaine Chambers was here. Somehow, my Mum had managed to get through to the public payphone of the staff accommodation. I ran to the phone, worried sick that something had happened to her or Wendy on the train journey back home. Mum was beside herself and virtually shrieked down the phone, 'You've got it! You've got it!'

I didn't know what the hell she was on about. 'What? What are you talking about Mum? Are you OK?'

She was laughing and clearly *very* excited, eventually managing to take a breath and explain to me that not long after she'd got home, Lieutenant Colonel McManus had taken the very unusual step of ringing my family home. This had been in case I'd gone there because of having had a day off to come to London for the board. She had known how important it was for me to try to get commissioned *before* my birthday, so she had wanted to tell me two wonderful bits of news: a) I'd passed the board and b) I would be joining Student Officer Basic Course No.40 (SOBC 40), which started at the QA Training Centre on 27 October 1986, just *one day* before my 26th birthday!

Shortly before I was commissioned

Further shrieking, squealing and laughter ensued – I couldn't believe it! *I* was going to become a QA officer – Lieutenant Chambers! The little nerdy, geeky, 'speccy four eyes', 'Chambers of horrors', 'Daddy Long Legs', 'Brainbox', bullied-at-junior-school kid had made it! Despite having had a comparatively poor start in life – born illegitimately in 1960, when such things did still matter; living in a council house when all my grammar school friends seemed very rich and privileged, at least in my eyes; failing dismally to get decent exam results at both school and sixth form college, despite having the ability to do well; being utterly clueless as to what to *do* with my life – suddenly my future seemed incredibly bright! I was *so* proud that day. Mum's delighted response to the news was music to my ears: I'd finally done something to make my parents and family proud of me. I was way beyond excited when, having hung up the phone, I raced back to the room to tell Claire and the others my incredible news.

The next morning, we girls went to Dover and got on the cross-channel ferry to spend the day in Calais. Ben, who had a massive hangover, was working so couldn't join us. Claire had a car, so we were planning on stocking up with cheap booze at the *hypermarché* before our return. We had a fantastic day, just mooching around and then lunching in a nice restaurant. I was in such a great mood, still high as a kite after Mum's phone call. It was truly one of the best times of my life.

SOBC 40

Having already completed my initial basic training as a private, student officer basic training was a doddle in comparison. Apart from one other nurse from 'the ranks', a lovely sergeant called Jen Ritchie, who I knew through having briefly worked with her, all the others in our intake were direct entrant, NHS-trained. Being Army-trained was a huge advantage to Jen and me. We would often find ourselves being consulted about how best to 'bull' shoes, get the dreadful white number two blouses ironed correctly (they had *the* most awful pleats front and back that were total bastards to iron to a satisfactory standard to pass an inspection), shape the grey berets into something that didn't look too like a flying saucer or large felt pancake – I'd often do my Frank Spencer impersonation whilst modelling how *not* to wear it! We would find ourselves smiling at the others' indignant reactions to being chastised ever so politely if items of uniform weren't quite meeting the required standard. 'Was the iron switched on, ladies?' was met with affronted indignation that we found hilarious. They were completely staggered to hear our tales of uniforms being thrown out of windows onto muddy flowerbeds; bed linen stripped unceremoniously off beds and crumpled on the floor; waste bins that we'd been 'Too lazy to empty, eh?' tipped out over our beds or rugs! I think they honestly thought we were making it up to tease them! The difference was remarkable, not just an urban myth. Officers really were treated with kid gloves.

Frankly, I didn't enjoy it anywhere near as much as I had as a private. There was a much greater sense of camaraderie in the ranks. I think because most of the student officers were joining up as fully qualified nurses, they just hadn't experienced the same sense of belonging as we did as student nurses. We had all begun the same training together and were much more inclined to work together as a truly supportive team. When there were inspections due the following day, people would help one another out. Someone who was brilliant at bulling shoes to a fantastic mirror-like shine would sit watching *Top of the Pops* in the lounge, doing six pairs, hypnotically circling the yellow duster, filthy with Cherry Blossom and spit; whoever was best at ironing the bloody impossibly difficult creases in our white blouses might do two or three while the lousy ironer might whiten someone else's plimsolls… you get the picture.

The confidential report written on 8 December 1986, at the end of our course, consisted of two succinct elements. The Course Report, written by a major (senior instructor) described me thus: 'A quietly confident young officer who trained in the corps. She showed a mature approach to the Personal Development Module, making pertinent contributions.'

The Deputy Commandant, a Lieutenant Colonel wrote this: 'Commissioned from the ranks, Lt. Chambers presented as a very "young" officer, and was initially very apprehensive about the course, she settled well nevertheless and was a popular member of the group. She was physically fit and did very well at course assessment. Lt. Chambers goes to her posting a little reassured but still hesitant about her new role.'

One thing that I did enjoy just as much was my second passing out parade, in early December 1986. On this occasion, Dad had managed to get time off work so he, Mum, Nain and Aunty Wendy came to Aldershot.

It's impossible for me to convey the sense of pride and belonging that comes with completing a series of very specific, staged manoeuvres whilst marching in your smartest number two uniform, behind a full military band. Knowing that your family are straining to pick you out as the small platoon rounds the corner onto the drill square, each of us concentrating like crazy to keep in time with the band and one another, desperate to avoid being the classic clichéd 'spotty dog', marching out of step! And – even harder in some strange way – standing stark still as the commandant and other senior luminaries march along our lines during the inspection, occasionally stopping to exchange pleasantries. I'll never know how I didn't tap my foot when the accompanying music was inevitably a very upbeat and quite camp tune, such as 'Copacabana' or 'Downtown' – both remain firm favourites to this day and instantly transport me back.

Another difference from my first parade was the lunch laid on in the training centre for two invited guests to join each officer. Nain was really miffed at this, because it meant she and Wendy would have to find a way to pass some time while Mum and Dad joined me at one of the large tables. Mum nearly slapped her when, in the reception room after the parade and just before lunch, she opened her capacious handbag and went to pull out a massive foil-wrapped round of sandwiches for her and Wendy! It was unceremoniously shoved back in, with Mum hissing at her, 'What are you doing?! You'll have to go into town to have that!'

Mum seemed to be most aware of the status of my having been commissioned. She had always regretted not making more of an effort at school, and later in life undertook a few different courses. She was hankering for a more cultured and interesting life than Dad wanted, so, in a strange way, she wanted to 'do me proud' and not show me up by not knowing basic manners. One of those courses was cordon bleu cookery, so she was well aware of which cutlery to use for each course. Most of us there had paid attention to the sessions teaching us how to behave at a regimental dinner, so acquitted ourselves well.

The lunch was actually quite intimidating, because although under the guise of a nice touch for family, friends and loved ones, we all knew we would be observed to make sure we had fully understood the strict rules of etiquette.

The only slight embarrassment occurred when the commandant stood up to make her post-parade speech. The room fell silent, apart from one guest's cutlery sounding as if it were being magnified by a megaphone as it clicked and clattered on a not-yet-empty plate. Opposite me, Dad was happily and obliviously chomping away until

Mum elbowed him really sharply in his side. He turned his head to look at her askance, knife and fork in his hands, about to say 'What?!' with his mouth still full. Mum looked fit to kill him, but the commandant was really kind, making a gentle joke before starting. Oddly enough, although I did find myself reddening, it was poor Mum who seemed most angry and embarrassed.

My first posting as 'Sister' Chambers was to be Catterick in North Yorkshire. I was frankly gutted, having hoped, after nearly three years back in the UK, it might be time for a more desirable overseas posting. Jen had got Hannover and was equally disappointed, as her boyfriend was based in the north of England. We dared wonder if we should push our luck and ask whether we might swap? We were the only two Army-trained nurses, so had a similar background. Amazingly, our request was granted.

Hindsight being 20:20, I have often wondered how things might have turned out had I just accepted my originally-intended posting to Catterick. But if I hadn't asked to swap, I wouldn't have got to know one of my best friends, Gail, and my life would have been so much poorer without her.

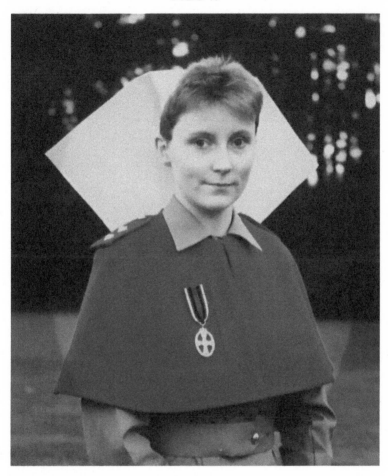

Sister Chambers

It All Started So Well

Before enlisting, in 1982, my life had had no order or focus to it, I had drifted into jobs and never really knew what I wanted to do with my life. The QAs had been like a family to me. I was a bit older when I joined up – most of my group were 18 or 19, I was over 21. When we first went to Germany, many of us hadn't lived away from our family homes before. When crises occurred, we had to support one another emotionally. It was true: training together ensured that bonds were made that could easily last for the rest of one's life.

I don't know if the other half of our group, who did all their three years' training in the UK, would disagree with what I'm about to say – and no offence is intended – but being away in Germany long before the days of easy, instant communication through emails, social media, iPads and mobiles meant we became really close as we couldn't easily ring home, let alone go home. We had little choice but to rely upon one another for succour, support and advice, whenever problems arose. Such close interdependence creates deep bonds that last forever.

This was also at a time when the Cold War threat was very real too – so there was a sense that life might be fragile. Knowing that the sheer weight and numbers of East German and Russian forces, who were very close by, would easily destroy our tactically superior weaponry within a very short period of time probably contributed to our 'eat, drink and be merry – for tomorrow we may die' attitude. There were a few pretty serious discussions about what the reality of an invasion would be. The knowledge that we were on the 'wrong' side of the very wide River Weser was quite alarming. We knew we would be expected to stay with any patients unable to be evacuated. Plus, the Army Air Corps, based at Detmold, a mere eight minutes' helicopter flying time away, would have been primed to come and blow the bridges up in order to slow the advance of any enemy ground troops. The infamous imagery of enemy soldiers in the Second World War as raping, pillaging, flame-throwing maniacs persisted long after that conflict had ended; the thought of trying to hold a horde of thuggish conscripts at bay with a 9mm Browning pistol was frankly ridiculous. We surmised that as women, it'd be easier for us to risk being shot for treason if we ditched our MOD90 ID cards, stole the fastest car from outside the officers' mess and made a run for it while it was still possible to get across the river. Male soldiers, with their short hair, would have been less likely to be able to 'pass' as civvies than perhaps we women could have done.

We had also talked about how we would end our lives if we ended up stuck in the hospital with no way to escape. The general consensus was a shedload of booze from the NAAFI, jukebox on at full whack, inject our patients then one another with insulin and slip into a lovely diabetic coma just as Ivan and Hans come crashing through the doors. I may have just shocked some of you, but these were very real fears we had. We all knew what we had signed up for, but the grim reality of war and conflict made us honestly question whether or not we would be able to carry out those duties if it came to the crunch. Despite our rare, heavy discussions, I honestly believe we all had enough conscience, honour and courage to do our duty. But I can't lie – I'm very glad we never had to find out.

The hypotheses we'd mulled over in Rinteln just a few years earlier were still as relevant after I was commissioned, arriving in Hannover just before Christmas 1986. Life there was just as intense an experience, and certainly the events that happened there shaped the rest of my life.

There was one person there to whom I was attracted, but she was resolutely straight and as she was a nurse in the ranks, our opportunities to socialise openly were rather limited. She was a corporal called Beth. I thought she was gorgeous and was delighted that we seemed to hit it off really well at work. She introduced me to the joys of attending German health clubs – not for the fainthearted! My inner prudish British schoolgirl who hated getting changed for PE because of being so boyishly flat-chested was in turmoil the first time we went. It was a club that had various areas – sauna, steam room, restaurant/bar, quiet 'rest' rooms, swimming pool, outdoor rooftop saunas (for rolling in the snow in winter!) and hot/cold plunge pools. Once I'd registered, we went to get changed but as I pulled my swimsuit out of my bag, Beth laughed and said, 'You won't be needing that – it's all naked!' My deep red face was due in part to thinking I'd be exhausted from breathing in to flatten my stomach, but also because I hardly knew where to look as she started stripping off in front of me. My surreptitious glances confirmed what I'd imagined – she had a lithe, toned, beautiful body. I was thankful I wasn't male as I'm pretty certain I'd have been having to think repellent thoughts in order to prevent an erection from springing out from behind my towel.

Any lascivious thoughts were soon driven away. Although I fancied her like mad, I knew she was unequivocally straight, so I just concentrated on enjoying her friendship. I made a point of only ever looking straight into her eyes whenever we were there. She was a warm and kind person and I was happy enough to simply appreciate being in good company.

Apart from the health club, our main ways of being able to socialise given our difference in rank related to sport. Hard as it is for me to believe now, I was once quite fit, healthy and slim. I always easily passed the basic fitness test: a six-monthly trial that, if failed, led to remedial physical training until it was passed. It consisted of a 'squadded' half mile – walking, running, walking, running – then a mile-and-a-half run individually against the clock, with the amount of time allowed adjusted according to one's age. For me the time allowed was 13 minutes and 45 seconds. One of my proudest achievements during basic training was coming first out of both squads in our final basic fitness test – taking only 10 minutes 51 seconds to complete my trial. I even managed to beat the A squad's star runner, Carla Indes. Then, nearly three and a half years later, during my student officer basic training, I came first again at only five seconds slower: 10 minutes 56 seconds... if only I still could!

In Hannover, a midwife captain, Emmie Fry, lived in the room next door to mine. We'd met when I was at the QATC, and I was pleasantly surprised when she indicated that she was hoping to put me forward to replace her as the QA Unit Sports Officer. There had been someone lined up, but in Emmie's opinion this candidate was well meaning but a little too old school 'jolly hockey sticks', like a latter-day Joyce Grenfell character. Emmie felt I'd have the ability to cross the bridge between ORs and officers, so asked if I was all right with her asking Matron. I was naturally delighted, especially as there tended to be a view that 'young' and recently commissioned officers needed to find their feet for at least two to three years before being allowed much extra-curricular responsibility.

I got the job and set to, thoroughly enjoying myself, even if my sporting prowess didn't really extend much further than running. I loved trying to get people through their BFT, especially those who were very unfit and struggling. It was always such a relief when they just made it and knew they had six months' reprieve until the next ordeal.

Most of my happiest social events there were sport-related. A team was put together to attend the Army Medical Services, British Army of the Rhine games in Münster. Beth and I eschewed the hired coach and went in her lovely classic sports car, with Chris Rea (huge in Germany in the 1980s) blaring from the tape deck... simple pleasures! To this day 'On the Beach' immediately transports me back to Hannover. Afterwards I went back on the charabanc, though, as I think Beth may have been going away for the weekend with her husband-to-be, Roy. The drinks and sing-songs carried on in the sports club well into the wee small hours.

There was also a 24-hour jogathon, initiated to try to raise funds for a much needed colposcope for Gynae Outpatients. I felt very proud to be given a trophy in the Junior Ranks Club as the officer (female) who covered the most laps – somewhere in the region of 46, I think, believed to have been roughly equivalent to 15 miles.

One other good thing about Hannover, as I mentioned earlier, was becoming close to a 25-year-old midwife from Blackpool named Gail, who became my best friend in the mess. She had been in my SOBC group. We weren't especially close during training, but when we were posted together to Hannover we got to know one other quite well. Gail is one of the loveliest, most open and honest people I know, though she can sometimes be almost too honest for her own good, not always thinking things through before speaking. It can be a charming trait, but it was to inadvertently cause me a problem later on.

Gail and I arrived in Hannover just a day or two before Christmas, when many people were away on annual leave, so we naturally stuck together. We went out into town for a drink and decided we'd try to make it a regular event, at least once a fortnight. Not too long into the posting, we were getting along famously – we would discuss anything and everything, very intently, often disagreeing but always respecting one another's opinions. She was great fun to be with, I loved her energy and direct approach to everything.

One evening, as we discussed relationships, I was yet again weighing up the pros and cons of telling her my 'secret'. Being me, I of course did, and she gave it some thought before rather nervously asking, 'You don't fancy *me*, do you?' She was clearly embarrassed to ask, and I was at great pains to assure her that, no, much as I thought the world of her, I had no romantic or lustful feeling towards her at all. She seemed reassured by this and I thought no more of it. The next time we were quaffing beers in the Ernst August Brauerei she took a long swig, looked at me quizzically and asked, '*Why* don't you fancy me? What's wrong with me?!'

Looking back, I had a lot of fun in Hannover and settled in quickly. I was thoroughly enjoying the transition from private to lieutenant. The ward staff were great people to work with: excellent professionals, trained to the highest standards, yet able to really let their hair down during their off-duty moments. Although I would sometimes get a bit peeved with a minority of the NHS direct entrant officers, who would be quite critical of some aspects of the military ways of doing things, I was just incredibly proud to be a QA. It crossed my mind that the one or two who whined about the strict, regimented way in which things were done tended to be those who seemed either a wee bit lazy or, worse still, who had no intention of staying longer than it would take to find a rich doctor or Household Cavalry officer to put a ring on their fingers. I know that perhaps sounds bitchy but, for a few, it was true. The vast majority were just fabulous though, great nurses and fun people with whom to work and spend quality time.

Life was good, and I had no idea how things were about to change.

Mel – Friday 12 June 1987

I was settling in well at Hannover and had been there for six months before the two events happened that were to change the course of my life. Both episodes were direct results of alcohol-fuelled impetuosity. I am perhaps going to risk sounding as if I am offering excuses here, so, in for a penny…

The Army has always been heavily influenced by a culture of 'work hard, play hard' and the Army Medical Services were no different from the toughest corps and regiments. 'Our' pub in Aldershot, the Royal Exchange, had two bars: the left side was the Cambridge's, the right belonged to 3 Para – we drank with the best! In fact, here's an interesting and rather telling nugget of information, or do I mean another 'urban myth'? Apparently, it was decided that student nurses were no longer allowed to go to Germany for the second 18 months of their three-year training course. Why? Because the incredibly cheap price of booze in the NAAFI meant that course work wasn't being completed in time and people were failing practical assessments due to being so hung-over from way too much socialising!

I remember when we arrived in Rinteln, and I first went to buy a drink in the NAAFI bar. I was wondering why the barmaid was filling my highball glass with two shots of spirits. I said, 'I'm sorry, I didn't ask for a double.'

To which she replied, smiling, 'That's not a double, love – that's a standard measure here!'

I said, 'So, a double would be *four* shots?!'

'That's right, welcome to Rinteln!'

When I returned later, she asked 'Same again?' But I said, 'No, I'll try something different,' and began to work my way across the optics. The price was staggeringly cheap – one Deutschmark, about 25p at the time, for a double *with* mixer. This was around a quarter of what the price would have been back in the average UK pub at the time. No wonder there was such a high level of alcoholism in the Army. The main reason for patients to be 'casevaced' (casualty evacuation – a medical transfer for treatment elsewhere) back to the UK was to dry out in the psychiatric wing at QEMH Woolwich.

I am recounting this to illustrate the prevalent way of socialising then. As I read back over the record of my interrogations about that time, I find myself cringing because the way in which I was questioned seems intent on portraying me as a lech and a lush! Taken independently, it might seem as if I was spending most of my time out socialising, drinking heavily and snogging colleagues left, right and centre. Sadly, that's quite an exaggeration and all of my peers, regardless of their sexual preferences, were enjoying the hedonistic lifestyle every bit as much as I was.

So, this is what happened – if you're hoping for some depraved, really heavy lesbian pornography then look away now. This is not 'Fifty Shades of Gay' or even 'Scarlet and Grey', those being the QA colours. What you're about to read will shock you, but in an altogether different way.

I had been made duty officer at very short notice for the third time in about a week and was heartily fed up. As a junior officer, this sort of thing was utterly tedious and came around with all too regular monotony. It was ostensibly a position of some responsibility but in real terms was just a total drag as you held keys and had to stay sober and on site, missing out on all the fun. On this occasion, the reason I was so miffed was because it was a busy Friday night in the mess, with not just one, but two functions running in tandem – Anglo-German night and an Italian pasta themed dinner. Once the meals had ended, many of my friends were off into town for a night out.

I had joined a few others in a couple of small glasses of wine in Mel's room before the meal and really felt in the mood to join everyone. Mel was a fellow officer, one of a little 'gang' of friends who all got on very well. She was nice enough, fairly quiet and innocuous, but friendly and seemed to have a good sense of humour. Luckily for me, another friend, Sandra, offered to hold the keys – that is, take over my role as duty officer for the night – as she didn't fancy going out due to working early the next day. The further fact that I had days off that weekend and had been intending to visit Sadie, now based in another military hospital in Germany, just made the offer too tempting to refuse.

We went into the heart of Hannover which, it being a Friday night, was buzzing. After a few beers in the Ernst August microbrewery, we then went off to the Rajneesh Disco. There were initially about eight or ten of us, then our numbers dwindled. After a few bops on the dance floor, I found myself in fairly deep conversation with Captain Matthew Sillitoe. He was viewed by some as a 'bit of a prat', but I found myself quite pleasantly surprised by his humour and intelligence. He was showing a softer, more human side – a rare and welcome change from his sometimes puerile humour, sexist comments and minor bragging. He had a very powerful motorbike and loved to get QA officers to accept offers of a 'little spin', then would rev it up, open the throttle wide and hurtle down the road with the dippy woman screaming her head off, clinging to him for dear life. We'd often rather cruelly joked that it was the only way he'd ever be able to get any woman to put her arms round him.

During a quiet moment in our discussion, we found ourselves playing the childish game of trying to out-stare one another without blinking. As the seconds passed and we both attempted to stifle a fit of serious giggling it seemed completely natural to lean into one another for a kiss… which was a very pleasant surprise and led to quite a prolonged 'necking session'. When we came up for air, we both blushed, as neither of us had ever really taken much notice of the other before then. Also, because the rest of the party were back from the dance floor, and were ribbing us mercilessly – 'For Christ's sake, get a room you two!'

When we all decided to call it a night and return to the mess, I remember that Matthew and I got a cab together, while the others went separately from us. On the short drive back, instant sobriety, of the 'Oh shit, I don't want to sleep with him!' sort, set in and I felt increasingly anxious as to how to turn down any such offer, should it, ahem, arise...

Luckily, as we pulled up near the annexe, where he lived, the others were arriving and began their cat-calling again. As Matthew sorted out the cab fare and indulged in mutual joshing with the other men, I seized my chance and dashed to the back door of the mess. I ran upstairs ahead of everyone else and took up position looking over the bannisters from the second floor, down to the entrance hall. This was adjacent to the bar, where they were headed for a last nightcap. I heard them come in, the ribaldry giving way to confusion then disappointment – 'Looks like she's blown you out, old chap! Probably gone to bed, never mind eh?!' After a few more moments, I realised the others were on the way up. Suddenly feeling immensely foolish, I decided to hide, so made my way up into the attic until silence fell.

As I left my hiding place, I suddenly felt wide awake again and wanted to tell someone where I'd been. As I wobbled along the corridor towards my room, I saw that the light was still on in Mel's room. This was much to my surprise as I felt as if I'd been ensconced for ages – it was probably only 10–15 minutes all told.

I gently tapped on her door and she answered immediately, albeit in a quiet voice, 'Who is it?'

'It's me, Elaine.'

'Oh, OK, hold on a minute,' followed by soft footsteps and the sound of the lock being turned. 'Give me a minute...' More footsteps, quicker this time then, 'OK, you can come in now.'

As I opened the door, I immediately felt awkward. The room was lit soft and subtly pink and the fact that she was in bed made me realise she had already turned in for the night – well, what little there was left of it. 'Oh, I'm sorry Mel, I saw your light was on and I'm wide awake – I didn't mean to disturb you – I'll go to bed.'

She smiled and beckoned me over. 'No, don't worry, I wasn't asleep yet... Anyway, I want to know, where on earth did *you* get to?'

I went over and sat down on the floor by the head of her single bed and began telling her my saga, revealing where I'd hidden from Matthew. She seemed surprised as it had looked as if we had been getting on very well at the disco. We laughed a bit about it: who'd have thought it, Captain Sillitoe being less of a tosser than we'd all thought. I then explained that I liked him well enough, but I just didn't want things to be uncomfortable if I'd accepted his offer to go to his room in the annexe 'for coffee', only to have to find a polite excuse for *not* staying the night *if* that was what he was hoping for. It was at this point, as we silently mused on the night's unforeseen events, I remember her saying something that totally blew me away: 'And what would you say if *I* asked you to stay the night?'

The twinkle in her eyes told me that I wasn't imagining it, nor did my ears need syringing. It was the strangest of moments, almost surreal, because it was so completely unexpected. No anticipation, no intimation of the bombshell that had just been dropped into my unsuspecting lap: thirteen little words, just out there, awaiting an answer…

In the few seconds it took before I uttered my bewildered reply, I considered the fact that I didn't really even fancy her as such – I liked her socially, she wasn't a very close friend, but she seemed like fun and wasn't unattractive. So far, my experience with women was a great deal more limited than that with men, so I found myself replying, in a somewhat smiley, amused and surprised voice, 'I think I'd probably say… "Yes".'

She laughed, and said with a big, suddenly oddly appealing grin, 'Get your kit off then!'

I got undressed in a very ungainly manner, still sitting on the floor by her bed – a bit like trying to get changed under a towel at the beach. She lifted the duvet to let me slide into the cramped, narrow bed beside her. There wasn't really enough room to lie comfortably side by side, so we were almost compelled into the missionary position, with me above her as we leaned in to start making love. I was momentarily surprised to realise she was also naked, then twigged that it might have been why she'd asked me to 'wait a minute' before letting me come in.

The sex, even without the added wisdom of hindsight, was hardly earth moving. Neither of us was experienced; we'd both had a fair amount to drink and there had been no seductive lead up to the unexpected invite. But, once again, for only the second time in my life, I knew I'd 'come home'. I had once read a line in Rita Mae Brown's 'coming out' classic, *Rubyfruit Jungle*, that summed it up – something like, 'It's like the difference between a Ferrari and roller skates.' Even second-rate sex with a woman was so much better than the best I'd ever had with any man. It held more *meaning*. Although neither of us orgasmed, I was more aroused than I'd ever been with anyone since my revelatory experiences with Sadie.

What happened was pretty vanilla and almost 1950s 'straight'. Start with French kissing; touch breasts; lick, kiss and nibble breasts; mutually masturbate/finger fuck one another... realise neither is going to come, so cuddle whilst falling asleep. The only thing I 'did' to her that she didn't reciprocate was to begin my first ever attempt at cunnilingus, mainly because she was guiding my head that way! I had never done it before and being drunk, gave it up as a bad job – my tongue wasn't too labile and my jaw was beginning to ache, so I resurfaced before we dozed off.

Although it hadn't been that fabulous, I did think the taste was much sweeter than the saltiness of fellatio. Another thing that really shocked me was the fact that she was actually pretty vocal and in my opinion wasn't backward at initiating things. As I recall it, she was the one who asked me to stay; she touched me first, and most surprisingly of all (and somewhat off-putting if truth be told), she kept repeating over and over, even when focused elsewhere, 'Your tits, your tits!'. She certainly didn't strike me as someone averse to what happened between us.

When we awoke later that morning, the sun streaming in through the thin, standard issue curtains, I felt confused but mildly elated – was this to be the start of something?

Yes, it was, but not a tender, mutually satisfying exploration of female sexuality. No – as I began to come to and wonder where on earth my contact lens had disappeared to in my haste to pop it out onto her bedside table, she brought me coffee and rejection in the same breath.

I was lying face down, fuzzy headed but content. She put the mug down and sat on the side of the bed – she laid a tender kiss upon my bare right shoulder then began the tentative speech. Whilst she had really *enjoyed* what had happened between us and it had been fun, it wasn't really her thing, although she freely admitted you wouldn't have thought so, judging by the noise she'd made! But she wanted to thank me as it had helped clear some things in her mind! She even threw in a little anecdote of a gay male friend of hers who had slept with women (herself included, I think) in an attempt to convince himself his homosexuality was a phase. I didn't fully get the point she was trying to make, but I think she was suggesting that she'd thought maybe she had lesbian tendencies or was perhaps bisexual. Was she deliberately cruel and insensitive in intimating that whilst it had been fun, it had served mainly to reassure her in reinforcing her heterosexuality?

My God(dess), what a kick in the bloody teeth! I knew my sexual technique, burgeoning as it was, may not have been enough to earn me a female Casanova tag, but blimey, talk about a double whammy rejection! I was utterly gobsmacked and not a little angry, to say the least. To say that I felt I had been used was an understatement.

Ironically, a day or two before this had happened, she had offered to give me a lift to the station. I was going to see Sadie, who had by now switched back to men, and had recently got married. Although I had felt as if I had been utterly in love with her and truly devastated by her affairs with other women and men, at least she had been totally honest in her approach to life, love and the sharing of her body. My obsession with her had by then faded to an acceptance that we would never be anything more than what we'd had: a brief dalliance. The last time I'd seen her was when I'd been out with her on her hen night. She had become a good friend and had introduced me to the truth of my sexual orientation, even if I didn't fully accept it until many years later.

Mel continued her little explanation with a caveat: 'We'll keep this to ourselves, eh? No need to let the others know.'

A bubbling ferment of rage was knotting my innards, but once again outwardly I was all equanimity. 'No, of course not – there's nothing to tell anyway.'

As my clothes were in a crumpled heap on the floor by her bed, she found a Japanese-style, knee-length, pale jade dressing gown for me to put on, so I could make a discreet dash to my room, just a few feet away around the corner. She refilled my coffee mug to start my hangover therapy, then peeped into the corridor to check that the coast was clear. As I struggled along, clothes pell-mell over my arm, coffee mug at a precarious angle as I tried to fit my keys into the lock, along came another neighbour, Captain Martha Diggory. I know I had a 'guilty' look of illicit sex written all over my increasingly reddened cheeks. I managed an embarrassed nod of my head in reply to her chirpy 'Good morning!'

As far as I was concerned, that was the end of the matter and I tried not to dwell on it. In any case, just seven weeks later, another event took place which took my mind off any thoughts of Mel...

Mags – Tuesday 4 August 1987

As far as the degree of physical intimacy is concerned, the next, equally unforeseen incident was far less of a 'sin' in the eyes of the military, as we didn't actually spend the night together, but of the two it was, for me anyway, much more erotic.

A small group of us had spent the evening down in the mess bar. As this is in what is known as the public rooms, we were at that time obliged to wear either skirts or dresses after 7pm: trousers were not permitted for the ladies! As it got late and most of the others had gone up to bed, only three of us were left: me, Gail, my closest friend and confidante officer-wise, and Mags, another ward sister. The conversation turned to a fellow officer, Celia. Mags was telling us that she had been spreading malicious rumours and suggesting that people thought I might be 'queer'. Gail and Mags knew someone who had recently arrived from CMH Aldershot. She had started the rumour mill turning and now Celia apparently felt it was incumbent upon her to bring it to the attention of her fellow officers.

Gail was fully aware of my pre-existent 'confusion' so we both laughed it off as stupid gossip and tried to play it down. Mags, however, really had the bit between her teeth, to the point that you would have thought they'd been badmouthing *her*. It was odd and made me wonder if there was more to her response than met the eye; a case of 'methinks the lady doth protest too much'. But I also knew she'd had boyfriends, so didn't linger long on that particular musing.

We were drinking Grolsch, a fairly potent beer, and enjoying the banter, but Gail decided it was time to turn in. As always, being a night owl, I really wasn't ready for bed and thought she was being a party pooper. To this day, no matter how exhausted I might be, it's as if a switch clicks in my head at 9pm and boom: I'm wide awake, raring to go! It's why I've always preferred night shifts to days – I especially disliked early shifts.

Mags left about 10–15 minutes after Gail, amidst much ribbing about what a wussy wimp she was being. Her parting shot was that I was always welcome to pop in for a natter later, as long as I brought some Grolsch with me – she knew I'd just added a six pack to my bar tab! She'd also said that she'd been having difficulty sleeping recently, although it wasn't until later that I found out the reason why.

After downing another bottle, I decided to go up. As I mounted the stairs, I was inwardly bemoaning the fact that most of my officer friends seemed to be early bird wimps, unlike us Army-trained nurses. These direct entry NHS girls just weren't as much fun; bloody lightweights!

Mags' light was on as I neared her door, so I thought 'Sod it!' and knocked. She immediately asked, 'Who is it?', then said to come in once I'd said it was me.

The room was in subdued light and she had the soundtrack to *The Rocky Horror Picture Show* playing in the background. Earlier in the evening we'd had a fairly deep and intense discussion about the film, and particularly its open attitude towards sexuality and experimentation. I've always loved musicals, but it was my best friend from school, Viv, who'd introduced me to this cult hit. Listening to her LP was quite an eye-opener at the time! We saw one of the earliest stage productions at the Comedy Theatre in London.

Mags motioned me to come over and sit beside her on her bed. She was lying under her quilt, wearing a T-shirt. I offered her a Grolsch and she laughed before saying, 'Fuck it, why not?!'

We sat, companionably listening and then quietly singing along to the songs until that famous refrain – 'Don't dream it – be it' – about being true to who you are started. There was a palpable tension in the air and, for what felt like minutes, we kept looking at one another quite intently, then looking away as if embarrassed or afraid of what might happen if we kept staring. Our eyes were scanning one another's features – whizzing from eyes to lips, jawline, hair, back to mouth, tongues nervously licking increasingly dry lips. The moment that we eventually leaned in to one another and began to kiss was utterly natural and wholly mutual. Neither of us 'initiated' it – it just happened. I would later discover that her statement of events read very differently to mine. But to my dying day I can only speak *my* truth.

Because there had been a bit of a lead up and some sexual tension prior to our mouths locking, I did find myself feeling turned on by the reciprocal degree of passion. She was a good kisser and we spent many minutes just freely exploring one another's mouths, our kisses becoming increasingly urgent as time moved on. This led me to feeling emboldened as we both seemed to be well and truly into what was happening. When she snaked one arm around my neck and the other around my waist, pulling me even closer to her and easing herself up from the bed so as to be almost in a sitting-up position in my arms, I felt I was safe to gently ease up her top. My right hand went under the T-shirt to touch her waist, brushing against the top of her knickers. She became even more passionate in her kissing, so I began to caress and fondle her left breast, feeling her nipple harden between my fingers as she let out a little groan of pleasure. I could hardly believe my luck, then she pulled away, looking down and saying, 'God, this is moving too fast for me!' I leaned away, confused. She continued, 'I've never done anything like this before – I'm enjoying it, but it's just going too fast for me!'

Of course, I'd stopped right away. In fact, I was immediately thinking there must be some sort of bloody epidemic in the QAs: so-called straight women who are desperate to see what it's like to be fucked by another woman, yet dare not admit it to themselves. So, how best to fulfil that particular brand of masturbation fantasy? Oh yes, find someone you think/hope is a bona fide dyke, convince her you're interested, then chicken out!

Part of me really couldn't quite believe it, a mere couple of months after the brush off from mammary-fixated Mel – here we go again! Apparently drawn in by a mutual adoration of hyper-ambiguous Tim Curry as Frank 'n' Furter, a cross-dressing transsexual who'll give and gain sexual pleasure to and from anyone and everyone. Yet, when it comes to the crunch, quickly apply the brakes, declare the need to keep our 'little secret' and you have one very bewildered person. I mean me, by the way, although I think maybe she was a little more confused than her vehement protestations to the Special Investigation Branch investigator would have you believe.

So, yet again, I found myself apologising, as if the 'too fast' progression was entirely down to me! Er, no love, it takes two to tango.

In the sober light of later that morning, yet another little card was written (I'd written a note to Mel after our interlude nearly two months earlier, assuring her that yes, I'd keep 'our' secret and that she didn't have to worry). At least the local stationery shops weren't going to go out of business anytime soon.

On the surface, things went back to normal. However, after that incident it often felt to me as if Mags was most definitely playing games. On a number of occasions when we were standing in a circle in a noisy bar, I thought she was deliberately moving very close to me, pressing her thigh against my leg, and sometimes brushing against me as she leaned across in front of me to retrieve her drinks.

She also began flirting shamelessly with a guy called Melvin, whose reputation in the mess was that of affable loser, chinless wonder and really nothing special to write home about. Mags was also friends with an officer called Reggie, based nearby, and she was very insistent that it would be a great idea for me to meet him, a sort of 'blind date', so that we could go out as a foursome. Reggie was a lovely man; charming, well-educated, well off, funny, quite handsome, despite a wobbly upper lip line. He seemed mildly pretentious for a young man, but I enjoyed his company, even though we never got further than a couple of dates. He was chivalrous and there was no physical involvement at all.

The Big Reveal

Two things would leave me totally perplexed after all the events played out as they did: firstly, why people I'd thought of as friends seemed to suddenly turn against me and secondly, how my two 'secrets' came to be revealed. It took me a very long time to fully understand the strange chain of events that led to *that* moment in August 1987, when my life would be forever changed.

Everything leads back to one person who, although not directly involved in my story, had a massive impact upon how I came to find myself accused.

She was called Elspeth, and was a friend of Mags and Mel.

Elspeth had apparently been a victim of deeply traumatic events when she was a young girl. This had naturally affected her enormously and she was increasingly troubled by dreadful, extraordinarily vivid and deeply disturbing nightmares as a significant anniversary approached. Mags and Mel were doing their best to help her get through this stressful time but were increasingly worried about her sometimes erratic behaviour. They would therefore take turns to either sleep on the floor in her room or get her to stay in their rooms so they could comfort and reassure her if she became distressed. Elspeth's heartbreaking trauma was affecting all three of them – they were becoming exhausted by their efforts to protect her.

Mel and Mags had been really struggling to cover for Elspeth, whose unpredictable behaviour had begun to be noticed by colleagues at work and in the mess. They were fearful as to how to help without putting her into a compromising situation. In those days, and in that environment, it wasn't possible to just ring in sick. You had to report to sick parade and see the duty doctor if you felt too unwell to work. There was stigma about not coping. As they hadn't wanted to report/refer Elspeth to the medical officer for a psychiatric opinion, they decided, fatefully, to talk to her boss.

Major Pam Harrold was well-liked and respected. She was known for having a good sense of humour and the staff on her ward seemed to be very happy working as part of her team. She was also widely believed to be part of what was known as the Grey Mafia. There were differing viewpoints as to what that actually meant. Some said it was a generic term for the more 'old school', senior QA officers – career women in it for the long haul. Others felt it referred to some of the closeted senior officers. There was a tacit understanding that many of the older, higher ranking QA officers were ostensibly single, classic 'spinsters of this parish' – wed to the job. It was often known that they were in fact lesbian, but no one would ever say anything openly.

I recall that Pam would often try to feign heterosexuality; for example, if a handsome young subaltern came into the dining room as a group of us sat at the table finishing lunch, she would smile conspiratorially then say in a not so *sotto voce* manner, 'Wash that boy and send him to my room!'. These comments simply made anyone hearing them feel uncomfortable. It was a painful mix of embarrassment, pity and sadness that she felt she had to do that.

After they'd filled her in on the appalling history, Major Harrold wondered out loud whether all her terrible experiences might make her susceptible towards developing lesbian tendencies? I was told that it was then that Mags said, 'Oh no, if anyone in the mess has lesbian tendencies, then it's Elaine.'

Thirteen very unlucky words – that's really all it took to initiate the process that ended my career.

Pam Harrold immediately asked Mags to explain her remark, reminding her that she should be careful about saying such things as they could have potentially serious ramifications.

Pam was insistent and so Mags told her – according to the statement she later made to WO2 Lentman, the SIB investigating officer – that she was, 'in bed one evening having had a few drinks in the bar with other mess members and was asleep. I was woken up to find someone lying over me and kissing me with her bloody hand up my T-shirt.'

Pam asked Mags why she'd waited more than two weeks to tell anyone about such a serious matter. Mags initially said she'd been so horribly shocked and traumatised that she preferred not to think about it. She had been so utterly disgusted and ashamed. She said she'd also thought it had been an isolated incident, but when she had confided in Mel, she had been stunned to be told, 'Oh my god, Mags! That's awful! The same thing happened to me too!' And it was then that they decided they ought to do something to make sure no other women in the mess would have to endure such an assault.

Having established that there was possibly a lust-filled, predatory dyke at loose in a mess full of innocent, resolutely heterosexual, uniformly irresistible young women (yeah, right!), Pam felt compelled to take action.

What she *could* have done:

As this shocking information had come to light at the weekend, in my view she could have handed it over to the duty matron to deal with. This was Major Firman, whose own specialism meant she was very well-placed to sort out human conflict and emotional issues. I subsequently found out from talking with her 'off the record' one evening that she would have brought my accusers and me together in a room, asked them to look me in the eye and tell me to my face what their accusations were. She seemed to believe they wouldn't have done that, so we could have talked it through, kept it to ourselves and gone our separate ways. This was a possible way to deal with it, and would have been desirable, especially as Mel was due imminently to leave to commence a long-awaited course back in the UK and I wasn't due to leave for more than a year, so problem solved. There would be time for things to blow over; I could learn to curb my burgeoning drinking habit and concentrate on becoming a better Sister.

What she *did*: went and reported it to Matron, one of the most straight-laced, pious, unsmiling, serious, 'Christian' women ever.

Tarot Prediction

In July 1987, about a month before I was called into Matron's office – after the night with Mel and before the incident with Mags – something rather strange happened. I was, yet again, on night duty as the night superintendent. During a quiet spell in the wee small hours I was in the office of Surgical Ward chatting with the staff. One of the nurses had a pack of tarot cards and explained that she was teaching herself how to use the pack so as to do readings for people. We were all intrigued and, as I had never had a reading before, I happily volunteered to let her practise on me.

As I shuffled the cards and she began to lay them out, she explained that people sometimes get mistakenly anxious if certain 'negative' cards come up. She cited 'Death' as an example, explaining that it didn't necessarily always mean the physical dying, but might refer to a symbolic death, such as that of a relationship or the end of a job.

Sure enough, the very first card that came up, which supposedly referred to the prevalent state of my life now was, you guessed it, Death.

About a week later I went home on annual leave. Whilst there, my younger brother Ian rang me from our local boozer, the Letchford Arms, asking me to come and join him for a drink. Mum and Dad were out at the Memorial Club so it was just me, Nain and our family dog Wooffer, a mad cross between a brindle terrier and a border collie, at home. Initially I refused, saying I was too tired and didn't really fancy it, so he gave up. About ten minutes later, he rang back – 'Aw, come on Sis, we don't see one another much these days, come and have a drink!' Nain was in the kitchen and got the gist, so mouthed at me 'Why not go?'. I told him that I'd pop round but wasn't going to stay late.

At first, he was charm itself, telling all his pals that I was his big 'Sis' and buying me a drink, arm around my shoulder, swaying a bit as he put his weight on me. He was pretty pissed but luckily still amicable at this stage. A large part of my hesitancy in deciding to go and meet him was that he was an alcoholic and totally unpredictable – it was impossible to know which drink would be the one to effect the horrific transformation from sweet-natured baby bruv to evil, destructive psychopath.

Ian's addiction had started whilst still at school, which he left at 15, without taking any exams. He earned a living doing odd jobs here and there, but was a professed anarchist, railing against the 'system' and determined to somehow survive without succumbing to societal expectation. He was bright, intelligent, difficult – basically a mass of contradictions.

Oddly enough, it was a friend and neighbour who proved the catalyst on this calamitous occasion. Terry Jonson, a lad who had been in the same year as Ian at school, joined us and made the very stupid mistake of talking about a joint birthday party we'd had at our house just under two years previously. It had started brilliantly, with loads of my mates travelling from Aldershot and Woolwich to doss over, and as Ian's birthday was only three days earlier than mine, he had invited a number of his friends along too. Oddly enough, this potentially volatile mix of military types and anarchist punks seemed to be getting along all right. But then, after Mum and Dad had gone up to bed, it turned nasty, with a fist fight breaking out amongst some of the men. One of Ian's less lovely mates had a lead pipe down his trouser leg and was duly chased away down the road, amongst a great deal of swearing and yelling. I became very upset and found myself screaming and crying in the middle of the front room 'IF YOU CAN'T FUCKING WELL GET ALONG THEN FUCKING WELL FUCK OFF AND *GET OUT!!!!!*'

Sadie, one of the dozens of friends who'd come along, told me I was very close to being given a slap to stop my hysteria, but I then just burst into tears.

Apart from one decorative plate falling off the wall and being smashed, no one was badly hurt and the punks didn't return, so the next day the party continued after I'd made the world's largest quantity of spag bol to combat the hangover!

Terry probably thought he was being funny when he brought the subject up, but Ian instantly became Mr Hyde – he started ranting about some of my military friends who had been at the party and this led to him berating me for belonging to such a vile and disgusting thing as the Army in the first place. How sick was I to help fix men up only for them to have to go back out to be shot at again? What kind of ignorant moron would even think it was OK to put on a uniform and serve a Queen who had no right to be there?

My attempts to placate him and make light of everything were falling on very drunk, deaf ears. I tried to calm him and was initially very gentle, just saying hey, that was *ages* ago, Ian – please let's not rake up the past, but he was having none of it: the anarchist bit was well and truly between his teeth. I could have happily murdered Terry but instead told Ian that I was going to go home as he was sadly ruining what had started out as a very promising evening.

That should have been an end to it, but no, he stormed after me, ranting and yelling – a stream-of-consciousness tirade of very angry and abusive insults, denigrating me for just about anything and everything that came into his crazed head. He was virtually screaming in my ear.

Then something very weird happened. Having always obediently obeyed numerous bits of well-intentioned advice, mostly for dealing with bullies – 'Just ignore them, love', 'Show you're better than them', 'Rise above it, Ellie, they're just jealous' – something inside me snapped. I was sick to the back teeth of always having to be the sensible, calm, patient, *sweet* sibling.

I could imagine Mum's voice – 'You're older, show him you know better'. I started yelling back at him and it felt *good*, very cathartic. By the time we got to the front door we were both shouting like a pair of deranged banshees. Coming into the hallway, poor Nain and Wooffer didn't know where to turn: the dog was confused as all hell – who to attack, who to defend? – so instead jumped up and down between the two of us, barking his head off. Nain was trying to intervene too: 'What on earth's the matter?! Stop it! *Please* stop it!'

It was sheer pandemonium, and suddenly Ian lashed out at me with a flailing right hook, but I was able to raise my left forearm up and block the punch. He kept trying to hit me in the face, but luckily for me was too drunk to be very effective. After the fourth or fifth block I'd just about had it with the odious little pisshead, so curled my own right hand into a tight fist and landed one on the left jawline, causing him to crash against the hall mirror at the bottom of the stairs – he screamed and stumbled upstairs into his bedroom, just as my bewildered parents came through the front door.

'What the bloody hell's going on?!' yelled Mum, as Wooffer kept barking.

Nain and I were both sobbing our hearts out and Ian was smashing his bedroom furniture again. 'He's not my fucking brother!' I cried. 'I'm sick to death of walking on fucking eggshells! I'm sorry, I *know* I shouldn't have bitten back, but he pushed me too far!'

The next day Ian went out early and I didn't see him again before I went back to Germany. I apologised to Mum, Dad and Nain for having acted as I did. I think we had all been quite stunned, as I really had always been so incredibly patient up to that point, but I wouldn't agree to retract my assertion that as far as I was concerned, I wanted nothing further to do with him and he wasn't my brother. Nain was incredibly upset by all of this.

Only two days after returning to Hannover, I was asked to take a call at reception and was shocked to hear Mum at the other end: 'Don't worry love, but I thought you'd want to know that Nain hasn't been very well' – my heart lurched – 'she's all right, but she went to the doctor on Monday, you know how much she hates to go' – yes I did, she'd once proudly told me that her GP had said to her 'Mrs Swift, you have the thinnest set of notes of any 84-year-old I know!'

Mum continued, 'Well, she'd been a bit short of breath for a day or two and that cough of hers seems worse than usual… well, he thinks she may have had a small heart attack and a stroke.'

I couldn't believe my ears. What the hell had my brother and I done? I was in total shock, mixed with a huge dollop of guilt – this was all our fault. I said as much to Mum, but she was lovely, trying to assure me that it was apparently minor and they hadn't even taken her to hospital after all, so it couldn't really be that serious, could it? I asked if I should try to come back, but she was adamant that it wasn't going to be necessary. She promised she'd contact the GP if there was any problem. Of course, I couldn't talk to Nain, as this was pre portable handsets and mobiles, so I had to trust that what Mum was telling me was true and asked her to *please* send Nain *all* my love and apologies.

Just six days later, on 10 August 1987, I was called to the phone again – Nain had died peacefully at home. To say I was devastated comes nowhere near describing how I felt, so I won't even try to convey those emotions.

I returned home again for the funeral, which happened very quickly, only four days after she'd died and just six days after poor Mum's 46th birthday. Ian and I did talk and made a tentative peace. We both felt utterly distraught to think that our actions seemed to have at best contributed to Nain's death, at worst caused it, but Mum seemed very calm and accepting of it. She said she was sure there must have been an underlying health problem and that we shouldn't forget that she'd had a troublesome productive cough for a very long time. I wasn't convinced.

So, a day or two after the funeral I returned to Hannover. Despite my ongoing grief about Nain, and the strange realisation that the Tarot had been right, day-to-day life returned to normal for, ooh let's see now… about four or five days.

Because...

I was on a 2–5 or 'split' shift, working on the Families Ward. I was in charge that day, Friday 21 August 1987, because the captain was away on leave. Everything was running smoothly, as always. We had a good team who all knew what they were doing and could be relied upon to get on with it.

I was working on the rota in the Sister's Office when the telephone rang. I heard Matron's cold, clipped tones in the receiver – 'Ah, Lieutenant Chambers, I need you to come to my office immediately.' I began to say that it would leave no cover, but she was very curt: 'That doesn't matter, come straight away.'

As I knocked, then went in, I genuinely hadn't the foggiest idea of why she wanted to see me so urgently. It even crossed my mind that something dreadful had happened at home with Ian. His alcoholism was getting worse by the day and he had attempted suicide before. But I was soon sitting, stunned to hear what she had to say.

She started by asking if I knew why I was here. Of course I didn't, so she told me, wearing a deeply pained and disgusted expression on her face. 'It has come to my attention that you may have made unwanted advances to two of your fellow officers – what have you got to say for yourself?'

I felt myself blushing beetroot and could feel the blood pumping in my neck – I just couldn't believe what I was hearing! I tried to calm my pounding heart, taking a deep breath and frantically attempting to compute things. I said that it absolutely wasn't true and that I was totally shocked by what she was saying. I then asked her which two officers and what exactly they had said, but she refused to tell me, saying that she had to speak to me first before deciding what course of action to take. Although I knew I had undoubtedly broken military law, I also knew that I most certainly had assaulted no one! Christ! My technique might well leave a lot to be desired, but I felt what had happened had been mutually consensual, and in Mel's case, as far as I was concerned, *she* had been the instigator! My mind was reeling...

'So, are you denying the allegations, Lieutenant Chambers?'

'Yes, of course I am. It's absolutely *not* true.'

'Well, I'm afraid there will have to be an investigation. You are dismissed.'

I returned to the ward and must have looked as if I'd seen a ghost. The staff on duty looked worried. 'Are you all right?' – 'You look a bit pale' – 'What did the old cow want?'

Of course I couldn't tell them, so I fobbed them off and, as it was nearly one o'clock, went straight to my room in the mess.

I knew I didn't have long to gather together any 'evidence' that would prove anything at all to do with homosexuality. Time was of the essence, but more importantly, where would I put it? There was no way I could destroy stuff other than by burning it and there was no access to a shredder, so I thought my best bet would be to hide anything at all that might be in even the slightest way incriminatory. I started frantically filling two carrier bags with anything that might be deemed as fitting the Sapphic bill: my diaries, letters, one or two books (*The Color Purple* and *Rubyfruit Jungle*), a newsletter from the Golden Wheel lesbian dating agency (along with a couple of letters I'd received in Aldershot from other subscribers – I was no longer on their list at that time, so why on earth had I kept it?!).

The way in which *Rubyfruit Jungle* came to be in my possession is worth mentioning. In 1983, Julie Walters played the eponymous star of the film *Educating Rita*. I've always been an avid film and theatre buff and this story was a particular favourite. In one scene, Michael Caine's character, a professor of English Literature who she is hoping will accept her into his class, asks why her character, whose real name is Susan, calls herself Rita. She pulls a paperback book from her bag and tells him it's after Rita Mae Brown. She is surprised he doesn't know her book, *Rubyfruit Jungle*.

Well, having adored the film, I blithely popped into WH Smith in Aldershot to seek it out, half expecting it to have been a fictional creation of Willy Russell's screenplay. I had not the faintest idea of what it might be about. It wasn't in stock, so, my curiosity having been well and truly piqued, it was duly ordered for me. I was shocked and delighted in equal measure when I collected it. The woman who served me gave me a rather snooty and disapproving look, which mystified me. I couldn't help but smile when I pulled it out from the paper bag to read: 'A novel about being different and loving it' on the front cover, and a summary on the back that proclaimed 'Being different isn't really so different'. To top it all, the heroine was described in the blurb as being 'a full-blooded, all-American, 100 per cent true-blue gay – and proud of it!'

The author photo showed a very attractive woman with short dark hair. I later discovered she and the tennis player Martina Navratilova had been lovers. It struck me as funny that this historic piece of lesbian literature had found its way into my life in such an innocuous way, yet would be assumed to have been a sure sign of my having deliberately sought out perverse filth!

As it was by now the middle of a Friday afternoon, I had made the fatal mistake of thinking any investigation involving the Royal Military Police's Special Investigation Branch (SIB) wouldn't start before Monday. They were based quite some miles away and it was POETS day ('Piss Off Early, Tomorrow's Saturday'), so I left the bags on my bed and went round to see if Gail was in. She was also on a split shift that day but had gone into town, probably to meet her young civilian boyfriend, Kai. The only other person I would have trusted, Nessa, was away on annual leave. I toyed with the idea of seeing if I could put the bags in the attic but decided against it because, being the afternoon, there were too many people around and I was likely to attract attention if I was seen acting suspiciously. It was a very small hospital of only five wards and an even smaller, mixed mess. So, thinking I'd catch Gail later, I naively went back to work.

Just half an hour into the second part of the shift, Matron rang and told me to come to her office. Once again, I had to tell my staff that I had to see Matron and leave the ward without RGN cover, but without telling them why. Everyone would soon be jumping to wild conclusions.

This time as I entered her office, she wasn't alone. A stocky man, probably in his forties, and a very young-looking woman, perhaps in her early twenties, were standing by her impressive desk. My heart sank. Goddammit! The khaki number two dress uniforms gave no clue, but their bright red forage caps did. Military police. Didn't these people have homes to go to?!

Introductions were made, all very charming and polite, then the allegations were repeated and I was asked if I had anything I'd like to say. I was advised that I wasn't being charged with anything at this stage, merely that they needed to know what my response was. Once again, I refuted the allegations most vehemently. This time I was told the names of my accusers: Captain Melanie Benn and Lieutenant Margaret Taft. I was then given a brief outline of what they were saying had happened.

Because I instantly *knew* my career was at an end, right at that very moment, I understood as clearly as anything that I was now fighting to defend my reputation in order to avoid being punished for an offence I *had not* committed. So, I looked WO2 Lentman in the eye and told him in a firm and steady voice that I was being painted as some kind of heavy-handed dyke (Matron visibly flinched) and that it simply was *not* true and that I had assaulted no one. I felt overwhelmed by the adrenaline born of a potent mix of fear, anger and indignation.

He then advised me that, due to my denying the allegations, he would have to carry out an official investigation. He said that, due to the lateness of the hour, he would leave the questioning until after the weekend. I breathed a sigh of relief. 'But,' he said, 'I would like to go to your room in order to conduct a search of your personal effects.'

Oh my God! The image of two full bags of 'evidence' sitting waiting on my bed almost caused me to laugh out loud. I was frantically trying to think of some sort of stalling tactic. I told him my room key was in my bag back in the ward office. I was hoping I might be able to chummily smile and say, 'It's a bit of a mess, will you give me five minutes and I'll meet you there?' Another barmy notion, given I'd been the fastest runner at basic fitness training, was to race ahead to my room and throw the bags out of the window. Before I could give voice to any such crazed thoughts, he said, 'That's fine, we'll come with you.'

Everyone saw me get my handbag from the office, accompanied by two 'Redcaps' and Matron – what on earth they thought at that moment I'll never know, but some of the rumours that later surfaced were nothing short of hilarious. Gail told me about them: I'd stolen 'controlled' drugs; I was a drug addict; I'd stolen petty cash from the mess bar; I had somehow 'fiddled' my expenses or mess bills; I had had an affair with a senior, married male officer.

Not one was even remotely near the truth, so a few weeks into the subsequent investigation I asked everyone I worked with in the ward to meet in the ward kitchen. Even though WO2 Lentman had made it very clear that I shouldn't talk about the case to anyone, I *knew* I'd be leaving the Army when it was over, and I was determined that such ludicrous rumours were going to be dispelled.

So, without going into all the details, I basically told them the essential stuff, which to my mind was the fact that they had enough evidence to prove I had previously had liaisons with women. Not one member of staff was bothered by this. In fact, if anything, it led to my having more support. I was given beautiful bouquets with lovely messages; cards were sent from across the ranks and in the mess.

Nearly everyone who showed me such immense kindness professed their shock at the stupidity of the ban. The vast majority of my colleagues were heterosexual, and these were the very personnel that high-ranking officers constantly claimed would 'leave in protest' if openly gay people were allowed to serve alongside them. These patronising proclamations, assuming that the rank and file servicemen or women held the same archaic, irrational homophobic beliefs as those who voiced them, were utterly offensive and presumptuous. I had experienced none of the reactions that were cited with regular, predictable monotony over the subsequent years of battle against such ignorant bigotry.

Conduct Unbecoming

When I re-read my diaries after they were given back to me, in January 1988, nearly six months after they were bagged up as 'exhibits', I was quite surprised to realise how terribly tormented I had felt whilst battling to accept my sexuality. They had finally been returned to me back at home in Harrow Weald, after I had returned to 'civvy street', delivered personally by two men who I presume must have been plain clothes Royal Military policemen. I didn't enquire or invite them in for a cuppa.

I felt a need to exorcise the mental image that had manifested itself in my mind – gruff, blokey SIB officers laughing themselves stupid at my most intimate yearnings and pinings, right back to early adolescence. They had taken *all* of my diaries, even those pre-dating my joining the Forces by many years. What possible relevance could they have had to present-day accusations of assault? Did they truly believe there would be some pertinent evidence to support my detractors' bullshit? That I would have taken great delight in writing a blow by blow account of how aroused and powerful I had felt as I ravished these poor defenceless women against their will?

Luckily, I hadn't recorded any of the details about my first truly revelatory lesbian experience with Sadie. Sure, there was mention of vaguely erotic dreams I'd had about my unrequited crushes, along with some fairly lame, non-sexual 'poetry', but nothing solid enough for them to extend their sordid witch hunt. However, sadly the letters I'd kept had led them straight to their target.

My first interrogation took place on Monday 24 August 1987.

117

Very embarrassingly, it was carried out in a room in the hospital. Being such a small unit, with only five wards, it was inconceivable that my friends and colleagues wouldn't have been aware that something significant was happening. Unusually, given the seriousness of the allegations I was facing, I was not suspended and was expected to continue carrying out my usual full-time duties – such as being second in charge of the Families Ward, unit sports officer and, often, continuing to act as the night superintendent.

The late 1980s was a time of technological innovations, such as CD players, mobile phones, Walkmans and the like, so imagine my shock when I realised that there was no equipment to record the interview! Whilst this may sound archaically funny, in reality it was incredibly annoying and frustrating. Mr Lentman would pose a question and then expect me to answer... slowly... enough... to... let... him... write... it... down... in... long... hand! When one is attempting to prove one's innocence in relation to allegations of indecent assault and give an account of what happened, this is just ludicrous, because the train of thought gets well and truly lost whilst waiting for the scribe to catch up. He wasn't even able to write in shorthand! I was totally gobsmacked. It also made the whole process hellishly laborious and time-consuming. I cannot help but imagine it was a deliberate ploy of the investigation branch, designed specifically to wear people down.

I had been offered the opportunity to have another officer present, but, knowing I was about to be asked about deeply intimate matters, I declined. So there were three of us in a room on the ground floor: me, Lentman and the female SIB sergeant. There were windows to the grounds outside, but thankfully no way for anyone passing along the corridor to see in.

Without knowing what exactly I had supposedly done, I was asked to recount the events of two evenings. So that – unbelievably in hindsight – is exactly what I did. My openness would really cost me.

I had been utterly naïve when the whole thing kicked off. My legal counsel, who had basically been assigned to me, rather like a duty solicitor would be to any accused person, had said I must be completely honest about everything. She told me that this was because the evidence alone (that they had gathered from searching my room) was more than enough to prove I had 'lesbian tendencies'. Therefore, even if the allegations were disproved and no actual *charges* were levelled against me, I was certain to lose my Army career regardless.

I had been falsely accused of 'indecent assault against a female aged 16 or over' and 'making advances of a sexual nature' – neither of which were offences exclusively nor solely applicable to a military environment. Offences tried in military courts can also be brought to civilian courts, and as I fully understood the devastating seriousness of the allegations, I was absolutely terrified of this, which I believed was a possibility. This unbearable prospect had been explained to me by my legal counsel, over the telephone. I'd asked as many questions as I could think of. But my head was all over the place, a complete maelstrom of chaotic thoughts crashing around. How much I really retained or even understood is a moot point.

So, I complied to the letter, giving as detailed an account as I possibly could of what had occurred on the two occasions. Although these allegations had completely flummoxed and mystified me, the one thing that kept me going throughout the entire time was the knowledge that I *knew* I was telling the whole truth – despite the mortal embarrassment of having to do so v-e-r-y s-l-o-w-l-y so that Mr Lentman could write it all down!

My honesty was to cost me dear. Hindsight always being 20-20, I'm stunned at my complete stupidity, but can only put it down to the fear. I really believed I was being questioned purely to establish whether or not there would be any hard evidence to convert mere allegation into full blown, answerable-in-court, conviction-carrying charges. I therefore concentrated on doing exactly as I had been advised.

I told them that after I'd left Mel's room that fateful morning, I had gone, as planned, to visit Sadie and her husband. Perhaps I subconsciously thought that as she had got married by now, she had the perfect alibi and cover for being completely, utterly and resolutely heterosexual. Lentman wanted to know all about Sadie, who she was, how we knew one another.

He was a skilled interrogator, persistent, insistent, oh-so-quietly-spoken. I eventually found myself admitting that she was the person with whom I'd realised I probably was in fact gay. Even as I write those words, I find myself staring at them in disbelief. What on earth was I thinking? The line of questioning instantly crashed into a wholly unrelated direction. Suddenly, my innocence in the face of possible assault charges seemed irrelevant, forgotten – he seemed hell-bent on gaining other scalps and was like a terrier with a rag.

Mr Lentman had wanted to know to what degree we were involved, when and where things happened between us and what we'd done sexually. Because our very brief liaisons had happened more than four years previously, I suppose I honestly didn't think there was a relevance to my case, which is why I told him. I obviously wasn't thinking very clearly.

I immediately realised I'd totally fucked everything up and was *desperate* to get to the phone to ring Sadie and warn her. And of course, that's exactly what I did. Sadie was naturally completely incensed at how bloody stupid I was; she even went so far as to ask if I'd deliberately dropped her in it as some sort of revenge! I pleaded with her, trying desperately to explain how hard it was being questioned in this stilted, stop–start fashion, unable to really get to grips with what I wanted to say. She wasn't interested and seemed very concerned that I hadn't mentioned the name of her last long-term female relationship prior to her having got married. I assured her truthfully, that no, I absolutely never mentioned the woman with whom she'd been involved.

I later heard that, as a result of my words, two SIB officers arrived at her married quarters. I suppose she was prepared for them, thanks to my phone call. Although they apparently searched the entire flat from top to bottom, nothing was found that could be bagged and tagged.

I only spoke to her once more after that fateful call and mistakenly believed for many long years that she too would have been forced to leave the corps after admitting that we had been involved. She had been shown part of my statement by the SIB, the legality of which (showing another person my statement, I mean) I was unsure about even then. The police had said it was to warn her that if she said I'd lied about things that had happened between us in the past, it would add weight to the case against me. When I had visited her that day (after my night with Mel), I had of course told her everything about what happened and how hurt and confused I was about it all.

Later, I was told that Sadie had in fact, at huge risk to herself, corroborated my story about our brief 'affair'. In one way, Sadie's statement should have been supportive of my version of events, but alas, Lentman saw it differently. When I was next summoned to see him, he tore a strip off me. I was quite shocked at his vehemence and found myself blushing shamefacedly as he berated me for jeopardising everything – didn't I realise I could be charged with deliberately suborning witnesses?! I'd never even heard that word before.

In any case, Sadie had told Lentman that she knew I'd been accused of indecent assault but that she knew I hadn't done it. When he asked her how she knew, she said, 'She's not that kind of person. She is too nice. She's afraid of rejection. She couldn't indecently assault anybody.'

Lowest Ebb

During the first week or two of the investigation, as Lentman began extending his enquiries elsewhere, I was in a chaotic state of shock, my mind frantically trying to make sense of what had happened. I just could not understand why, if Mel and Mags had genuinely felt so repulsed by what had happened, they had continued to interact with me, socialise with me and still treat me as a friend. None of it made any sense. I went over and over things in my head, trying to figure out *why?* and scribbling notes in a little book. I was desperate to find anything that might help prove that I was the only one telling the truth.

My friends and colleagues were amazingly supportive and I somehow kept going. Only Gail, Ness and Sue knew more about what was going on. Others would have heard plenty of rumour and supposition through the usual gossipy grapevine. And I had no idea what my accusers were telling their friends. I could only hope that the nature of the accusations might be a little too embarrassing for them to freely share with anyone endeavouring to find out. But the stress of not knowing what was happening behind the scenes was really getting to me.

When things had first kicked off I had known I would, at some point, probably sooner rather than later (little did I know how lengthy the investigation would be), need to go home to my parents – I knew I had to tell them. It being such a long-winded and convoluted story, I realised it would be impossible to try to telephone them and talk them through it. I'd never have gathered enough 5DM coins and there was no guarantee of privacy as the phone was stuck on the wall in a corridor of the mess. I had therefore written a very long letter – it ran to 21 sides of A5 sheets of Basildon Bond – because I really felt I needed to fully try to explain the background to what had happened. After posting it, I was sick with worry – what if they disowned me? Or were so ashamed and disappointed in me that they didn't want me home? With Nain's death having happened after I'd finally flipped out and fought with Ian, I kept thinking they'd hate me. This was one more proof of my failure as a daughter. Or worse still, what if they bought into the whole 'no smoke without fire' notion? I was beside myself with anxiety, yet was still expected to work throughout the whole process on my own.

I was so angry that I was deemed to be incompatible with Army life, yet more than capable of being effectively responsible for the smooth running of the entire hospital whilst acting as 'Night Super'. In this very responsible role, one is, in effect, acting in lieu of the commanding officer overnight! It made no sense whatsoever. I was still the unit sports officer, theoretically able to shower with other women after running BFTs, yet ostensibly a sick pervert who couldn't control her randy urges to pounce on unsuspecting women!

Having seen the consultant psychiatrist – evaluation of one's mental state was considered essential, as homosexuality was still viewed as 'unnatural' by the Forces – I had managed to get him to prescribe enough Temazepam to put an end to my life. I had been outwardly calm, rational, even perhaps 'accepting' of my fate. I told him, truthfully, that I was struggling to sleep at night. Understandable given what was going on.

On one particular evening I was at absolutely my lowest ebb and I got horribly drunk. I'd had enough of trying to maintain a level of impeccable professionalism whilst at work, yet having to deal with knowing that *everyone* was aware, to some degree or other, of what was going on. I was also terrified that I might end up facing actual charges rather than mere allegations and be taken to court martial. What if I was found guilty? It was two against one – my word against theirs. Matron seemed to have made up her mind about me, so what was to say the SIB wouldn't too? I didn't know if that would mean a jail term or, even worse still, that due to the nature of the 'offence', I might be struck off the nurses' register. How on earth would I ever work anywhere again if I had a criminal record? I hadn't realised that officers weren't put into the 'glasshouse' (prison). Having spent four and a half years in the ranks, I was none the wiser.

I was lying in bed, the room beginning to spin a little, when I opened the bottle of Temazepam. I was considering whether or not to write a last letter to Mum and Dad, but I'd heard nothing from them following my 21-page revelation, so they'd clearly made their minds up too. Well, if they didn't want me, nothing else mattered. I was about to grab a handful of the little yellow and white rugby balls when there was a knock at my door.

I staggered over to open it to find Geoff, who also lived in the mess and I knew socially, standing there. I must have looked a frightful mess, bleary-eyed from so much beer, but he just put his arms out to hold me. I fell into them and started weeping.

He told me he was going to take me to his room. When we got there, I was somewhat taken aback to see his civilian girlfriend. This was most definitely against regulations. He had in effect saved my life by knocking when he did – how can I ever sum up how grateful I am that fate threw him my way at that precise moment? As the three of us talked about the iniquity of what was happening, he started offering his views about sex and how what people did with their bodies behind closed doors was no one's business but their own.

I wasn't really saying much at this stage, feeling very rough and just wondering what was happening to my life. We each had a bottle of Grolsch; not that I needed anything more to drink. I was struggling to focus and my head felt very swimmy. Geoff's discourse, a distant mumbling in my distracted head, came into sharp relief when I realised he was delivering his theories about bodily intimacy whilst holding his prick, which was now clearly visible as his dressing gown had parted. Cath didn't seem in the slightest bit perturbed by this and I was actually quite fascinated and surprised that this not particularly tall man had such a large, fat dick! He wasn't masturbating, rather holding it and moving it about, as if to illustrate his point, rather like a phallic light stick. I must have stared a little too long, because he seemed to take this to mean I was up for a little diversionary threesome. Much as he was a very funny and likeable guy, I certainly didn't find him or his girlfriend remotely attractive. They were clearly 'swingers' and she seemed very keen to kiss and touch me, but it wasn't reciprocated at all. As I realised where they were hoping to take things, I decided it was time to leave. Their protestations rang in my ears as I nearly bounced off the walls and stumbled back to the safety of my room, door locked!

The unbelievable hypocrisy of it all was beginning to make me mad. Here was I, accused of forcing unwanted attention of an unnatural kind onto unsuspecting friends and colleagues. Yet a heterosexual colleague, ostensibly concerned for my welfare, takes me to his room and tries to persuade me that I can take my mind off thoughts of suicide by joining him and his girlfriend in bed! I was being treated as if I was the worst kind of obscene pervert, yet right under the same roof were utterly reprehensible, opportunistic hedonists, bent (ahem) upon getting their rocks off at my expense.

The next day (well, later that morning actually!) was the first and only time I ever overslept and didn't go into work. Looking and feeling like the proverbial wreck of the Hesperus, I opened my door to a very angry Lieutenant Colonel Andrews, Deputy Matron. It was mid-morning and I must have stunk like a brewery. There was an empty Grolsch bottle and the spilled Temazepam clearly visible on my bedside table – did that engender any sympathy or concern? Of course not. I was severely reprimanded and ordered to sort myself out immediately!

Although I was still incredulous about what had happened, Lieutenant Colonel Andrews' pep talk did the trick. I totally got a grip of myself and determined that from that moment forward I would be an exemplary officer. I would act impeccably and do everything by the book. If I was going to be made to leave, I would do so in a way that would make them admit their ridiculous rules were causing them to lose a bloody good QA!

I was true to my word and worked harder than ever. I continued to carry out all my usual nursing and sports officer duties and was still allowed to be night superintendent. Part of this role was to give a handover verbal report to whichever senior officer was acting as duty matron when they came on shift in the morning. Most duty matrons were fine, very relaxed, but just one always struck terror into everyone's hearts. She was Major Eleanor Henderson, then in post as the in-service training officer (ISTO).

I knew her from CMH Aldershot, where she had been the sister in charge of the ward on which I qualified as a staff nurse. She had a fearsome reputation for being a vicious old cow, known for taking great delight in trying to reduce at least one person per day to tears – patient or staff, she was egalitarian in her cruelty! But she had always been fine with me when I was in the ranks. I think that was because on the first occasion that her voice boomed along the ward at me, only a day or two after I'd first started there, I hadn't shown any nervousness. Our first exchange went along these lines:

Major H: 'Nurse! What on earth is THAT doing there?!' ('That' was a holdall belonging to a patient, which was sticking out from beside his locker.)

Me: 'I think it's Corporal Brown's holdall, ma'am. Shall I put it in his locker?' I was standing tall, looking straight at her heavily made up eyes; her vicious thin lips a too dark shade of red that we ORs would never have been allowed to wear whilst in uniform.

Major H (clearly surprised that I hadn't replied in a tremulous, nervous voice): 'Yes. And make sure everywhere else is tidy, it's matron's round later today!'

Me (outwardly smiling happily): 'Yes Ma'am!'

Thereafter she was no trouble to me at all. In fact, she would certainly back her staff if she felt that other wards or departments weren't behaving appropriately. If there had been a bit of an issue with, let's say, Theatres, she would be straight on the telephone to them, ripping their poor ears off!

And yet she had been utterly awful to me from the minute I arrived at Hannover. It was a complete mystery to me as to what had changed since I left the ranks to become an officer. Nothing was ever good enough for her and she was always trying to nit-pick about ridiculous things. More than once she would stop me in the corridor, make a great issue about 'inspecting' my uniform, which was always immaculate, then order me to get my tippet adjusted as it wasn't sitting right on my shoulders, or insist that it should be sent to the tailors for alterations that were not necessary. The only thing that kept me from becoming wholly paranoid was the fact that I knew it wasn't only me being bullied in this way. I took it upon myself to always 'beat' her at her own game, readying myself with well-rehearsed retorts for whatever ridiculous 'issue' she would throw at me. I would virtually memorise the entire histories of every patient and their families, ready for the inevitable, tedious grilling that happened whenever she was duty matron and I was night super. It became a bit of a battle of wills, that for the most part I felt I was winning, but it was inordinately irksome and frustrating.

Oddly enough, her attitude towards me seemed to soften once the investigation was underway. She eased off slightly, but I find it hard to imagine she felt sorry for me. I was grateful though, as her nastiness was one more thing I could well have done without at that time.

As Major Henderson was our ISTO, the request I had been intending to make for some time to be put forward to do midwifery training would have to be approved by her. So I went to see her. Needless to say, she declined to put me forward, but she did say that it was because I needed to gain more experience in my comparatively 'new' role of junior officer and that I should wait for another year or two. She was almost showing me some kindness, not saying it in her usual, acid-tongued fashion.

Had things turned out differently, I knew what trajectory I wanted my QA life to take. There was already a waiting list of 12–18 months to start the course, then 18 months doing the course, followed by a 'pay back' of three years (twice the length of the course that they had funded). I worked out that by then I would be around seven years into the maximum eight years of my Short Service Commission. Once that time is reached, one either leaves or applies for a Regular Commission.

I had already made up my mind that nursing in the Army was the career for me. It was a way of life that suited me very well. I knew that once I'd got a Regular Commission my job would be secure until retirement at the age of 55 (October 2015), by which time I would certainly have attained the rank of major, maybe even lieutenant colonel, who knows? Either way, it felt like that would give me plenty of time to get out and have fun, especially given the huge pension and tax-free gratuity that would be the reward for 33 years serving Queen and country. But of course, now this dream was over – utterly destroyed.

As the investigation lumbered slowly on, I began to feel calmer. My tactic of working as hard as possible and doing everything by the book was really helping – I began to sleep better and decided that, as I knew what had *really* happened, I had absolutely nothing of which to be ashamed. I knew that many of my friends and colleagues found the rules as completely nonsensical as I did, so I was going to walk tall. I can't deny that the first time I went into the downstairs mess lounge for afternoon tea at 4pm I was shaking inside, convinced that I would be shunned. How wrong was I?! It was very telling that I always found people either joining me or waving me over to sit with them as we tucked into the freshly baked pastries, home-made dainty sandwiches and sipped tea from bone china services. Often, I would see Mel at the opposite corner of the lounge, looking increasingly pale and drawn, with bags and dark circles beneath her eyes, and she had definitely lost weight. It simply served to further strengthen my resolve. It looked as if she was the one under investigation!

I soon understood why Mel was particularly stressed. Her version of events was unravelling – and so it seemed to me was she, sadly. As I was walking back to the mess from my second, much shorter (only nine hours this time) interrogation – the first having been an epic 15 hours – she walked past me on her way to a second grilling by Mr Lentman, accompanied by Deputy Matron. Both looked very solemn and I felt a tiny twinge of sadness at what had happened. I had always liked her and had relished the thought of her being a friend.

Due to the odd way in which the second lot of questioning had gone, with the focus shifting away from my supposed assaults, I already had a good inkling that she too was being called in for a second grilling by Warrant Officer Lentman. He was beginning to realise that the case wasn't quite as cut and dried as he had probably first imagined. I had been asked at great length not only about my past membership of a lesbian postal dating agency, but he'd also started trying to get me to incriminate other potential lesbian servicewomen and officers. I began to get a bit more savvy and resistant – admittedly a bit too late, alas. I was shocked and angry that my case was clearly going to be used as a springboard to seek out other undesirable women with unnatural proclivities. The lengths to which these people were prepared to go, in order to rid the forces of perfectly excellent personnel, was a revelation of the most distasteful kind.

It seemed that Mel wasn't the only one regretting things around this time. One night, Major Pam Harrold came and knocked at my door. It was a few weeks into the investigation, so I had by then begun to figure out certain pieces of the puzzle. None of my facial muscles moved as I looked right into her eyes. She looked very uncomfortable but tried to smile and said, 'I just wanted to see how you are, Elaine.'

I was standing tall and motionless in the doorway. I'd have given one of those statue street entertainers at Covent Garden a good run for their money. She had thought I – as a junior officer – would move to one side and allow her through, so when I hadn't followed the unspoken rules of politesse, she was visibly squirming. My implacable, intense staring into her eyes was proving incredibly unnerving to her. She was unusually lost for words and kept dropping her gaze to the floor. My heart was thudding like a bloody jackhammer in my chest, but I remained completely unmoving and unmoved – Botox would have rendered my stony face more expressive.

She started nervously, 'I've been worried about you... we all have...'

Although it was barely discernible, I know she heard the sarcastic snort of breath through my now flaring nostrils. I continued with my immutable stare, unable and unwilling to disguise the utter contempt I felt for her. My upper lip began to snarl in a passable tribute to Elvis.

'I mean, well, er, is there anything I can do for you, Elaine?' Her

soft voice was hardly audible. Outwardly, I continued the face off;
inwardly I was screaming, 'Anything *you* can do for *me*? I think
you've already fucking well done it!' The reply she heard, delivered
in the calmest, most firmly polite monotone I could muster, was 'No
thank you, I'm fine.'

She mumbled an embarrassed, 'Well, if you're sure – you know
where to find me,' before finally taking the hint, then her leave.

After closing my door very carefully, I waited for a moment then
looked for something, anything – yes, that'll do: a large, not quite
empty coffee mug was grabbed from my dressing table and hurtled
with such fury at the sink in the corner of the room, some feet away,
that the force smashed a huge hole in it. The cold coffee dribbled
down the wall, an organic imitation of Pollock.

Nain's Candlewick Saves the Day!

One of the most surreal and laughable aspects of the whole investigation also happened to signal an important turning point for me. Not long after I saw Mel and Lieutenant Colonel Andrews on their way to the hospital, I had been asked to see Lentman again. Half expecting to be berated for disobeying orders – perhaps he'd got wind of the fact that I'd talked to the staff on Families Ward – I went in ready to blow. I was by now heartily sick of the length of time it was taking and simply wanted to leave. I was also having to try to deal with the increasing horror of realising that others, completely uninvolved, were now implicated due to my letters and diaries having been taken.

I had told Lentman I'd snuck back to my room the morning after sleeping with Mel – and had been seen by another officer. But I was taken aback when he asked if I was still in possession of my usual dressing gown. I asked if he meant the long blue candlewick number that my grandmother had given me? He said 'Yes, if that's the one you would usually wear.' He then wanted me to try to give him as detailed a description as he possibly could of the one that Mel had lent me after our night together.

I found myself describing it as best I could, wondering exactly why he wanted to know. Once he had again laboriously written... down... the... details... pale... green... nylon-y... sort of... Japanese-y... looking... design... belted... knee-length, he took us to the large MFO (Military Forces Overseas) packing boxes outside Mel's room. She had already packed most of her things as she was shortly due to be posted out to a long-awaited course. She wasn't around, so it felt very intrusive to watch as he prised open the lids and began searching. It didn't take him very long to find something fitting the description.

'Is this it?' he asked, holding it aloft for me to take a closer look.

'Yes, it is.'

'Good – can I please have your dressing gown now, ma'am?'

I was bewildered as to the significance, and slightly amused if truth be told, but I duly took him around the corner to my room, took Nain's Christmas present to me off the hook on the back of my door and handed it over. He wrote some numbers on a label and 'bagged and tagged' my old-fashioned but very warm and snuggly 'exhibit'.

I can only surmise as to Captain Diggory's thoughts, on 26 August 1987, when she was asked to answer Mr Lentman's questions. Did she recall seeing Lieutenant Chambers on the morning of Saturday 13 June 1987? Could she recall what she was wearing? Describe it? Did she know what Lieutenant Chambers' usual dressing gown looks like? Describe it? You get the picture, I'm sure. Incredibly luckily for me, her statement says this:

I do not consider her a friend, more of an acquaintance. I see her daily, usually, and in the preceding months, by observation, believe her to own a light blue dressing gown of thick material. It may even have a pile to it. On reflection, I cannot be absolutely certain of its colour, but I am positive that it is of thick material, of wrap-around design and ankle length.

I have been asked by WO2 Lentman, RMP (SIB), whether I can recall ever seeing Lt. Chambers in any other dressing gown, and specifically a light green one which he has shown me today, attached to which is an exhibit label endorsed MKM/15.

I have signed and dated that label.

In answer, I should like to state the following: I believe I do recall seeing Lt. Chambers on a single occasion in a dressing gown other than the one I normally associate her with. I cannot specify what time of day or what day or month this would have been. The only registering fact is that on the occasion I saw her, she wore a 'different' dressing gown. It may even have been that exhibited as MKM/15. Certainly, the one she wore was of thin material on that single occasion.

WO2 Lentman has explained to me that I am alleged to have

encountered Lt. Chambers in the corridor outside her room in the Mess on the morning of Sat 13 Jun 87, clutching her clothing and wearing the garment exhibited as MKM/15.

I can offer no comment on whether or not that is so, but once again cannot deny the possibility of it.

The fact that she was clutching her clothing would have little impression upon me as I would automatically associate that with a recent visit on the part of Lt. Chambers to the nearby drying room to collect laundered clothing, a common enough sight in all states of dress.

And the following day Captain Diggory was interviewed again and shown my dressing gown. She said:

Further to my statement of even [sic] reference dated 26 Aug 87, I have today been shown a light blue dressing gown by WO2 Lentman, RMP (SIB), attached to which is an exhibit label endorsed CMC/1.

I have signed and dated that label.

That garment is the item I referred to, and with which I associate Lt. Chambers' normal dressing gown, in my statement of yesterday. I recognise it as such.

As a result of this marvellous piece of sleuthing to rival that of Miss Marple herself, events were to take a sudden turn in my favour.

Because I'd been so graphically descriptive about our lovemaking – along with details of losing my contact lens, the borrowed dressing gown – Lentman had known that her story made no sense. Mel had initially told him that I had come to her room one evening, very upset about something and a bit drunk. We were sitting side by side on her bed, both fully dressed. As she tried to comfort and calm me by putting an arm around my shoulder, I had apparently 'lunged' at her, grabbing a breast! She had pushed me off, told me off and sent me off to my room, tail between my legs. She also made much of the fact that we were *not* friends and that I apparently had a very intimidating way of staring intently into people's eyes when talking to them. What can I do? It's a Scorpio trait! Seriously – I look into people's eyes because I am genuinely interested in what they're saying. Is that a sin?

I was quite mortified to later learn that he had read my statement to her, with Deputy Matron listening in! As her version of events was so completely different, he had pursued the dressing gown line as it proved I had stayed the night, rather than having popped round, made my assault, then been sent away in shame!

Captain Diggory's awareness of my usual attire, along with the discovery of the two bits of nightwear was beginning to reveal the fabrication. Mel must have mulled it over for a number of days, but was looking increasingly pale, pasty and drawn... When she did the honourable thing she saved my bacon, but also cooked her own goose, because it cost her very dear.

I will never know what happened to make Mel decide to come clean a couple of weeks later, on 9 September 1987, but thank God she did! I only got to read what she had eventually admitted to Lentman some ten years after the event. She had also made a heavily amended confessional statement, which was in the file I received after requesting copies of all paperwork connected with my case. Some of what she said broke my heart when I finally read it all those years later. The tragedy and waste hit home once again, stronger than ever. For the sake of one night, that no one else had even known about, she lost her career. It was devastating to read, amongst many pages:

> I kept thinking back on my incident with Lt. Chambers, and almost convinced myself that something very bad had been pushed on me.
>
> In my haste, and in trying to protect myself, in case anyone thought I was a lesbian, the facts from my previous statement were given. These being untrue. I never said to Maj Harrold at this point that Elaine Chambers had assaulted me.
>
> Following this statement, I wish to put into writing that I never realised [what] the outcome of my lies would be. I now realise to the full and deeply regret what I have done.
>
> I do not believe the label of 'lesbian' should be given to Lt. Chambers. I feel this officer has had mixed preferences for some years which has never, to my knowledge, affected her work. I believe from what many people have said and what I myself have seen of Lt. Chambers in the Army environment, that she is a very good Army officer. I understand the Army reasons for such rules on sexuality but also realise in situations as this, they risk losing very good people.

Despite her remorse, she was deemed to have acted in a manner unbecoming of an officer, by lying to protect herself and thus condemning me. She was reported for 'alleged unnatural conduct' and 'alleged attempting to pervert the course of justice'.

I only discovered this and much more when my data protection request, ten years after I was discharged, led to a delivery of a massive file of records not only of my statements, but those of everyone else who had been caught up in the investigation and its far-reaching fallout. I was staggered to receive this information and to discover some of the hateful things that had been said and written about me. Yet, amongst the pain of reliving such awful times, there were beautiful nuggets of love, support and protection too. It was certainly an eye-opening, yet ultimately heartbreaking, testament to the humanity we share, despite our differences and travails.

Although I was terribly sad about what had happened to her, Mel's action in coming clean really was vitally important to me, saving me from a much more damning and potentially life-threatening outcome. I truly believe there would have been a distinct possibility of my committing suicide if I had faced trial and been found guilty of such a disgusting offence.

Caught Up in the Web

Although Mel's admission was of course incredibly useful to me, it transpired that the SIB was prepared to invest even more of its resources in the investigation, resulting in another couple of scalps. Because a number of letters and cards had been taken following their search of my room, this had in turn meant other investigations were initiated elsewhere.

When I came to Hannover, I had got along really well with a nurse I'd worked with there. Claudia was a lovely person, an absolutely excellent nurse and an all-round good egg. She had a cracking sense of humour and we just naturally clicked. We were quite drawn to one another – I believe by what would now be termed a mutual 'gaydar'! I was as sure as I could be that she was gay and there was most definitely an element of subliminal flirting going on between the two of us.

After a few months at Hannover, despite the fact that socialising (other than at official 'cross rank' functions) between officers and other ranks was not allowed, we arranged to meet up on the edge of town one evening. We went to a bar for a few beers and, having clearly recognised one another as being 'of the faith' we began to tentatively open up. Although I knew what we were doing was not permitted, this transgression wasn't done in a thrill-seeking, rebellious way. I think even then, I genuinely couldn't understand the preoccupation with such a hierarchical structure in terms of rank. It was quite anathema to us – we were taught, as nurses, to think independently and to make conscious, considered, deliberate efforts to care for every patient in a holistic manner. To see each person as an individual and to try to anticipate and consider their needs. Yet, once I had made the transition from private (the lowest rank in the QAs) to lieutenant, I could no longer socialise with close friends who were still in the ranks. I understood and recognised the need for order and structure whilst at work, but I found it hard to see the logic in my being allowed to go out with fellow officers, many of whom, being NHS-trained nurses, were from the same backgrounds in terms of class and social mobility as any of my closest friends in the ranks. Yet a meal in a restaurant with Nessa, for example – one of my closest friends from nurse training – had to be treated like a clandestine sortie. It made no sense to me.

I think for both Claudia and me it was an enormous relief to feel a sense of mutual trust. Ultimately, trying to discover or accept your true authentic self in an environment that condemned that same self was so incredibly stressful. It was just crazy to think that an Army that made people leave if they got pregnant was also ejecting the very type of women who were most likely to be able to commit long term to Forces life. Lesbians were not going to be getting married (this was the 1980s, don't forget), nor to be dropping sprogs every 18 months or so! We were perfectly suited to long term careers in HM Forces.

Claudia was soon to be posted to Hong Kong and, after another surreptitious evening at the bar we did a bold, nay, reckless thing. There was a bit of a bash going on in the sergeants' mess and we went along with me as her guest. As was very much the norm for everyone in those days, mucho vino de collapso was quaffed and I was, as we used to say, absolutely minging, to the point of doing a pseudo strip tease routine (which was apparently caught on someone's cine camera!). I didn't actually remove any clothing, but was showing off like crazy, loving the laughs, wolf whistles and applause. I *so* should have joined an am-dram group – what an exhibitionist!

As dawn approached, we ended up in a clinch in the toilets. Nothing else happened then but a very few days before she left, she sneaked with me to my room in the mess. Again, nothing more than a bit of kissing and cuddling occurred, mainly due to two things. Firstly, I really *liked* her, but I didn't actually fancy her. Secondly, she was way too nervous about being caught, so decided to go back to her room. This had happened more than four months before the fateful night in Mel's room.

A few weeks into my own investigation, Claudia sent me a letter from Hong Kong, even though she knew she wasn't meant to communicate with me. When the SIB had searched her room, they uncovered cards, letters and correspondence between her and an ex-partner, Alma. I had only served for nearly six years – Claudia had nearly 20 years' exemplary service under her belt and Alma, a WO2 at another German base with the highest level of security clearance, had completed even longer than that. Now, because they had been inadvertently caught up in my investigation, both Alma and Claudia were being investigated themselves and would subsequently be forced to leave the Army.

I felt ashamed that my having kept correspondence and diaries was now going to cost others their livelihoods. Claudia's letter to me nearly broke my heart – she was so incredibly kind and didn't even seem to blame me for what had happened.

Amazingly, a few weeks into the investigation, Alma rang me in the mess. Like Claudia, she did not remonstrate with me for having caused such chaos and havoc. I was incredibly humbled by their kindness and the fact that, as much as anything, they were expressing concern as to how *I* was coping! Their incredible selflessness, sensitivity, compassion and concern for others was astounding to me. I was utterly blown away by such dignity in the face of unbelievable stress and humiliation. And none of it through their own doing. They were exhibiting exactly the qualities that the Forces hope for! The degree of guilt and shame I felt at having cost these courageous women their careers, simply by keeping letters and cards that had been sent to me, was utterly overwhelming and unbearable. It was like the ripple in a fetid pond, the poison swilling out to Special Investigation Branch policemen and women at military units around the world. Their assiduous tenacity and determined intent to weed out any and all personnel exhibiting even the tiniest hint of homosexual tendencies was impressive and consistent.

Claudia and Alma had around 40 years of exemplary service

between them. Both with unblemished records; both very well respected and admired. The madness of losing their skill, experience, knowledge and dedication makes no sense whatsoever. It took me many years to begin to deal with it and to finally stop blaming myself.

The outcome of the investigation for Claudia and Alma was particularly outrageous compared to the more lenient treatment of my by now married former lover Sadie. Despite Sadie's 'Result of Proceedings' paperwork being annotated with the EXACT same 'offence' for which Claudia Appleby and Alma Loftus were made to leave, Sadie was only punished with a written warning and allowed to stay in the service. Sadie's bisexuality meant she was deemed as being just as 'guilty' of a criminal, dismissable offence as the rest of us. Yet I believe, by virtue of having got married, the supposedly unbreakable rules were apparently ignored in her case!

Sadie had made it very clear to me when we had last spoken on the telephone that she wanted absolutely nothing further to do with me. As I had mistakenly believed she would also have been forced to leave, due to having admitted to homosexual liaisons with me, I carried that misplaced burden of guilt for far too many years. If only I knew sooner that she had been allowed to stay.

Only one other friend abandoned me. We'd met when both student nurses. Nothing had ever happened between us, but I did have quite a crush on her. I'm pretty certain that she was aware of this, even though I never told her. In amongst my bagged evidence were some rather lame attempts at poetry, written to 'Marcella' but never sent. Lentman tried very hard to push me to tell him who 'Marcella' was, but I steadfastly refused. I was now going my own way, regardless of being told to tell them everything, as per my legal advice. I do not know if he ever worked out who she was and had her questioned. There were no records of anything amongst the paperwork I eventually received, but she would not talk to me when I tried once or twice to ring her, and she never replied to the letter I sent to her family home.

The lengths to which the SIB was prepared to go to weed out possible lesbians and gays can be no better illustrated than by one last story.

My friend Debra had left the QAs and was living in the south of England with her then girlfriend, Sam. They had met in Rinteln and I got to know Sam when they were both posted back to Aldershot. This was in 1985, as I approached the end of my training and qualified as a staff nurse. I really appreciated having friends I truly trusted and in whom I could confide. They had been very supportive of me and, because they were happy together, were hoping that I might one day find someone too. They once took me out to a gay pub in Guildford, the Greyhound. It was well known as a favourite haunt for lesbians in the WRAC. I was *so* nervous about going – not because I was afraid we'd get raided and caught, more because of my preconceptions about what a lesbian might look like or how one might behave. I'm cringing as I type that, but it is, I'm ashamed to say, true.

I imagine that any younger LGBT reader might be shocked at what I'm saying. But my only impressions of lesbians as I hit my teenage years, in the early 1970s, were very negative and clichéd. Films such as the infamous *Killing of Sister George* reinforced the butch/femme image that of course helped perpetuate much of straight society's feeling that in a lesbian couple, one *must* be acting as the man! So I was as guilty as the next person of imagining gay people in the most extremely hackneyed terms ever – either very masculine women, or effeminate men, with little room for the reality of a vast spectrum of exciting diversity!

Sam drove us to the Greyhound. Being a bit older than us, she had the luxury of owning a car. I sat in the back, wittering in a very deranged and excitable manner until we finally arrived. The place itself was a bit of a dive but absolutely packed to the gunwales with dykes of every shape, size and sensibility. I was quite astonished and a bit intimidated. Yes, the majority of women there certainly fitted the stereotypical image of lesbians at that time, but there were a fair number of more girly, feminine types too – quite a revelation, and enthralling. There was one very attractive young woman there and Sam knew her! We were introduced. She was a civilian called Roxie, shorter than me, very slim and androgynous, with short black hair and a lovely aquiline profile. I couldn't believe my luck later in the evening, when she asked me to dance as a slowie came on – Bryan Ferry's appropriately titled 'Slave to Love'. I was so nervous, taking my lead from her as to which rhythmic beat to follow as we swayed our hips from side to side and began to turn in our slow circle. This was the first time in my life that I'd ever danced like this with a woman. I felt overwhelmed. It was wonderful as she wrapped her arms around me and held me close.

As the evening wore on, I became aware of a very solid, über-butch woman giving me the evil eye. It was very unnerving and I couldn't figure out what her problem was. When we decided to leave it had begun to rain. Roxie had been kissing lots of people on the cheek as she left; she seemed to know everyone. Debra and Sam ran to the car and, as Roxie caught up with me, I heard myself blurting out, 'Do I get a goodnight kiss then?'

'Yeah, course you do!' and she leaned in for what I thought would be the same as everyone else's, a hug and a peck on the cheek. What a very welcome surprise! A lovely 'Frenchie', then a cheeky grin and a wink as she turned and ran to her car, waving her hand. I was enraptured, but nothing came of it. I heard from Sam just a few days later that Roxie and Storm, the glowering butch, were now an item.

When I'd been languishing in Welbeck, in February 1986, Debra had written me a very long, funny, gossipy letter. It was a great fillip and really tickled me. One of the more interesting snippets concerned something that she'd heard about from another lesbian friend of ours, Jacquie, who was at Queen Elizabeth Military Hospital, Woolwich, for the second 18 months of her training.

What she'd told Debra and Sam was that, due to there apparently being a bit of an 'outbreak' of lesbianism there, an officer had undertaken an informal enquiry. It was felt that some of the women were just trying it for a bit of a laugh, almost getting onto a faddy gay bandwagon, but some QAs had apparently taken to wearing small badges under the collars of their ward dresses. A bit like a sort of secret code or signal. If they felt they were being a bit outnumbered by the real and pseudo lezzers, they'd lift the collar to a fellow 'hettie'. They had the letters SQAS on them, indicating membership of the 'Straight QA Society'. Unbelievable!

My having kept this one letter led to the SIB turning up at Debra's *civilian* home on 1 October 1987 and asking to question her. They had the jurisdiction to do so because she had left the service less than six months before (by only a matter of weeks).

I was beyond shocked when I found out about it. They were initially very interested in trying to ask all about the assertions about the 'investigating officer' at QEMH Woolwich! It transpires that the poor woman was questioned by the SIB because of Debra's letter, but denied any impropriety – 'I would like to add that I am not a lesbian, have no lesbian tendencies and that the allegation made against me in the letter exhibit MKM/7 is unfounded'. This statement is dated 3 December 1987, nearly four months after my investigation began. I was at home by the time this was happening. What an incredible waste of time and resources. And all because of a letter that had been written nearly two years earlier! Does anyone reading this still believe the McCarthyist witch hunt analogy to be inappropriate or overblown? Of course, Debra refused to let them come in, so they never got the chance to grill her. I'm pleased to say they didn't pursue it further. I'm still slack-jawed with incredulity at their dogged determination.

Λ

Further Questioning

During the first round of questioning, on 24 August 1987, I had been completely compliant, as advised by my appointed legal counsel. But the second round, focusing almost wholly upon old correspondence, left me feeling furious. In particular, Lentman was interested in four letters that had been forwarded to me by a contact/dating agency called the Golden Wheel. How incredibly ironic that, rather than the episodes of 'flaunting' my depravity at public venues such as the Greyhound pub in Guildford, my discreet attempts at exploring and understanding my sexuality were of *such* great interest to my interrogator.

Apart from the fact that the letters were completely innocent, sometimes charming, sometimes quite prosaic and boring introductions from other members, they had no relevance whatsoever to the case in hand. I told Lentman the very dull and rather sad, in my view, story of the only woman I actually met in person as a result of my brief time as a member. I had replied to a letter from the woman politely, but she had not taken the hint and turned up in Aldershot one afternoon on an unsolicited visit. She must have been quite a determined character to have found out the telephone number of the QA billets, because somehow or other she got through to Alexandra House and I was shocked to be called to the phone.

I reluctantly agreed to meet her at the station, then walk to some parkland. We sat on a bench and I very carefully and as sensitively as I could, given the difficult circumstances, made it very clear that

I was not attracted to her, did not want a relationship with her and wasn't too happy at her just pitching up unannounced like that. She eventually appeared to have understood and accepted why I had been pretty miffed and took her leave. It scared the bejesus out of me, as I had realised how dangerous it could have been for me if she had managed to find her way to the billets. I felt really sorry for her though, because I completely understood her desperate need to meet other women and to find someone special with whom to share her life.

Shortly after this episode, I had written to the Golden Wheel to cancel my membership. Lentman even commented upon the fact that I'd kept a copy of the cancellation letter, thanking them for their 'indispensable' services. I explained to him that I had been brought up properly, taught to write 'thank you' letters after Christmas and birthdays, so I was simply doing what came naturally to me, being polite.

Interestingly enough, many years after this occurred, I was shocked to discover the first of a number of what I thought seemed like discrepancies in the records. I'd always recalled the initial interrogation as running to a mind-boggling 15 hours. This second round of questioning seemed more reasonable, at just nine hours. Although I did initial each page of the statement copy to indicate it was a 'true' record of what had been said, I was in fact utterly past the point of caring by that time and simply wanted it to be over. Maybe it just felt that long, but the times recorded didn't match my later recollection.

One of the statement copies I eventually received shows Lentman recording this at the end of that second interrogation:

> I said, 'You are now given the opportunity to read over the Record of Interview. As you do so, would you sign the bottom of each page, indicating that you have read it, agreed with the contents and make a written note against anything you consider to be inaccurate. You are also invited to place your initials against each question and answer. Do you wish to read the Record of Interview?'

> She replied, 'No.'

I said, 'Pardon?'

She replied, 'No.'

Between 1257 hrs and 1329 hrs I therefore read over my Record of Interview to Lt. Chambers after which I asked her, 'Do you agree that I have read you an accurate account of this morning's interview?'

She replied, 'Yes.'

The interview terminated that same day. At my request, Cpl Wells [a new side kick] then read over the Record of Interview appending the last page thereof with her signature.

I attached an exhibit label to that Record endorsed KM/3 which I have signed and dated.

That exhibit I now produce.

K LENTMAN
WO2
RMP (SIB)

I've included this snippet to illustrate the ludicrous, outmoded and frankly unbearable manner in which the whole process was undertaken. Try to imagine 32 minutes listening to him reading back to me what I'd just bloody well told him – and what he'd then spent bloody *hours* laboriously writing down. As he did so, the urge to say at the end, 'No, I don't agree' and force him to start writing again was an overwhelming temptation, but I was honestly beginning to lose the will to live. Staying calm and polite in the face of such painstakingly slow bureaucracy was driving me crazy; the urge to let out a primal scream, then a stream of choice expletives that would have made a sailor blush was becoming increasingly overwhelming. I genuinely just wanted it to end before implosion or worse, finding myself facing an actual charge, that of grievous bodily harm!

Throughout every interview, I had fully complied with what I increasingly felt was not especially helpful advice. I was cooperative and gave very detailed accounts of what had happened between myself and the two purported victims. I had realised almost immediately that I was fighting to save my reputation, but perhaps more importantly, I was at risk of losing my livelihood. No one in their right mind would employ a nurse who couldn't control her filthy urges! That was the risk – if the allegations became what were believed to be substantiated charges, I could have found myself in a court martial situation. With two accusers, the odds were stacked against me. I have never been so terrified in my life. There was so much at stake.

Of course, when I was first questioned, I wasn't privy to what Mel and Mags had said. I only knew that I had been reported for 'alleged indecent assault on a female over 16 years' and 'alleged unnatural conduct', but exactly what form these alleged incidents were supposed to have taken was unknown to me. And I couldn't even begin to fathom why, if they were so certain they had been assaulted or attacked, they had waited 10 weeks and 16 days, respectively, after their devastating experiences, to report that there was a rampant lesbian sex maniac on the loose in the mess. None of it made any sense at all, especially as we'd all been attending numerous mess events together and often having drinks in each other's rooms pre and post various social occasions. I was utterly mystified, confused and, frankly, very hurt. I was facing incredible accusations and about to lose absolutely everything I'd worked so hard to gain. I couldn't begin to imagine why these people, whom I'd begun to think of as friends until those fateful evenings, could clearly hate me enough to destroy me.

It would take more than 10 years before I was able to begin to unravel the complex web that had trapped them into turning against me. In fact, even after I'd read through all the statements, still I would learn new things years down the line, mainly through reconnecting with former colleagues through Facebook. People would privately message me about their own recollections of that time. The impact had been massive – not only for those of us directly involved by being questioned, but also our friends, partners, work colleagues and other mess members.

Friends and acquaintances could see Mel slowly cracking up under the strain, yet felt scared to get too involved. The fear of being tainted by association was an insidiously evil result of living in such close proximity to one another, yet being expected to conform to rigid hierarchical, class and social strata. Almost a parody of the stiff upper lip maxim. We were nurses, doctors, care assistants, midwives; our whole ethos was primarily focused upon caring for people. The patients in our care – service men and women, their families, civilians – all were to be given the very best care that only military hospitals could provide. Yet, despite that renowned camaraderie and preparedness to die for our comrades, when it came to the crunch, there was neither care nor consideration afforded to me by the Army. My unnaturalness excluded me.

The irony was that, had there never been a ban in place, none of the pain and suffering need ever have happened. For the root cause of my ordeal stemmed from one woman's desire to try to hide or cover up her own homosexual proclivity. It has to be remembered that *any* sexual activity, even in the privacy of one's own room would be frowned upon. And yet if a heterosexual officer had been accused of assault such as this and had, as was my situation, eventually established their innocence and that any sexual activity had been mutually consensual, they would *not* have lost their career. They would have been severely chastised and possibly given a formal written warning, but nothing more.

I recalled the many occasions on Monday mornings back in Aldershot when there would be a fairly lengthy queue of QAs outside the personnel officer's office, awaiting their punishment for having been caught with a man in their room during a spot check of the billets at the weekend. These could be married men, senior officers, cross-rank affairs, one-night stands, regular boyfriends (often becoming husbands at a later date) – but the worst punishment would be accepted then forgotten.

If a woman had been found in another woman's room? Questioning, witch hunts, expulsion.

And gay men often had it much worse. They were sometimes forced into humiliating physical examinations, including checking anal reflexes, with MOs having to follow standing orders giving instruction as to what 'signs' to look out for to help spot any possible homosexuals. These included notes about possible indications of make-up being worn! Many would be jailed when the investigation began or put under either mess or house arrest and instructed to be incommunicado.

The hypocrisy of Army morals really was breathtaking. There were all manner of transgressions occurring on a regular basis, many of which I would argue were considerably worse than my own. Just to give a few examples, I could mention the illegal drinking dens in the bowels of the hospital cellars, with 'skimmed off' supplies of alcohol and food being provided at *very* subsidised rates – only invited, favoured 'members' allowed!

Or how about the male nurse who was known as a serial sexual harasser of young, female student nurses? The only consequence was that his wife eventually divorced him.

Or how about the numerous extramarital affairs causing difficult break-ups, affecting morale and causing stress and tensions galore? In one especially galling case a woman, working for the Red Cross, single (therefore theoretically free to sleep with whomever she should choose) was sent away from Hannover in a 'punishment posting' because she was the mistress of a very high-ranking male officer, married with children.

Then there were some alcohol-dependent people serving, often being posted back to the QEMH 'P' Wing to dry out, on full pay. Sadly, many would return to the booze time and again, occasionally becoming a liability to their colleagues when on duty.

And that's not to mention the underhand wheeler-dealing going on in the mess. Allegedly some favoured mess members were able to buy sides of meat and various food and drinks at cut price 'mates' rates' for cash. These completely illegal transactions did not show up on their mess bills (which were paid at source from one's monthly salary).

I could go on but won't. I know that the equivalent sort of things go on throughout the corporate and business worlds. The point I am trying to make is that, although I was far from perfect, when I was in uniform, at work, I was always 100 per cent committed to being the best that I could be. I was a team player who had been trained to the highest standards in the world. I was so incredibly proud to wear my QA uniform and to be able to serve Queen and country. My patients were cared for in a wholly professional manner.

The other most important thing was the fact that, as in civilian society, the vast majority of people with whom we lived and worked really couldn't give a monkey's about another person's sexual orientation. Sure, some would joke about it, there's always talk about 'banter' even to this day. The men especially would usually say things like, 'Well, as long as they don't try it on with me.' Some would be cruder – 'Backs against the wall, lads!' when showering after sports – but as a general rule, most people really were not bothered.

The WRAC was full of very obviously gay women but they were not routinely investigated. Why? Probably because the powers that be would have known that the services would have been totally decimated overnight had they made the effort to find out officially. There was also the fact that the longer-serving, wilier dykes knew not to have any 'evidence' of any sort. Even if it was a widely known, 'open' secret, as long as nothing occurred for which the SIB could be called, the status quo remained unchanged, with no detrimental effect upon the running of military units.

I have to admit that the very fact that the archaic rules existed did sometimes serve to excite me – I liked the danger and risk of being caught. It might cause some people to think: this was a reckless young woman who deserved to be thrown out; look at how irresponsible and foolhardy she was. But it must be remembered that the events recounted here amount to a handful of episodes during a period of just under six years of Army service. They all took place during off-duty time and were, as was eventually established, mutually consensual and either behind closed doors or unwitnessed.

Unfortunately, my case had been thrust into the spotlight, and there was now no avoiding the scrutiny.

As the investigation expanded all round the globe, I knew my fate was sealed. Although Lentman had shocked and terrified me when he'd told me he hadn't believed my version of events, he had then utterly confused me by not charging me. Throughout the whole process, I had never been suspended. I had been expected to carry on fulfilling my work duties to my usual high standards. Exactly as one would expect an Army-trained nurse to do. None of it was making any sense to me.

I was advised in a written notification from Colonel Warrington, Hannover's commanding officer, that my punishment was to be to resign my commission. I would not be facing the possibility of court martial, which was, of course, a huge relief, but I was not being allowed to get on with my life. It was totally farcical and frankly outrageous. I was being made to give up my commission because my genetic makeup, my very *existence* was deemed to be wholly incompatible with military life. Yet here I was, expected to continue working in the role I was apparently no longer fit to undertake – I was never suspended during the investigation. It is the perfect illustration of how utterly pathetic and out of touch the powers that be had become.

Knowing my fate, yet expected to carry on working as if nothing had changed, it was impossible for me to apply for potential jobs because no one was able to tell me when my leaving date would be. I'd rather foolishly hoped that, decision made, I'd be allowed to go quickly. Lesbian tendencies having been treated as something akin to the most base and depraved perversion imaginable, you'd think they'd have been keen to get rid.

Although I was of course heartbroken at losing my chosen career, I just wanted to leave. It had dragged on and on, metamorphosing into a sickening witch hunt. The pressure of the all-consuming self-loathing and guilt I felt in respect of what had happened to Claudia and Alma, and what I'd erroneously believed would have happened to Sadie, was becoming way too much to bear.

When I'd learned that Lentman had apparently believed Mags' version of events, I was baffled. If this was true, and he really thought that I had molested her against her will, then why wasn't I charged? I can only surmise that it was because he knew it would be a classic case of 'her word against mine' and would never be provable either way. As time had passed and I'd gradually filled in the gaps, I came to the view that there were many strange anomalies and I couldn't

believe that it wasn't obvious to him that I was telling the whole truth
and nothing but. However, his conclusion was as follows:

> I have found elements of your account regarding the allegation of assault
> by [sic] Lieutenant Taft to be untrue on your part and must assume your
> fabrication of those parts of the evidence were designed to rebutt [sic]
> the allegation. Accordingly, I am reporting you for the indecent assault
> upon Lieutenant Taft. All of these matters are offences under the Service
> Disciplinary Acts and I believe prosecution of the same will succeed. A
> report will be submitted to your commanding officer and other relevant
> service authority. You do not have to say anything unless you wish to
> do so but what you say may be given in evidence.

Despite this report, I was not charged, but told I must resign my
commission, as per my CO's recommendation.

Eventually, nearly three months after it began, in November 1987,
I was told I was finally going to be allowed to leave BMH Hannover
and fly home to the UK.

My last few weeks in Germany were extremely tough. I felt more
and more angry and indignant at how I seemed to be viewed as a
degenerate pervert. Having been cast as 'accused of "unnatural acts"'
and behaviour, I sometimes felt like giving them what they expected.
A rebellious streak would sometimes emerge, making me behave in
deliberately provocative ways.

I had always liked slightly zany and quirky clothes, but had of
course followed, to the letter, archaic rules about how female officers
should dress. On a couple of occasions as the end of my time there
approached, I brazenly walked out of the mess wearing a fabulous
pair of heavy black 'peg' trousers with a blue stripe down the sides,
shiny black men's brogues, a white shirt and black leather tie, a
fantastic charity-shop-special oversized Pierre Cardin men's khaki
gabardine trench coat, my hair gelled up into quasi-punk/Morrissey
spikes, contact lenses in and eyes made up with a heavier-than-usual
line of Siouxsie and the Banshees kohl beneath the lower lid. I'd also
been playing records loudly in my room to get into a party mood

before going out – I was almost daring anyone to come and knock at my door to complain.

Once I had been told the date of my flight back to Blighty from RAF Gütersloh, I set about organising some farewell soirees. My campaign manager for my social calendar was my friend Sue Hunt, a lovely nurse I'd worked with on Families Ward, who, because she was a civilian, could freely socialise with me without Army constraints about mixing with officers. She played a big part in many of my best nights out.

By this stage, most of my friends and colleagues knew exactly what had been going on, because I'd told them the truth. I honestly believe, judging by the cards, notes, flowers, personal comments and large numbers who attended my two leaving do's, that they understood how I felt. Everybody kept saying what a crazy waste it was and how stupid the whole situation had been.

One very poignant evening out occurred when Sue and I went to see The Communards in concert. They had just released their *Red* album and we were hearing some songs for the very first time. It was an amazing show, with Sarah Jane Morris there accompanying them, but especially brilliant on 'Never Can Say Goodbye', which Sue had already adopted, along with 'Don't Leave Me This Way' as a farewell song. The most poignant song of the whole evening for me was T.M.T.L T.B.M.G – 'There's more to love than boy meets girl'. Ain't that the truth?!

In total, it was an incredible five very long months before I was allowed to leave the Army. I didn't leave Hannover until three months after things first came to light. They had intended to make me await my discharge date at the QATC in Aldershot, but in a rare moment of compassion, they sent me home on full pay until two months later. My commission was officially resigned on 18 January 1988.

Luckily my parents were very supportive – though Mum had taken her time to finally reply to the 21-page life history I wrote when I first told her what had happened! She wrote me a lovely, loving letter explaining that the tardy response was due to having been 'knocked for six' by what I'd told them. She had, after all, not only lost her mother very unexpectedly; she and Dad were also trying to deal with their alcoholic young son when her daughter then dropped such an incredible bombshell! My room would *always* be there for me and she and Dad would *always* be there for me too. I was so lucky to have that family support.

The only time I nearly cried in front of anyone in QA officialdom was in Aldershot. It was 13 January 1988. I'd had to go there to return items of kit and uniform, undergo a final medical and complete various paperwork connected with having been subject to the Official Secrets Act. In hindsight, I think they should have presented me with a specially created medal for outstanding acting – how the hell I passed the 'stability' (emotional) element of my discharge medical is beyond me! I was utterly frazzled, exhausted, stressed and anxious.

The commandant spoke briefly with me and was the only senior ranking QA officer to show me any kindness. Rather than chastising or condemning me, she expressed her regret that my career should end in this way, particularly in light of the fact that I had been trained in the QAs. Most QA officers were direct entrant NHS-trained nurses – the number of QA-trained nurses being commissioned from the ranks was much smaller. She then wished me well for the future. Her sincerity and clearly kind, compassionate face led to her being the only person in a position of authority to whom I offered a truly heartfelt apology for the trouble and inconvenience my behaviour had caused. For the first time, in direct response to being shown some tender kindness, I felt ashamed and embarrassed at having blown it. Allowing myself to get drunk and follow my heart, rather than exercise self-discipline and stick to the rules, had cost me the career I had loved. Falling foul of my perceived base desire had marked me out as an egotistical, lust-filled young woman whose own needs had caused her to break rules and take risks.

What nearly made me weep was when her last words to me were these, 'Well, Lieutenant Chambers, I'd like to take this opportunity to thank you for the time you've given to the corps'.

I thanked her, and left the Royal Pavilion, beginning the long walk down the drive, now effectively a civvy again. My mind was awash with so many memories. I remembered the times we were yelled at on the drill square, desperately trying to master the manoeuvres required to make us look great when our families came to proudly watch us march in our passing out parades. I thought of the incredible swelling of emotion in my chest and up to my throat as I rounded the corner onto the square – once as a private and again as a student officer – concentrating like crazy not to lose the rhythm of the band leading us on... left, right, left, right. To this day, the sound of the initial drum beat of a military band brings up a maelstrom of different emotions just as powerfully as it did then.

Walking the 'wrong' way down the drive, away from the place where I'd experienced my proudest moments, made friends I'd love forever, found a family and a way of life that I'd thought was mine to live until 2015, the floodgates finally opened and the tears fell freely. I headed into an uncertain future.

High Anxiety

If ever I was tempted to help increase the Special Investigation Branch's tally of Sapphic scalps, the day I was summonsed to see our then Brigadier, Rachel Brandon, came closest. Her office was in the heart of Holborn, spitting distance from Tavistock Place and the hotel I had worked in years before. It was in January 1988, a day or two before my commission was officially resigned, and just after I had seen the QATC commandant in Aldershot. This was to be my last official appointment as a serving QA officer.

I never really understood exactly what the intended purpose of our meeting was, but I had gone in best bib and tucker, wearing my most expensive, 'special occasions' skirt suit, blouse crisply ironed, looking as smart as I possibly could. I wasn't offered a seat, so found myself standing in front of the brigadier's very impressive desk, to be told, in no uncertain terms, that I was an utter disgrace and had let the corps down! I was shaking inside, enraged at the incredible hypocrisy of knowing that she was surrounded by 'old school' career officers, many of whom had had a great deal more experience of a Sapphic nature than I could ever imagine. I stood proud and tall, in the manner I'd been taught during basic training, nearly six years earlier – shoulders back, chest out, bottom tucked in, back straight. I looked her right in the eye. She really seemed to despise me, glowering as if I were the worst example of human depravity.

'Well, ma'am, I'm sorry you feel that way, but I don't agree – I think the corps has let *me* down.'

She was apoplectic, but also at a loss for words, probably due to shock at my temerity. Not only answering back, but daring to disagree with her. There was nothing more that either of us was prepared to say, so I was duly dismissed, both literally and figuratively.

There were no tears as I walked back along Southampton Row to Euston. My all-consuming sense of rage at the injustice and hypocrisy of it all had left me dry-eyed. As my anger slowly subsided, it was replaced with the most desolate sense of emptiness and sorrow. I passed the hotel where my working life had begun, and thought about popping in to see if Rose or Pat were on duty but decided against it. My low mood was hardly conducive to a sociable reunion. A whole raft of memories flooded back all at once, crowding my head with 'what ifs' and 'if onlys'. I glanced down Tavistock Place towards the third-floor room that had been my first home away from home... what on earth was I going to do next?

Home Again

After I'd received my letter from the MOD, on 21 December 1987 (not the best Christmas present), telling me that the Army Board had decided I should resign my commission, I found myself at a crossroads. I had decided against taking my case to court martial, because I knew my case was unwinnable. By then, four months after it began, I just wanted it to be over. There was a choice though, albeit one that had Hobson written all over it – the final paragraph said:

> Should she neglect or refuse to submit an unqualified application to resign within 14 days of the date she is officially notified of the Army Board's decision, the Ministry of Defence, Army Department (PS2a (Army)), should be informed and action will be taken to terminate her Commission with effect from the same date that her resignation would have been effective.

So, as part of the termination paperwork done at the QATC, in the traditional style of 'service writing' that we had been taught during officer training, I had sent in my handwritten letter.

On 18 January 1988 I was once again a civilian.

I had finally left the QAs. Nearly five months after my world had fallen apart. And nearly six years after it had all begun, so full of promise.

I tried to set things back on course. The trouble was, having lost absolutely everything, I simply didn't have a clue as to what to do or where to go. I had no plan whatsoever, because until that point I had genuinely believed I had embarked upon a career for life. Now

I needed to find a new job fast, as I'd made no provision for my future financial security at that stage. I was only 26 years old when the investigation began, now I was 27 – what need had I at that stage in my life to set up savings accounts? I had been given absolutely no resettlement courses or advice whatsoever prior to leaving and, once I'd returned all my uniform and kit, I was given the princely sum of £775 as a final payment to send me on my way. The usual 'going rate' was somewhere closer to £1,900. I was also advised I would no longer be eligible for any pension due to the nature of the cause of my enforced resignation. Five years and ten months of loyal service, for what?!

QARANC Training Centre
Farnborough Road
ALDERSHOT
GU11 1PZ

Ministry of Defence (DNS(A))
First Avenue House
High Holborn
LONDON
WC1V 6HE

13 January 1988

Madam,

APPLICATION TO RESIGN MY COMMISSION

I have the honour to submit an unqualified application to resign my Commission with effect from 18 January 1988.

I have the honour to be, Madam,

Your obedient servant
(Signature)
E.M.CHAMBERS
LIEUTENANT (526031)

I was incredibly lucky that I was able to return home to Harrow Weald – many people were rejected by their families and viewed as having disgraced them if the circumstances of their return to civvy street became known.

In fact, it was pretty tough for all of us when I came home, but not for the reasons one might have imagined. Yes, my unexpected departure after nearly six years would be tough enough to explain. Mum had said that all she would tell any curious family, friends, neighbours or work colleagues was that I'd simply decided I didn't like life as an officer and had therefore decided to quit. I really wasn't all that bothered about people known to me being aware of the real reason – I knew I was innocent of the allegations and had done *nothing* wrong. It's easy to feel right is on your side when in that type of situation. No, the bigger concern was how to explain the sudden departure to potential employers without arousing suspicion?

One small blessing was the fact that, due to having been commissioned from the ranks, my service record, the Regular Army Certificate of Service, had not been marked SNLR – 'Services No Longer Required'. This slender red card booklet contains a rundown of your service history for personnel below officer rank – detailing when and where you enlisted, assessments of military conduct and character, Army service (when and where you've served, medals, mentions in dispatches, etc.), certificate of discharge. They were often deemed useful to show to potential employers after leaving the Forces and returning to civvy street as a positive endorsement of a person's character and capability. Unless of course the final entry in the book was SNLR, services no longer required. It was virtually impossible to explain to someone why your assessments and military conduct history were often filled with positive comments and gradings one and two (exemplary; very good) yet the final entry was military speak for having been fired. How to explain that one away without outing oneself?

However, because I had left the ranks to become an officer, mine was marked thus:

Date of Discharge: 26 October 1986
Rank on Discharge: Private
Cause of Discharge: On appointment to a commission
Corps from which Discharged: QARANC

Although all notifications of officer occurrences are recorded in the *London Gazette*, my exit in disgrace would simply show as 'resigned commission'. So, yes, RHIP – 'rank has its privileges' – certainly held true and was yet another thing about Forces life that I didn't think fair. But it would help me as I could think of evasive or non-committal answers when asked why I'd decided to resign.

Again, to younger readers, this may seem irrelevant, but this was the era of Mrs Thatcher's much-hated Section 28, which became law on 24 May 1988. This was a clause to the Local Government Act, stating that a local authority (council) 'shall not intentionally promote homosexuality or publish material with the intention of promoting homosexuality' or 'promote the teaching in any maintained school of the acceptability of homosexuality as a pretended family relationship'.

It's hard to believe this came into being only 30 years ago. It was a very difficult time to be openly LGBT, because our government was effectively pandering to rising negative attitudes following the outbreak of HIV/AIDS. In 1987, the year before the legislation was enacted, the British Social Attitudes Survey revealed that 75 per cent of the population said that homosexual activity was 'always or almost always wrong'.

It was clear, then, that it would be better if I kept potential employers in the dark as to my reasons for leaving the Army. I knew I would have to tread carefully in interviews. As it happened, this was all perhaps less worrisome than I might have imagined – having pretty much sailed through the rigours of the intense process of gaining a commission, I had become unusually immune to interview nerves. In fact, I can honestly say that as the years have passed, I have come to quite enjoy being interviewed. Some friends deem that as just plain weird or even perverse, but it is what it is. Probably a good thing too, because I've certainly had more than enough practice since then.

Having been lucky enough to have been trained to 'Be the best!', finding nursing work via agencies was very easy. I soon found myself not only getting as much work as I wanted or needed, but even being 'chased' to cover shifts on particular wards. Being reliable, punctual, knowledgeable and competent was reaping its rewards.

Agency nursing pay was pretty good (a bone of contention to this day, as the hourly rates are considerably higher than those of the regular ward staff one is drafted in to assist, when covering shifts). But I certainly earned my money. Most shifts were of course on the heaviest and most difficult wards, mainly medical and elderly care. An endless round of washing, cleaning, changing and transferring doubly incontinent, immobile patients. Many had Alzheimer's, making communication especially difficult and frustrating. I worked wherever they needed me to go – Watford, Guy's, St Thomas's, Mount Vernon, Hillingdon – but most often at Northwick Park in Harrow. I also opted mainly for night shifts as the pay was better and my body clock had always been better suited to them.

After nearly six years nursing in military hospitals, the NHS was a *huge* shock and disappointment. I'd had a little NHS experience before, working briefly in two NHS hospitals during my training. The first was Park Prewett in Basingstoke, where I did my eight-week psychiatry placement. Military 'P' wings were deemed too limited to match civilian nurses' experiences, being mostly filled with alcoholics on 'drying out' programmes, so we were fielded out on secondment. It was the same for geriatrics, so that eight weeks was spent at Hydestile Hospital in Godalming, which soon became known as 'God-awful', due to it being a series of old Nissen huts that had been adapted after the war.

The agency work at Northwick Park was especially grisly, with a number of the regular ward staff being miserable, jaded and downright nasty to many of their poor unfortunate patients. Many times I'd ask for help to clean some frail old lady who'd been incontinent and was shivering in a cold, wet bed only to be told, 'Oh, she does that on purpose, tell her to wait!' It was a thankless role, with all attempts at being friendly and helpful roundly snubbed. There were too many embittered harridans who resented what we were earning, yet who wouldn't or couldn't be bothered to improve their own situation by working for promotion or leaving to find a better position elsewhere. It was such a shock after having had the great privilege of learning my craft in the well-staffed atmosphere of historic and impressive buildings such as the Cambridge Military Hospital in Aldershot.

NHS students were often part of intakes of dozens or even hundreds. In most QA groups' final year of training, the numbers of students would often be in single figures. There were only five in our class. That's a pretty fantastic tutor/student ratio, I think you'd agree?

I had been used to having a small number of patients for whose care I was responsible, so this was very different. Whilst I was able to understand the reason behind the obvious resentment, I still found it disgusting that so-called nurses could be so cruel to the poor unfortunates under their 'care'.

There were other differences too. Many tasks were carried out alone, due to the simple fact that wards were often very short-staffed, hence the need to use agency nurses. We had always worked in pairs in the Army if tasked to do dressings. One nurse would do the actual dressing, always aseptically, using two forceps in the 'no touch' manner, and the other was known as the 'dirty nurse'. Not an aspersion upon her personal hygiene, rather the fact that she'd act as an assistant, opening packs and passing you things so that you didn't sully your aseptic hands. It worked extremely well, reducing the amount of time that you'd have needed if alone, due to having to wash your hands every time you stopped to open something. It was *the* cardinal sin if you ever touched the sterile field of the opened dressing pack on top of the trolley, or if the forceps of the 'clean' hand touched those of the 'dirty' – never the twain shall meet! Even cleaning the trolleys before and after every dressing (how often is that done these days I wonder?) was carried out in a very strict fashion: wipe with cleaning agent from back to front, side to side, never going back over where you've just wiped, then down each leg, never coming back up, then the supporting bars, then the bottom shelf, also from back to front in a side to side movement, then down to the wheels themselves. Then repeat with the rinsing wipes. Then dry. Every time. Before and after. While this regime was undoubtedly time-consuming, I can honestly say that we very rarely saw any cases of what are now known as HAIs, or hospital acquired infections. And when we did, they had usually been acquired at another hospital, prior to transfer to the safety of the military establishment.

More than anything, I missed the companionship and camaraderie of Army life. Living and working in such close quarters builds bonds that are honestly unbreakable. I know that probably reads as a bit twee, but I swear it's true. Always being part of a team whose members, especially in the ranks, have gone through the same experiences – going from basic training to nurse or stewardess (equivalent to today's health care assistants); training, military exercises, playing sport and socialising together; forming relationships – this engenders *such* a deep sense of pride and cohesion. My QA and RAMC friends, colleagues and I were of course very different, coming from all parts of the UK, all classes and social groups, but we all felt that connection of shared experience. It was something that is impossible to explain to anyone who hasn't been through it themselves.

Switzerland

After a few months of assignments in and around London, the agency Medic International told me they had a position coming up that might be of interest. It was a one-year post as a staff nurse in Lausanne in the French-speaking canton of Vaud in Switzerland. The Centre Hospitalier Universitaire Vaudois (CHUV), a huge university teaching hospital, was recruiting for a number of different wards. Seventy per cent of their 9,000 employees was made up of foreign nationals as, for most Swiss workers, nursing was not viewed as a very lucrative career (which is pretty much the case worldwide, hence there always being work for a trained nurse; one of its redeeming features as a career choice). I wasn't convinced that my O level French, unpractised since leaving school nearly 11 years earlier, would be up to it. Nevertheless, I was encouraged to come for an informal assessment/interview.

Amazingly, they told me they thought I'd be fine, and offered me a place on a four-week French course for which I would pay £150. In return, there would be mornings (Monday to Fridays) spent in the lovely Hampstead home of an older lady teacher called Nelly, followed by afternoons in the Harrow office, concentrating more on the medical terminology. There was also a guarantee that they would only send us to Lausanne once they were happy that we would pass the written and oral tests there. It wasn't in anyone's interest to send someone who might fail, as anything less than 80 per cent in either test meant a seat on the first flight back home – game over!

I was in a lovely group with two other staff nurses, Dave and

Allison, and a physio from Ireland called Patsy. Nelly was a hoot and her methods worked well. The moment you got through the door you were only allowed to speak French. We discussed all manner of subjects and would sometimes watch French films – she'd cover the English subtitles with a strip of paper taped over the bottom of the TV screen, then ask us questions about the story afterwards.

The medical learning back at the office was made slightly easier by the fact that many terms are Latin in origin, so apart from being pronounced slightly differently, often the roots of the words were similar, making it easier to learn. The only other difference is the way that abbreviated terms such as AIDS would become SIDA in French, due to words often being transposed in translation.

After a whirlwind month, we were all deemed ready to go over for the tests!

By the time I was due to go, I had finally learned to drive and had committed myself to the first of life's big purchases: I had a lovely, brand new black Renault 5GTS which I was paying for in instalments, thanks to my regular agency work. I loved the freedom that owning 'Elijah' gave me. The name wasn't due to a sudden conversion to Christianity, having renounced the error of my perverse ways; it was inspired by the letters in the number plate: E520 JLA.

So, I decided to take the car with me, thinking of the opportunity it would afford me to explore such a beautiful part of the world. My good friend from Hannover, Sue Hunt, was going to accompany me from Harwich to Hamburg. I would drop her off at her married quarters in Hannover before continuing through East Germany to visit Gail in Berlin, then driving down to Switzerland.

We started the trip from Harrow with me carefully driving Elijah to Harwich, and onto the overnight ferry to Hamburg. Once onboard, naturally we headed immediately to the bar, which was pretty empty as it was still early, and sat enjoying a couple of beers. Before we had even finished our first drinks, two more beers were delivered to our table by the smiling barman. We looked around, trying to figure out who'd sent them over. I was frankly a bit miffed – I simply wanted to relax with my friend, have something to eat then get a good night's sleep, ready for the drive to Hannover the next morning. Still, encouraged by Sue – 'Aww, come on Chamberoony, the night's still young!' – we accepted them and proceeded to drink a fair few more. As the intended meal hadn't materialised, I soon felt quite squiffy. Along with the motion of a fairly choppy North Sea, I found myself, quite unusually for me, feeling a bit seasick. Sue found my newly civilian wimpishness highly amusing, nearly wetting herself laughing in the ladies' loo as I proceeded to throw up what seemed to be mainly the frothy heads of umpteen German lagers!

Any thoughts of an early night were quickly ditched when Mrs Hunt decided the best cure for my green gills would be some diversional therapy – let's go to the disco! So, off we staggered, ship rolling erratically. Before the deejay took over, a live band covering the usual pop, rock and disco classics entertained the crowd. They were pretty good, so I joined in the fun on the dancefloor. When we sat at a table as the interval had been announced, we were approached by the barman and his friend who'd sent us the earlier beers. They looked familiar – they explained that they were doubling up as the in-house band! They were Hungarians, clearly set upon some fun once their shift had finished. They were incredibly persistent, plying us with drinks, flirting outrageously and teaching us how to say something that was pronounced 'Egg – is – sheer – gad – dray'. We were assured it was just the Hungarian word meaning 'cheers' or 'good health', but I wasn't entirely convinced. On one visit to the loo, I said to Sue that I bet it really meant something akin to, 'Yes, of course I'd love to have unprotected sex with you and your friends!'

I really wasn't comfortable with the way things were going, but we agreed, after the disco had closed, to one last 'nightcap' in one of their cabins. It was way down in the bowels of the ship and I was seriously concerned that Sue might bugger off and leave me to fend for myself. She was of course married, so there was no way the 'boys from the band' were going to strike lucky with her. Obviously, although Sue knew why I'd left Hannover, they didn't, and were blissfully unaware that I was the wrong tree up which to be barking!

We politely quaffed yet another shot and the guy who seemed

most interested in me was getting just a little too close for comfort. The cabin being so tiny meant we had nowhere to sit other than on the lower bunks. He was squashed up against my thigh and kept putting his arm around my shoulder. My attempts to persuade him that we ought to get to our cabin as it was getting late were met with much cajoling: 'Just one more, Ell-ain, come on, you know you vont too. Sue does – Egeshirgedray!' Telling him *Sue* wasn't the one driving, *I* was, also fell on deaf ears, so I glowered at her on the opposite bunk with his little pal. 'Well, just one more then, but we need to go to the loo first – where is it?' Having given us directions, we squeezed awkwardly out of the cabin, my suitor reaching up with his free hand (the other was clutching a shot glass) to try to squeeze my arse. I forced an insincere rictus of a smile over my shoulder as I shoved Sue out into the corridor.

Sue was in hysterics, howling like a hyena. I couldn't help but smile but I then said, 'Come on, let's make a run for it!' We tottered as fast as we could, which was probably not all that fast, given the amount of drink we'd had and the fact that the ship was lurching quite badly in every direction. The corridor seemed interminably long but we reached the end without any sign of our admirers following behind. We ran and stumbled our way round what felt like miles of identical corridors, unable to find our deck, let alone the bloody cabin! We began to giggle uncontrollably. After one last lap of the entire ship, with still no sign of our priapic musicians, we found our cabin – halle-bloody-lujah! One last look up and down the length of the corridor – phew – no one to be seen.

We sat on the bunks, Sue still with a beer bottle in her hand. A moment later, still laughing about the evening's events, there was a gentle but rapidly insistent knocking at the cabin door! We nearly died on the spot, our eyes wide in amazement.

'Ell-ain, Ell-ain – please come out – I know you are in zere! Vye you are hidink from me?'

We were both about to burst out laughing or shriek. I frantically signalled to Sue to keep quiet. Amazingly, given the situation, she succeeded for a moment before dropping the beer bottle with an almighty crash to the floor! Bloody Nora, just a bit of a giveaway!

The imploring recommenced, but I just whispered to Sue that surely he'd *have* to give up soon, otherwise the poor sods in the cabins next door would be likely to complain. Sure enough, after what felt like an eternity, he seemed to have finally got the message. His beseeching pleas had stopped and the whole ship was silent. We waited and waited. Eventually Sue crawled on her hands and knees to the door, then reached up and very gently pulled the handle down. She got onto her knees and put her head into position, ready to take a peek through the tiny gap – but as she gingerly pulled the door open a fraction, she nearly had a heart attack when she looked through and was eye-to-eye with my stalker!

Having shut and locked the door again, he finally got the hint. We couldn't understand how he had known which cabin we were in. We'd certainly not told him the number and he didn't know our surnames. There'd been no sign of him at all when we were dashing around like some weird comedy hybrid of Benny Hill and Jacques Tati's Monsieur Hulot, trying to find it ourselves. When we got up a few short hours later it was an enormous relief to open the door to an empty corridor – and also to find his extended roles didn't include serving breakfast!

Somehow or other, we finally made it to Sue's married quarters in Hannover. It was bittersweet being back there so soon after my enforced departure. The next day I was to continue on to Berlin. Gail had been suddenly posted out of Hannover, just a few months after my departure. She took the famous military train to British Military Hospital Berlin on 28 March 1988. As the more usual length of any hospital-based posting was two years, she always feels in her heart that it was effectively a 'punishment' posting. She was also, as I have alluded, almost too honest for her own good sometimes. Of course, both of us can only surmise, we know we cannot prove our supposition to be true. But I find it very easy to imagine that the powers that be must have been very nervous about the possibility that, especially after a few glasses of wine, Lieutenant Bentley's loosened tongue might have had the potential to cause embarrassment to certain people known to have been affected by the investigation. It could have then seemed as though she may have been thought to pose a threat, so had to go.

Berlin is an amazing city and I know Gail enjoyed certain aspects of her time there, but she was very traumatised by the circumstances that seemed to have caused her transfer there. When we've discussed the events at Hannover, which we have many times in the 30 years since, she has always expressed her disgust and anger at the way in which the whole thing was handled. She acknowledges that she was a frightened and confused young officer when this happened. She'd been in the Army for less than 10 months when the SIB came to Hannover. She had also been questioned by Mr Lentman, mainly in the hopes of uncovering some discrepancies between mine and Mags' accounts, and had experienced the same thing I did, feeling when the written record of her statement was presented to her that it didn't properly reflect what she had said, but she just wanted it to be over.

As Gail had been in the bar on the night in question, she was potentially a key witness. Unfortunately, the record of the interview shows that Lentman felt what she said actually strengthened the case *against* me. This was because we had different recollections of who had gone to bed first, Mags or Gail. I never really understood exactly *why* that should be so significant, but it was there in black and white.

I had later learned from Gail that on the morning that it all blew up, Mel had come to her room in a dreadfully distressed state. She had told her that she should 'look out for Elaine' because I would need her support and friendship. I wonder if her concern was perhaps another indication that her statements may have belied her true feelings towards me. I'm not suggesting that she wanted any relationship or was a closet case, merely that she seemed to care a little about me.

Then, later in the inquiry, I managed to get a message to her. I wanted to speak to her directly, in an attempt to at the very least make sense of *why* she had done such a cruel and hurtful thing to me. It was a mammoth risk. Lentman would have thrown the book at me had he ever found out.

Gail acted as intermediary and we met away from the hospital, near some woods. Mel was in her car and I sat in the passenger seat. Oddly enough, there wasn't really that much tension between us, more a sense of sorrow, remorse and slight awkwardness. Although I had hoped to gain some understanding of how we had come to find ourselves in this mess, all she would tell me was that she had never meant for things to end up like this. There were complicated reasons behind it and she truly was sorry that it had all become so utterly crazy and fucked up. I asked her how she'd been treated by the SIB and she said they'd been polite enough. I also wondered if she knew what was likely to happen, but at that stage, comparatively early into what would eventually drag on for five very long months, she said she really didn't know. I think at that point she was probably hoping for a severe reprimand – perhaps some sort of written warning. She'd only recently got a promotion and a specialist course was now on hold for the foreseeable future. What a price to pay for one stupid mistake!

We didn't dare risk being seen together, so I left and walked back alone through the woods. All the meeting had done was to confuse me even more – she certainly wasn't acting like someone who was terrified I'd assault her. I later found out, yet again from Gail, that she had been astounded that I'd remembered so many tiny details about our night together. Gail, knowing me as well as she did by now, was able to clear it up for her. 'Mel, what happened between you really *meant* something to Elaine – it *mattered* – it wasn't just a bit of a laugh. She's struggling to accept who she is, to understand what makes her tick.'

So, my need to see Gail, before I started the new job in Lausanne, was complex but vitally important to me. She had been my mainstay and although I know she sometimes hated the 'role' that had been foisted upon her, she never let me down. Hindsight being a wonderful thing, I realise how invidious it was for her – she was literally a conduit between the three main points of this odd triangle. Not only had she worked with Mags and Elspeth, but Mel had come and told her things, asked her questions. I was trying, through her connections, to glean some sort of insight or understanding into *why* this had happened to me. Gail must also have been aware of the likelihood that if her friendship with me seemed too intense or close, she may well end up being erroneously tarred with the same Sapphic brush.

In fact, after I'd had my room searched, Matron had shown Lentman to Gail's room. I think he went to her because he'd discovered the card I'd written to her, but never delivered, asking her to hide my two carrier bags. Although I've never taken up smoking, I would occasionally try a cigarette. I happened to have a packet of what were Gail's preferred 'cancer sticks' at that time. I liked the elegant flip-lid box – they were menthol flavoured St Moritz – the glamorous image and name suiting my Francophile aspirations and a more upmarket take on Viv's Consulate. The pack was nearly full; I kept them in case Gail might want one when she popped by.

After she'd been questioned, she came racing into my room in a state of shock – 'What the bloody hell's going on, Elaine!' Amidst my tears and anger we managed an ironic smile – the idiot had remarked upon spotting the smokes in her room – 'Oh, that's funny – Lieutenant Chambers has some of those in her room too!' What a completely daft thing to say, as if only lesbians smoke foreign ciggies!

Despite my relative inexperience as a driver, I managed to safely negotiate the quite scary route from Hannover, then through East Germany without incident. I was well aware of the fact that there were immensely strict rules to undertaking this journey. It entailed passing directly through a Cold War 'enemy' country in order to reach Berlin, which in pre-reunification era Germany, was an isolated 'island' protected by the Western post-war axis nations. The long-awaited fall of the infamous Berlin Wall happened in November 1989, less than two years after I made this first trip.

One was expected to stick rigidly to the prescribed route, never going off any of the side roads. Petrol was only to be purchased from the service stations on the route. No deviations of any type were allowed. If you broke down, you just stopped safely and waited for assistance to arrive. You must never go above the speed limit of 55 mph.

There was also the fact that, as a former member of the military, I was still under the jurisdiction of the Official Secrets Act. As such,

I should have consulted the MOD about my intended trip. One of the discharge forms I had received prior to my ignominious ejection was MOD Form 138, the nattily titled 'Security reminder on travel to or through Communist countries: or use of Communist transport'. It stated that:

> You are reminded that certain hazards attend travel to Communist countries by anyone who is, or has been, in Government Service and who may possess, or be thought to possess any information of a classified nature. In order to protect such information and indeed for your own protection, if you propose travelling to or through a Communist country or by Communist country sponsored transport, you should first consult Ministry of Defence (SY(A)), Metropolis Building, Northumberland Avenue, London.

As the rights and privileges associated with military employment had been so unceremoniously stripped from me, I decided that as I was now a civilian I was therefore free to do as I pleased. I couldn't afford to fly, though even if I could, the restriction included 'travel to West Berlin *by whatever means*'. But I'd got the job lined up in Lausanne, and I wasn't prepared to let the MOD interfere in my life any further than it already had.

I was a little bit nervous as to what might happen to me if I had been stopped, but as I drove into the outskirts of West Berlin I felt utterly elated. I had booked myself a hotel, but without Satnav, Google maps and iPhone at my disposal, I managed to get lost. Having come unscathed through a Cold War country without any hiccups, I could see the funny side.

I was very impressed at how green and lush the city was, it really looked so lovely. As I slowly began to drive across an impressive iron bridge, I suddenly realised that there was no other traffic. I slowed down and as I looked ahead I saw a barrier and some soldiers... carrying rifles.

I decided it might be wise to do a test-standard three-point turn and go back. As I did so, I could see the guards staring towards me, doubtless seeing the GB number plate and the bewildered look upon the gormless tourist's face. I had managed to drive onto the infamous Glienicke 'Bridge of Spies' – site of all the most significant spy exchanges between the East and West throughout the entire Cold War era!

The couple of days in Berlin flew by – I managed to see Gail, very briefly. We had a couple of nights out and I was just so relieved not to have lost her after all she had suffered, through no fault of her own. She and I had a deep, unbreakable bond – we'd clicked pretty much immediately after our first couple of evenings out together following our posting to Hannover. But our shared experience served only to deepen and strengthen that bond. As I left the city for the long drive back across East Germany, down through France, then to Lausanne via Geneva, I had plenty of time to ruminate on the hand that fate had dealt me. Despite all the trauma and heartache, the embarrassment and loss, I'd been given one gift that couldn't be taken from me – I'd met one of the most wonderful people I've ever known. Her love and friendship means more to me than she could ever begin to imagine.

I think that the reason I had gone for the nursing job in Lausanne was because I was almost trying to prove to everyone that I was better than they knew. It was June 1988, less than six months after my ignominious expulsion from the QAs. Who needed the stupid Army? Not me! It was a metaphorical two fingers to them all: look at me! You tried to destroy me but I'm off to a fantastic new job, with great pay and conditions; driving a brand new, gorgeous, tinted-windowed little motor; speaking French fluently and living the high life.

If only. Things didn't quite work out as I'd hoped. After a mere 10 days in post, as a staff nurse in the surgical/transplant ward on the 15th floor, I managed to screw things up royally. Here's how. We'd just been paid our first salary, and everyone was up for a celebratory night out. I offered to drive down into Lausanne, which I duly did. We eventually found a back road in which to park and walked to the White Horse bar. Of course, the minute everyone started necking their beers, I wanted to join in. Allison, Dave and the others told me not to worry, saying we'd get a cab back and that I could pick the car up the next day. Great idea – cheers! A number of beers later and we want to go home but there's not a taxi to be found. Sadly, after much chuntering and wandering aimlessly around, we found my car. I told everyone to get in and promised that I'd be ultra careful, this was Switzy after all, land of control-freaks and humourless saddos...

Amazingly, we got back in one piece without attracting the attention of any *gendarmes* but ended up at an Irish nurse's room. Out came the whiskey and various other types of booze, which, I am deeply ashamed to confess, I did imbibe, liberally... And that's when the mad notion grabbed me – I had three days off, why not nip up to Hannover to see my old friends? I had the presence of mind to go back to our apartment block to pack some clothes, my camera and pick up my passport... Then off I went.

It was now gone 2am as I whizzed north. I noticed a couple of times that I was pretty tired and almost let go of the wheel, causing the car to jerk slightly to the right, but despite knowing this, I somehow couldn't bring myself to stop and turn around to go back and sleep it off. As I began to drive through Henniez, a small town known for its bottled mineral water, I clipped the base of some stone steps outside a bakery with my offside wheel – it was on a leftward bend and the car crashed at high speed into a lamp post on the opposite side of the road, then ran into a barrier outside a farmer's land, uprooting 70 metres of the metal fence before spinning into the middle of the road, then turning onto its roof before finally coming to a halt.

The odd thing was that, rather than seeing my whole life flash before me in the few seconds from initial impact to coming to a standstill, I experienced something else altogether. I clearly saw myself in a hospital bed in an intensive care unit, unconscious and bruised, cut, bloodied, and swollen, with wires, monitors, tubing galore. Mum and Dad were by my bed, crying and looking bewildered and upset – I distinctly remember thinking, 'Oh my God! How on earth will I explain this to them?!' and praying that I wouldn't die.

Once the car came to a standstill, I undid my seatbelt and pushed at the door, which luckily for me did open quite easily. I turned myself round onto my hands and knees (having been upside down) and crawled out over the broken glass of my window. As I attempted to stand up, I remember thinking 'Great! I haven't broken my legs!' Then my head felt as if it would explode – both temples were throbbing and I was in so much pain. As I put both hands up to the sides of my head, thinking, 'My arms are OK too!' I looked at my now very wet hands and was a bit surprised to see they were covered in blood.

A small crowd of people had gathered and I was being offered a chair to sit on and a blanket because I was suddenly shivering uncontrollably, my teeth chattering very audibly; dental castanets. I heard myself saying, in perfect French, 'No, no – I'm not cold, it's because I'm in a state of shock.' It really did feel like an out of body experience. The most awful thing about it all, apart from the fact that I could have hurt or killed someone other than my own idiotic self, was the fact that the ambulance took me straight back to A&E at the CHUV! Bloods were taken before I was allowed to go home. Incredibly, I just needed three stitches to the wound above my left ear. The bruises round my eyes would fade... and although I was allowed to remain in post, my new boss clearly thought me the most disgusting, reprehensible, irresponsible drunken lout she'd ever known. It wasn't an auspicious start, and in her eyes at least, she had no reason to enquire as to *why* I would have done something quite so stupid, so soon after landing such a plum job.

Nothing I ever did during my year there was good enough for her. I tried so damned hard to make amends, to show her what a good nurse I was. I hoped, in vain, that she would eventually, with the passage of time and the consistency of my application to demonstrating the excellence of British military nurse training, relent a little. But it wasn't to be. I often wanted to let her know that I was still really in a state of grieving for all that I'd lost in Hannover, but it never happened. Perhaps unsurprisingly, once my year on a *permis stagiaire* (temporary work permit) was over, I wasn't eligible to apply for the scarcer and much prized *permis B* which allowed one to stay on indefinitely. Many years later, another position arose there and I asked about applying, but was turned down flat, even though I'd explained to the owner of Medic International why I was actually in a very fragile and vulnerable state at that time. Apparently the CHUV contact there had described me in their feedback as having been a very 'mediocre' nurse. A spectacularly good drunk driver though. Ho hum...

Oddly enough, having survived a crash that most definitely would have killed me had I been in a right-hand drive car led to a bit of an epiphany. Having later received developed photos of my completely destroyed car (taken on my camera, presumably by the *gendarmes*, to shock me) caused me to become extraordinarily grateful for the tiniest things – the first time I got caught in an unexpected rainstorm, I relished getting soaked to the skin. I was simply grateful to be alive to *feel* the rain. I dashed back to my accommodation nearby and wrote dozens of very poor poems. I was so aware of the notion that someone or something up there liked me – it wasn't my time to die. I still had to earn my angel's wings. Thankfully, no one else was hurt or injured as a result of my incredible stupidity. Again, hindsight makes me believe I was still completely traumatised by what had happened to me. I think it would be agreed that I was suffering from post-traumatic stress disorder.

Crashed car

My joy at being alive didn't translate into a mad rush to exercise a new-found freedom to express myself, and therefore my sexuality, though. I hadn't come out to any of the nurses in my ward. My friends Allison and Etienne encouraged me to find out if there was any sort of scene in Lausanne. There was one women's bar, but I was terrified of going. Allison very kindly offered to go with me, but I only went right towards the end of my year there. Up until then, I socialised with work colleagues, Allison and Etienne and their friends. I had been well and truly stung by Hannover, so I was happy to focus on work, music gigs, cinema, theatre and visiting the beautiful country in which I was living.

About four to six weeks before I was due to return to the UK, one of my Swiss nurse colleagues, Genevieve, invited me to join her with some friends for an evening out. I was delighted, but felt immensely shy around her because I thought she was absolutely gorgeous. She picked me up from my room, driving very fast in her sporty car, a top-of-the-range black and red Renault 5GTI, CD player blaring Mory Kanté's 'Yé Ké Yé Ké' at top volume – I was in heaven! After we'd joined her two female friends at a bar, she explained that her boyfriend couldn't come along as he was a policeman on call that night, but they wondered if I'd like to join them at a nightclub? I asked the name, but they got a bit giggly and smiley, eventually fessing up that it was a gay club, but that they often went because the music and atmosphere were fantastic. Her best friend, also a nurse at the CHUV, somehow *looked* gay to me, in that completely unfathomable way that is sometimes referred to as gaydar. Nothing you can put your finger on, just an innate sense...

I was rather confused as to what exactly was going on here – I'd briefly met Genevieve's hunky, macho (another cliché, *n'est-ce pas?*) policeman at either a Siouxsie and the Banshees or Cure gig – they seemed very happy together, quite touchy-feely, and yet... and yet...

Her best mate, Jeanne, I was sure had the hots for Genevieve. I honestly couldn't figure it out.

Anyway, we went to the club and had a great time, but I was none the wiser as to what the score was. I think Genevieve was a bit of a flirt, to be honest. I remember just one particularly uncomfortable time at work that made me blush. It was during a team handover between shifts, when we would sit next to one another around a large table and wait to take our turn to report on our patients. On this particular occasion, Genevieve was sitting next to me, to the right. I was very attracted to her and I'm sure she instinctively knew it, despite my best efforts not to give her any clues. It felt as if she was being a bit of a tease that day, deliberately sitting much closer to me than she needed to. She got close enough to press her left thigh against my right. I moved away but she did it again, twice. What a provocative minx!

Back in the UK with Mum and Dad once again, in July 1989, I was completely at a loss as to what to do with myself. I managed to keep my drunkenness a secret from them, pretending that I'd merely fallen asleep at the wheel and crashed. Because it had happened so soon after my arrival, the fine was paid and the year-long ban was over by the time I was back, so it didn't affect my chance of driving again. Also, as Switzerland wasn't an EU member, the offence didn't show up on my UK licence – phew!

I started doing agency work initially then got a job as an administrative assistant with the Metropolitan Police Office, based with the Force Inspectorate at Tintagel House in Vauxhall, opposite the MI6 building. It was poorly paid but I got on fairly well with the other members of staff in our small team. The one aspect of the role that did appeal was having to proofread the reports. These were written by fairly senior police officers, many of whom were virtually illiterate. It was therefore great fun for me to précis their unwieldy sentences (paragraph-length at times). I relished the challenge of rendering pages of the utmost tedium at least marginally more readable.

Some of them were very happy for me to prune and tweak their work in this way and actually took the time to acknowledge my efforts. It was only going to make them look better after all. I wasn't going to really benefit other than in knowing I'd made an improvement of something so dry and boring. Others were far less gracious, often refusing to accept my alterations and insisting that their original garbage be taken to the printing room at New Scotland Yard. It would be nicely bound and covered before being presented to the Commissioner and DACs. Needless to say, the poor pay, frustration and boredom meant I didn't last long there.

My brief period working as an administrative officer with the Met, from May to November 1990, coincided with the start of a difficult time for my family. As if we hadn't had quite enough to deal with already! As the commute from home was a bit of a pain, I was considering moving out and renting somewhere nearer to work. And although I felt guilty about it, my brother Ian's antics were part of the reason too. One of the nicer Chief Superintendents at Tintagel House was looking for a tenant for a partly-furnished two-bedroomed flat in Beckenham, so the tenancy became mine.

By now, Ian was no longer living at home, but was still causing grave concern with his worsening behaviour due to his addiction to alcohol and drugs. He was clearly spiralling into a very destructive pattern. Despite his best efforts to stop, including paying for hypnotherapy sessions and trying Chinese medicine and acupuncture, he remained in their thrall – but especially alcohol.

After I had returned home, it was immediately evident how bad things had become. I was convinced that Ian didn't only have an addiction; his behaviour, increasingly erratic and bizarre, seemed reminiscent of paranoid schizophrenia. Of course, psychiatry was not my specialty. In fact, I had pretty much hated the eight-week secondment we spent at Park Prewett in Basingstoke.

However, I felt I had enough rudimentary knowledge to recognise possible symptoms. Mum, Dad and I would often find ourselves sitting in the front room with Ian. Ostensibly we'd all be watching a TV programme together – nothing unusual there, an innocuous family scene. But look a little closer and you'd see that Mum would be nervously chewing her already down-to-the-quick nails, whilst constantly glancing away from the screen, sideways, surreptitiously at her boy. Even from across the room, I would see the glistening film of unspilled tears in her eyes. Dad would be watching her, also trying to be discreet, clearly out of his depth, not knowing what on earth he could do in the face of so much tense emotion in one small space. He just wanted to get out and go, anywhere – the Memorial Club, the golf course, take the dog for a walk, anywhere but be sitting here... I would watch all three of them, while the main focus of our uncomfortable attention, Ian, would sit obliviously in the other armchair. His left leg would be bent up, his arm cradling his knee, while his right leg, foot on the carpet, would be jiggling up and down very rapidly. His body, from the waist up, would also be rocking back and forth – a constant rhythmic tattoo. His strikingly pale blue eyes, noticeable against his very pale skin and vivid copper-coloured hair, would be turned towards the TV screen. But look again and you'd see they were unfocused. This perfect audition for the part of an extra in *One Flew Over the Cuckoo's Nest* was made so much worse by his constant muttering and chuntering beneath his breath. Mostly it would be inaudible, but odd snippets would be horribly clear: 'Cunt!' – 'Shut up!' – 'I know... I know!'

Even as I watched, feeling completely at a loss as to what to do, I would find myself thinking: poor Mum's going to have a nervous breakdown before he does! She looked so close to it. Mum would interject softly, trying to sound steady: 'Ian... Ian... it's all right love.' The quavery wobble would nearly set me off. He would come back into the room, looking at us, taking a moment to recognise the three concerned faces looking at him so lovingly, so anxiously. But he was never back for long.

One day I talked with him and felt I might be making some sort of progress – he began to open up. When we heard him shouting out at night and rushed to his room, he told me he had been having the most horrifyingly vivid and real nightmares – either brutally killing people or being killed, and trying to escape. He looked at me with such fear and desperation as he explained that he had sometimes woken up and found himself under his bed or cowering in the bottom of his wardrobe, not even knowing how he got there – literally sleep *running*, not walking. It broke my heart. I tried to offer hope in the form of strategies, but before we could pursue this train of thought, it was too late.

One evening at home, he became very agitated. He was unable to sit still, constantly jumping out of the armchair and peeping through the curtains, and running into the hall to pick up the telephone, intently listening. We all took turns to try to gently persuade him to come and sit with us. His jumpiness was making us all very nervous; we all felt we were walking on eggshells. Although clearly he was very twitchy and distracted, he was not making us feel threatened. It was rather as if he was trying to make us understand, see things as he did.

'Don't worry Mum – I *know* they're out there. They were on the porch. I could hear them when I was in bed.'

'Who, love?' Mum looked ready to crack.

'The police! They've tapped the phone – I *know* they're there, Mum, I've just got to catch them!'

Eventually, having opened his bedroom window and shown him that the porch beneath was devoid of any rozzers, we persuaded him to go to bed. Amazingly, given the state we were all in – for this had gone on for a number of weeks now – we even managed to get a few hours of uninterrupted sleep. As daylight streamed through my bedroom window the next morning, I heard a very familiar sound. As we only had the one bathroom, if someone was in the bath and we only wanted to have a pee, we'd knock on the door and ask them to pull the shower curtain across. It wasn't ideal, but when needs must and all that. I'd vaguely heard someone running a bath as I was coming to, but had imagined it to be Mum. So I was a bit surprised to hear the gentle tap on the bathroom door followed by Mum saying, 'Ooh Ian love, can you pull the curtain over? – I'm desperate to spend a penny!'

The drag of the curtain rang along the rail, then the click of the lock being pulled back and the door opening – so far, so familiar – then came a heart-stopping, piercing scream. Mum was yelling over and over, 'God no! God no! God no!' Dad and I hurtled out from our respective rooms.

Mum was shaking violently, sobbing her heart out as Ian looked at her in bewilderment. 'It's all right, Mum,' he assured her, as calmly as anything, 'It'll be all right… but I *know* they're out there.'

Ian was sitting in the bath, wearing jeans but no top. The water, about a foot deep, was crimson red from the multiple slashes on his left forearm – the razor blade was still in his right hand. An instinctive response kicked in. Mum and Dad were frozen to the spot so I just took charge. Speaking very softly and calmly, realising I had to give Mum and Dad tasks so that I could try to get the blade away from Ian, I said, 'Dad, go and ring an ambulance please.' He scurried off.

'Mum.' Her trembling was still pretty violent and she was choking on paroxysmal sobs. 'Mum,' I repeated, my voice slightly more urgent now. She snapped out of it and looked at me like a lost child, our roles completely reversed. 'Can you get me a clean towel from the airing cupboard please?' With frantic little nods of her head, she ran out.

I got down onto my knees and rested my forearms on the edge of the bath, hands holding opposite elbows, as much as anything to stop myself from shaking. As is often the case with blood, especially when diluted in water, a little goes a long way. I'd instantly clocked the fact that, although the criss-cross pattern of slashes looked horrific, the wounds themselves were fortunately not deep and no major (or minor, for that matter) blood vessels had been damaged.

My baby bruv looked at me as if seeing me anew. He greeted me with a beatific smile – 'Sis!'

I lifted my hand to his, palm up, and just gave a barely perceptible nod as I looked from his eyes to the blade then to my hand, all in a fraction of a second. No words were needed, he understood. Mum watched from the landing, in my peripheral vision, clutching freshly-laundered tea towels, standing motionless, holding her breath. My heart was in my mouth... but he let me take the blade, which I put out of reach on the sink – then I helped him to stand up and get out of the bath. We wrapped his arm in the tea towels, then managed to persuade him to let us get him out of his wet clothes and helped to towel him dry.

The ambulance arrived quickly, but they were accompanied by a police car! I don't know if Dad's description of the event had been misinterpreted? Perhaps it was thought a suicidal young man with a 'weapon' was a danger to others? All I knew was that we would *never* get him to hospital if he saw 'them' outside. Cue some frantic, very rapid explanation through a barely-open front door, as to why it would be best if they *didn't* come in – whilst Mum distracted Ian as she helped him to get into some clean dry clothes.

The paramedics were, as always, absolutely fantastic, dealing with Ian so professionally and with such compassion. I wish I could say the same for the rest of the so-called medical profession. At A&E at Northwick Park, I felt as if the depth and severity of Ian's symptoms really weren't being taken seriously. I tried to speak to a doctor privately, away from Mum and Dad – I didn't want to worsen an already fraught and desperate situation by voicing my theory within earshot. It may have been because I was a staff nurse, but he wasn't at all interested in what I was saying, very much assuming a superior and patronising attitude. He practically laughed at my suggestion that there may be more to this than alcohol abuse. I was beginning to believe Ian might be schizophrenic, what with the increasing degree of paranoia.

'Oh no, I don't think so – it's almost certain to be entirely down to the level of toxins in his system. He'd have been diagnosed before now,' the doctor replied.

I could easily have found myself being carted out by a couple of burly security guards – I was tantalisingly close to whacking the condescending little prig!

Somehow or other, probably through sheer persistence, I managed to get him to admit Ian to the psychiatric ward for observation. What was worrying me every bit as much as Ian's state was that of my poor mother. I emphasised as heavily as I could that if we were sent home with Ian, there was a distinct possibility that any one or all of the rest of the Chambers family might be back later as we were all close to crisis point. What the doctor hadn't known was that Mum had a history of psychiatric problems and was wracked with anxiety and guilt that she might have in some way landed Ian with a horrific genetic legacy. No amount of assurance would ever truly dissuade her. It was all beyond heartbreaking.

After a few fairly pointless days as an inpatient, Ian was once again sent home. Dad and I went to his GP, virtually begging for help. I even said I would be prepared to sign a declaration that if they would just prescribe him something like Heminevrin to try to help him to withdraw, I would come to the surgery every single day for a prescription for a single bloody tablet if necessary! However, they were worried about giving him any form of medication due to his previous history of suicide attempts (read – 'cries for help'). It was through my own research that I found out about a specialist unit called St Bernard's at Ealing Hospital, so back I went – I was not going to let this go – and Ian was finally admitted as an inpatient to complete a properly structured 'drying out' programme. We all wept tears of joy and relief.

The next few months were nothing short of miraculous. Ian completed the programme and, after he was discharged, he moved into a bedsit above a shop in Brick Lane in East London. My parents once made the journey to visit him there and he delighted them by cooking them a delicious roast chicken dinner with all the trimmings. Seeing the 'old' Ian again – bright, warm, funny, intelligent – even managing to get the occasional spot of work, usually casual labouring, gave us all renewed hope. However, this hope was shattered just a short while later.

Living in London was too costly, so he came back to Harrow, this time renting a tiny bedsit above the parade of shops closest to Headstone Lane railway station. I was still at home then, mainly doing nights at accursed Northwick Park (I cannot tell you how much I have come to associate that grey concrete monstrosity with all that is bad and wrong about nursing these days!). On this occasion I had come back from a late shift. It was a cold, dark winter's evening. As I approached the house, I noticed all the lights were on but the car was missing. On the doorstep were numerous spots of what looked like congealed blood. I was trembling as I tried to get my key in the lock, terrified as to what I might find. I rushed in, hurtling from room to room like a maniac, yelling out, but it was soon clear there was no one home. The TV was on but no note had been left anywhere for me. I even ran into the back garden.

I rang Northwick Park and got put through to A&E. Eventually I managed to persuade someone to tell me that yes, an Ian Chambers *had* just come into the department, accompanied by his parents. Rather than faff about running to bus stops, I called a minicab and went straight back.

Ian had been out that evening at the Letchford Arms and had got very drunk, winding up other punters but, according to witnesses, just being a 'bit of a prat, really'. He hadn't been violent, just a bloody tosspot! After he left to stagger the short distance back to his bedsit, he had been viciously attacked from behind, his assailant slashing at his back, arms and throat with a Stanley knife. When he'd collapsed onto the snow-covered ground, his head had been kicked in like a football before he was left for dead.

Somehow, after who knows how long, he had come to and miraculously managed to make it back to Ufford Road, to my poor parents. These parents were the same saps he'd yelled and screamed at so many times over the years – humiliating them in the most public of ways. The neighbours' net curtains would be twitching like mad as he'd lurch wildly down the road in a drunken rage, berating them in the most vile and hateful manner, effing and blinding as he declared to the world in a snarling, rasping voice: 'You're PATHETIC! Working-class CUNTS who bought your stupid, shitty little council house from that fucking evil shit Thatcher – driving your stupid little car – what's WRONG with you? You fucking morons – I'm never gonna swallow that shit – I'm getting out of this shithole – I'm gonna DO something with my life!'

Despite all they had been through, every painful episode, all the anxiety and hurt, their love for their child was all that mattered. They somehow managed to bundle him into the car, covering him in winter coats and blankets as he was shaking uncontrollably and was freezing cold to the touch. He'd been lying unconscious in the snow, his leather jacket torn to shreds, literally hanging in ribbons over his back, which was now a mush of white flesh and bloodied, criss-crossed slash wounds. His eyes had swollen closed, his upper lip had been cut towards his nostril and was covered in congealed blood. Amazingly, his brain hadn't been damaged, but it was a very tense wait for the swelling to go down before they could safely scan him.

He did make a full recovery and his attacker was identified, brought to trial, found guilty and imprisoned. However, Ian's attempt to get some compensation from the Criminal Injuries Compensation Board was denied. The reason given was that as he (Ian) might have in some way provoked the attack, he would not therefore be deemed eligible for any compensation. This was despite the fact that his assailant had attacked him from behind, with such viciousness that the imprint from his boot was clearly visible on his cheek, and Ian had been a drunk, defenceless victim left alone to die. Mum was outraged by this decision. She had always railed against any form of injustice. I know my own loathing of injustice stems from her, as does my hatred of lies and being patronised.

My relationship with Ian had, despite these difficult episodes, improved greatly since I'd left the Army. I think this was down to a variety of reasons. Obviously, as an anarchist punk, it was far easier for him to relate to me now that I was no longer a part of the establishment, as he saw it. Also, I think he was secretly surprised and impressed to discover that I was gay. It added an allure, a sense of being different, an outsider. He hated what he saw as conformity. It was always a strong theme in the lyrics that he wrote for his punk band, Malice.

We shared a passionate love of music too – I had amassed an impressive collection of 7" and 12" singles, LPs and cassettes and we would often discuss our favourite bands and genres of music. We both had eclectic and very varied tastes and would swap singles and make 'compilation' cassettes for one another. I saw Malice perform their very first public gig, at Blackwell Secondary Modern School (now Hatch End High), the same school he had left at 15, without taking his CSE exams.

I thought the band were very good and I know there had been talk of a possible record deal a year or two into their existence. They began to get gigs in local pubs, then bigger 'music' pubs in London. After a small 'tour' north of the border, a Scottish fanzine did a fair-sized article and reviewed a gig very favourably. To this day I have two treasured 'demo' cassettes and hope to get them safely digitised. Ian was not only a songwriter but the lead vocalist and bassist, having taught himself how to play. He was also a talented artist, creating some excellent stencils for use with spray paint on walls, leather and denim jackets, guitar cases and speakers. Banksy, eat yer heart out! Sadly, though, his story didn't play out in the way we all hoped, though for now at least, we had a brief period of respite.

Coming Out, Moving On...

Having been forced to resign my commission in essence for being gay, I decided it really was about time to do something about it. This was after I'd come back from Lausanne, in July 1989. Although I had known deep down since I was a pubescent teenager, I had spent too many years trying to resist my true leanings. I'd been constantly trying to convince myself I was going through a phase, or maybe bisexual, or just a tad obsessive with certain people (all of whom happened to be women!). As a result, I was still quite confused about my feelings.

A week before I left Hannover, the resident psychiatrist, a charming major, had written me a letter to give to my GP if I felt I would benefit from some counselling, given the stress I had been under during the investigation. Although he was duty-bound to see me, because in those days anyone deemed to be homosexual had to have a psychiatric evaluation – it was treated as if it was an illness – he was in fact very sympathetic. He even admitted to me, off the record of course, that he thought the Army's whole approach was archaic and ridiculous.

11th November 1987

Dear Doctor,

Reference: Elaine Mari CHAMBERS, d.o.b. 28.10.60

Elaine Chambers is a nursing sister in this hospital and has been the subject of an investigation recently because of alleged homosexual activities and it is likely that this will culminate in her leaving the Army. It is possible that when she leaves the Army, she might feel the need for counselling of a psychosexual nature and I would be grateful if you could refer her to an appropriate agency if she requests this.

The military authorities view homosexuality in a serious way and it remains an offence within the Army although prosecution is unusual unless there are other factors such as abuse of rank, threats or blackmail. This is not so with Elaine and so it seems likely that she will just leave the Service. The investigation here within the hospital has been extremely traumatic as it has been carried out by the Special Investigation Branch of the Royal Military Police who have ended up interviewing many female members of the Mess in which Elaine lives. The Officers Mess, in which she lives, is a mixed mess but is largely full of female nurses.

Elaine has come and talked to me on a number of occasions and has been under a great deal of stress as the investigation has gone on in a small hospital involving many people with whom she lives and works. I think it will be much more appropriate and easier for her to look at all the issues involved after she has left the Army and is out of her current claustrophobic position. She has had a number of heterosexual relationships and a very limited number of homosexual relationships and feels extremely confused about her sexual identity. It is sad that she will have to leave Army nursing but this unfortunately is so and I am confident that she will be able to settle down into civilian life but might well find it useful to receive psychosexual counselling.

Yours sincerely,

Consultant Psychiatrist

When I asked my GP about this I was referred, wrongly, I now realise, to see someone at the Caryl Thomas Sexual Health Clinic in Wealdstone. The woman I saw was cold and very unhelpful. She even commented, when I said I wasn't entirely sure what my true feelings were, due to having had very nice boyfriends in the past, 'Well, you certainly seem to have made up your mind.' When I asked what she meant, she said 'Well, look at your choice of clothes.'

I was absolutely stunned! Had I been wearing dungarees, 18-hole DMs and a baseball cap over a grade 2 flat top I might have understood. However, my ensemble actually consisted of a blouse (yes, not a shirt), a very girly burgundy jacket and a pair of smart women's trousers over shoes with a lowish heel. I'm guessing it's the trews and shoes that were the tell-tale signs – that and the short nails and no make-up, perhaps. I was shocked, amused and angry in equal measure – ultimately, though, I thank her because she pushed me towards accepting my true identity quicker than might have been the case had I gone back for a second session.

I left in a fit of enraged pique, determined that, as soon as a suitable topic appeared, I would pluck up the courage and finally go through the doors of 'Gay's the Word' bookshop and join the weekly lesbian discussion group. It felt like it was the right time to go and meet some bona fide dykes and see if I fitted in.

Just a few weeks later I eagerly flicked to the 'Lesbian and Gay' pages of *Time Out* and lo! 'Coming out'! So, this is it, I thought. I am somewhat ashamed to say that, despite knowing the days of the notoriously infamous Gateways club were long gone, I was as bad as any ignorant homophobe. I imagined a lesbian discussion group would be bound to be full of Beryl Reid's *Killing of Sister George*-type ageing butch dykes, smoking cheroots and eagerly eyeing up any fresh meat!

But I decided to go anyway, and arrived early, wandering up and down outside, watching from a distance, trying to discreetly observe what 'type' of clientele this weekly event was attracting. Eventually, I took a deep breath and went in. There was a very mixed group of around 12 of us and the atmosphere was friendly and welcoming. The facilitator was Angie, a lovely woman with shoulder-length fair hair tied back in a ponytail, wearing glasses and with an open, smiling face.

After hearing a few stories, I took the plunge and offered up my sorry tale. Everyone was horrified that such treatment went on in this day and age – they were all incredulous. It felt so wonderful to be in the company of women who were fully at ease with their sexuality; I felt utterly liberated and immediately wished I'd been brave enough to attend years earlier! Afterwards, a number of us went to the sadly now defunct LLGC (London Lesbian & Gay Centre) in Cowcross Street, Farringdon, for a few beers and to continue the banter.

I soon became a regular at the Wednesday groups, in my old

haunt of Bloomsbury, eventually even acting as facilitator myself. Angie trusting me in this role every other week meant the world to me. The LLGC was also a home from home. Apart from post-discussion drinks, with the Gay's the Word attendees, there was a mixed disco on Friday nights, then the wonderful women-only disco in the basement on Saturdays, with DJ Ritu playing fantastic music, then the Sunday afternoon/evening tea dance/disco, full of drag queens, flamboyant poseur gay boys, butch and femme dykes galore and everyone in between! It was at this time, around autumn 1990, that I met Elaine McKenzie, renowned host of many fabulous women-only events and whose Glass Bar at Euston station was a must for me to visit whenever I could. Her infectious enthusiasm and sense of fun always raised a smile – such an inspirational person to know.

I absolutely loved those times but have to admit that I was probably overdoing it somewhat with the boozing. I suppose it was down to the heady mix of the excitement and freedom I was experiencing for the first time in my life.

One notable after-effect of the investigation was the way in which the whole experience had completely destroyed what little confidence I might have had as far as women were concerned. Even though the allegations had never been translated into charges, I carried an inbuilt fear of being falsely perceived as a lech or sleazebag if I dared to let anyone know I was attracted to them. I was absolutely wracked with insecurity. Even though I had always known I was completely innocent, I suppose I was fearful that people might ascribe my misfortune to the notion of there being 'no smoke without fire'.

My reticence eventually led to one amusing event at the LLGC. A young woman had been regularly attending the GtW discussion groups then joining us afterwards for drinks. She was a trainee solicitor, doing her articles in central London, clearly intelligent, articulate and confident. I enjoyed her company and input to the group and the ongoing discussions and debate, but wasn't attracted to her. She was always chatty and friendly, but I thought she was like this with everyone. On this occasion, as I came out of the loo into the corridor, about to return to the group at the bar, she bounded towards me, a wide smile on her face.

'All right?' I asked.

She came right up to me, standing in front of me, so I shifted to the left, to allow her to pass and go to the ladies. But she moved across too, once again standing in front of me, almost nose to nose. I raised an eyebrow quizzically and, being very British, said 'Sorry', thinking I'd misread her intention.

She laughed out loud and, grabbing me by the shoulders, pushed me against the wall and said, 'What have I got to do to get you to notice me?!'

Even though I of course knew what she meant, I was terrified, so said, 'Of course I've noticed you, you've been coming to the group for a while now.'

Once again, she half snorted, then said, 'I fancy you, you idiot! I've been hoping you'd ask me out!'

Before I could figure out how to respond, she kissed me; a not unpleasant surprise, but her insistence and self-confidence flummoxed me completely. Writing about this now, it seems ridiculous to say, but I was almost flattered into a relationship. It didn't work out, mainly because I simply wasn't attracted to her physically, but she did play an important part in helping me to slowly rebuild my own self-confidence. But it would take many years before I would feel confident enough to ever dare act upon what I thought was mutual attraction, or to even consider trying to initiate a courtship.

Mum and Dad were of course fully aware of my new 'lifestyle', and although outwardly they were very supportive of the life I was leading, I knew that Mum wasn't really comfortable with it. She had always been a very sexual being, loving to flirt with men and often edgy and jealous around other women. She was very proud of her looks and figure when she was younger, especially pointing out how good she thought her legs were – she'd often say, ironically using the gay men's secret language of 'Polari', 'I've got great lallies, haven't I?'

She had told me that she had never had any schoolgirl crushes or fantasies about women, and was honest about the fact that the thought of sex between women made her feel very uncomfortable. Although she was careful not to risk hurting my feelings by using really strong words, I knew she found the whole idea repugnant.

Despite this, she understood that my sexual orientation was not something about which there was any choice. We had always been very close, more like sisters or best friends than mother and daughter, so could talk very openly. I went to great pains to assure her and Dad that my preferences were nothing to do with my upbringing – the breakfast cereals they fed me, not having a strong male influence for the first few years of my life, going to an all-girls school, being treated badly by boyfriends... As far as I'm concerned, for whatever reason, genetic or otherwise, I am like just about every single one of the LGBT people I've ever met: I didn't choose to be gay – I just am. I truly believe, as Lady Gaga once sang, I was born this way. The only choice I ever made was to accept and embrace who I am and what makes me happy. Any righteous heterosexual who feels they can condemn me for who I am is completely deranged – I could no more change this inherent essence of my being than change the colour of my skin or eyes. And as for the religious fanatics? Well, I always ask them, why would their God deliberately create someone as a perverse aberration, to be mocked, derided, imprisoned, tortured, killed, then condemned to spend all eternity in hell? Not the kind of deity I'd want to worship, whatever my personal peccadilloes!

I asked Mum on a number of occasions through the years how she really felt about probably not having grandchildren. I'd only ever had the very vaguest of curiosity about how it would feel to be pregnant. And although I had intended to train as a midwife had I stayed in the Army, I never felt overly maternal myself. I do wonder if I'd have been a good parent, but on balance, I think remaining childless was the right choice for me. Mum always said she honestly didn't mind because it was a lousy world and she'd only be worried about them and their future. But I was never entirely convinced and, it transpires, with good reason. After Mum's death in 2009, my aunty Dora, her sister-in-law, told me that Mum was very upset about it but had never wanted to hurt my feelings by saying so. Even though this just confirmed a long-held suspicion, it still cut to the quick – feeling that mum was disgusted and repulsed by the expression of love that brought me the joy and pleasure to which any person aspires.

I think things were further compounded by the fact that my brother's last serious girlfriend had told Mum and Dad when she first became pregnant. At the time, Ian was being quite psychotic and was occasionally violent and aggressive towards her. One evening, poor Libby was at our house, crying in Mum's arms because she was so torn about what to do for the best. She was a very beautiful, vibrant and outgoing young woman. Her social background was quite different to his. Her family were not happy for her to be seeing a boy like Ian, an anarchist punk, more interested in obtaining fame as part of Malice than earning a respectable living! Our whole family really loved her – she was just such a lovely young woman. She stuck with Ian for as long as she could, but his behaviour, due to his alcoholism, was pushing things to a limit and she reluctantly decided to have an abortion. Their relationship couldn't survive that, so Ian eventually made a decision to get out of England ('No future!'). Obviously my mum was devastated at losing the chance of a grandchild – especially as she knew I would not provide her with one – but she knew it was for the best.

As it happened, Libby breaking up with Ian was a very significant turning point, leading him to make up his mind to leave the UK. Having constantly knocked Mum and Dad's 'boring' lives, he finally got around to doing something about his own – applying for his 10-year 'full' passport and saving money to go to Europe. It was to prove a fateful decision.

By the time he took the ferry to the Netherlands, I had settled into a new job in France. Medic International had contacted me about another opportunity, this time at a smaller privately-run hospital called the Polyclinique du Maine in Laval, the 'capital' of Mayenne, a department between Brittany and Normandy in the north-west of the country.

While I was working in Laval, Ian was meanwhile working his way from Amsterdam to Greece. From there, he then came to the south of France. He'd managed to lose his passport en route. Mum and Dad had given him my phone number, thinking I might be of assistance, as I was fluent in French. We spoke only twice and the last call saw him hang up on me. He was angry when I had hesitated to give him my address. I tried to start explaining that, as I was in a rented apartment, it was a bit risky to invite him to stay. I was skirting round, walking on eggshells once more, but I think we both knew I was saying I didn't want him to stay in case he got drunk and ruined things for me.

He phoned Mum and Dad after he'd spoken to me. He'd been trying to stay dry and had spoken of his sadness about past troubles, including our fight and Nain's death. He told Mum he felt hopeful though – he'd met some nice people and was going to hitchhike to Marseilles, where he had the chance to do some paid labouring.

It was their last conversation. Two days after he spoke to Mum, on Good Friday, 9 April 1993, whilst walking along a busy road with no pavement, just on the outskirts of Salon-de-Provence, he was killed instantly when he fell beneath the back wheels of a passing articulated lorry. We have no way of ever knowing whether it was suicide or a freak accident, but he definitely wouldn't have suffered.

I finally managed to visit last year, in 2018, and felt some small solace in seeing what a beautiful part of the world, in my all-time favourite country, had been his final destination.

In the Pink

In early 1991, before Ian's death, I was remaining busy with the Gay's the Word group, trying to find some stability and purpose. Inadvertently, this was the catalyst for my life taking on a whole new direction for the next decade or more.

One Wednesday evening at the LLGC, following a very animated discussion, I was fairly drunk after a number of pints of beer – yes, I was definitely more butch than femme in my beverage preferences at least. Someone picked up a copy of the *Pink Paper* and drew my attention to an article that she thought might be of interest to me. I gave it a quick once over but was a bit too gone to fully take it in.

'You should give him a ring,' she said.

'Yeah, I might do,' I slurred.

So, once home at my flat in Beckenham, I decided I'd go for it. Dutch courage I suppose, but he answered despite the lateness of the hour.

'He' was Robert Ely, a former Army bandmaster, and the article was a brief summary of what had happened to him, asking anyone with a similar story or experiences to contact him as he was hoping to gather evidence. He was due to appear as a witness before the Armed Forces Bill Select Committee at the House of Commons. This is a five-yearly review which looks at all issues surrounding the running of all three services of HM Forces. In this case, the review was looking at the experience of gay men and women in the Armed Forces, and Robert's own story was to be aired in public for the first time.

He had joined the Army as a boy soldier at the tender age of 17, in December 1966, and had completed nearly 20 years as a bandmaster. He had been serving with the Parachute Regiment, just packing his things to go on a tour in Germany in June 1986, when the SIB came knocking at his door. His investigation was instigated as a result of a soldier he'd never even met, but to whom he had been writing, as the soldier had been questioned and the letters discovered. Although they had never been involved in any type of relationship, the very nature of the content of the letters was enough to end his career almost immediately. He was placed under house arrest for five days and ordered not to discuss anything with anyone whilst the investigation got underway. During his interrogation, comments were made that he must sleep with his dog and even his own brothers. Prejudice, ignorance, stupidity and hateful behaviour all accepted as 'the norm' back then. Yet Robert was the one deemed to be incompatible with service life.

Eventually, in June 1986, he was dismissed 'SNLR' – 'services no longer required'. These four words blighted so many LGBT servicemen and women over many decades. Robert was suddenly out on the streets with no support, no resettlement programme to help prepare for a life in civvy street that was completely unknown to him. This extremely talented musician and composer lost his pension rights and all the many benefits that service life brings – free healthcare, heavily subsidised food, sports facilities, travel cards, uniform, training – and all at a time when everything had been going so well for him. He had been about to apply for a regular commission, having gone as far in the ranks as he could, as a warrant officer. It was all snatched from him without any warning. This was a man whose shock and revulsion at the IRA attack on the bandstand in Hyde Park had led him to create the appeal fund that would bring help to the devastated families of those bandsmen who had been killed and maimed. Who would offer him support and assistance now that he was to be thrown onto the streets? No one. Due to the cataclysmic expulsion from the only career he had ever had since being a teenager, he soon fell into financial difficulty. He not only had to give up Rags, his beautiful Old English Sheepdog, but even had to sell his home. Enforced life as a civvy has been extremely tough for him.

When he got over the surprise of answering the phone to a young, slightly slurred-sounding woman, we talked and talked and talked! It was so incredible to know that we weren't alone in what we'd been through. Each of us was stunned to hear the other's dreadful story and we determined that we must meet up as soon as possible. He was based in Bristol then, but we got together and decided we needed to try to do something about this totally ridiculous, outdated and barbaric situation.

The *Pink Paper* article had been written as a result of Robert having contacted Stonewall to see what help might be available to him. Stonewall was founded in 1989 by political activists such as Michael Cashman CBE, Lisa Power MBE and Sir Ian McKellen, who were lobbying against Section 28 of the Local Government Act. It is an LGBT rights charity that took its name from the Stonewall Inn in New York's Greenwich Village – the site of the Stonewall Riots of 1969, widely acknowledged as spawning the birth of the modern Gay Liberation movement. Today's pride parades are directly descended from this momentous site. Stonewall is still going strong, which is perhaps a sad indictment that there is still much to do before true equality is reached, but also shows that persistence, logic and cogent argument can reap reward. The progress that has been made, in the UK at least, is inspiring.

Robert met Michael, the actor famously known as having the first 'gay kiss' in EastEnders whilst playing the part of Colin Russell. BBC2 was looking for interesting topics for their frontwoman Joan Bakewell to cover in her series *Heart of the Matter* and Robert and I were enlisted to take part in an episode called 'Falling Out', which was broadcast on 30 June 1991.

This was a pretty significant event – for anyone not familiar with her work, Joan, a journalist and now Baroness Bakewell DBE, was once most famously referred to as 'the thinking man's crumpet' and was one of very few early women television presenters. Having such a high profile personality cover the issue was significant. (The programme we recorded is still available to watch on YouTube – just type 'gays in the military Heart of the Matter' into your browser.)

The episode discussed the military ban, offering viewpoints from both sides. Robert and I had decided to put our heads above the parapet, as it were, and had agreed to be filmed. Having unceremoniously lost everything we had loved and valued, we had nothing left to lose. However, before I confirmed my commitment I very hesitantly approached Mum and Dad. I owed it to them to let them know what was being proposed. I'm not entirely sure what I would have said or done if they had opposed my involvement, but thankfully, they actually seemed quite keen. I think their recognition of how unjustly we had been treated overrode any worries about people viewing it and discovering my secret. Even if Mum wasn't wholly comfortable with my orientation, she was determined to see justice done. She loathed unfairness with a passion. Both she and Dad also said they were simply worried that I might face some criticism or backlash. Ultimately, I was delighted to be able to tell the producer that I was happy to participate.

Robert and I did our filming on different days, so we had no idea of how we would come over after the editing was done. It was the first time I had been filmed and I was incredibly nervous. The day before I was due to go into town to meet Joan Bakewell, I had gone out to the LLGC. Knowing that I had an early start and would like to present an intelligent, articulate argument against the silly old duffers, I had of course accepted every one of the drinks bought for me by the rest of that evening's discussion group. I made the last train and dozed off in a drunken stupor, only to arrive at the end of the line, having snoozed past Beckenham Junction. Having just a few coppers in my purse and the last London-bound train having long gone I did yet another immensely stupid thing – do you detect a theme here, folks?! – I shared a minicab from St Mary Cray with a bloke in a similar state of inebriation to me. Luckily for me, he and the cabbie were both very sweet, not only *not* raping and murdering me, but paying for the cab and refusing to give me an address to which I could send a reimbursement cheque. I was dropped right outside my flat at stupid o'clock, the dawn chorus already chirruping away at top whack. When my alarm split my very hung-over head about 90 minutes later, I was momentarily wondering why I was waking up in a disco – I didn't remember picking up the yellow flashing road safety light from the pothole outside!

I was still feeling extraordinarily fragile after showering and dressing – the face in the mirror certainly wasn't ready for a close up, Mr DeMille! Bloodshot eyes, heavy bags and a bloody great cold sore that looked like an alien tumour on the middle of my lower lip. Aaaaaaagh! Then I nearly had a heart attack as I realised I didn't have enough cash for the train into town! This was long before Oyster cards and contactless payments, so I hurtled next door to Sloane House Nursing Home where I now worked. The night girls were still on duty, and there was no Matron to ask questions, thank goodness. Not one of them had enough cash to lend me; I couldn't believe it! Then Tracy suddenly thought of something – why not take a note out of a patient's envelope in the safe? Ethel wasn't going to need it and I could replace it when I got back, no one need be any the wiser – perfect! As I was absolutely desperate by then, I agreed, took the fiver and careered to the station at a rate of knots. Just as I was making my way to the tube at Victoria, I felt an agonisingly familiar, way-too-flaming-early cramp – oh joy, what a fantastic time to come on! Incredibly, I managed to reach the appointed rendezvous on time, despite having had to use up what little of Ethel's money was left on a tampon from the station toilet vending machine!

Joan was absolute charm itself, buying me a cappuccino in a cafe just opposite Gay's the Word, which was where we were going to film some of the shots. The main bulk of the interview was to be carried out in a flat belonging to the producer, Emma, which was just around the corner. It felt odd being back in my old stomping ground from the Bedford Hotel days.

Despite all the problems, filming went well. It took absolutely *ages* so I was very concerned as to how they would edit it. Three hours of filming was going to have to be pruned to fit a debate programme of only half an hour! We then went outside to film some 'walking' shots for a voiceover section. I found it very weird and unsettling to suddenly be incapable of doing something I never usually even thought about. We had to do about four takes! 'Too fast, Elaine!' – 'Better, but next time don't look at the camera!' – 'You look like you're marching; could you not swing your arms so much?!' That's why I have my hands jammed deep into my pockets and am looking down in the shot they eventually used.

Robert experienced a similar phenomenon during his distance shots, and we laughed ourselves silly when we finally got to see our respective end results. I still titter when I see him feeding the ducks in Regent's Park – he's throwing the bread so hard and fast it looks as if he's trying to kill the poor birds!

Joan, Emma and the crew seemed genuinely happy with what I'd given them, telling me that the way in which I'd told my story, calmly and unsensationally, made it all the more powerful and effective. I felt really excited as I went home.

The next day at work, having gone to the bank to draw out some cash to replenish Ethel's envelope, I came very close to being sacked from a second nursing role. Matron had been told about what had happened and was, quite rightly, absolutely furious with me. I had completely betrayed my position of trust – how dare I take a patient's personal spending money; it was utterly unconscionable! She was incandescent with rage. I was beyond mortified; my deep shame showed through my puce, burning cheeks. I immediately realised it was time to sort my life out and curb the now worryingly regular habit I had adopted of knocking back anywhere between four and seven pints when I was on a night out.

I took a massive risk and decided to explain to Matron why I felt I had no choice but to borrow the £5. I hadn't a clue as to how she would react, but once I had explained what the trip was for, she softened and was genuinely interested to know more about what had happened. She also told me that she thought I was one of the best sisters she had worked with at Sloane House and didn't want to lose me when I was such an asset to the team. I was close to tears; her praise meant a great deal to me, especially after I had been such a total fool.

All the staff were soon quite excited, wanting to know when the programme would be broadcast. It was probably for the best that the story came out amongst my colleagues, because there was at that time an increasing awareness of the issue. Articles about me and other Rank Outsiders had begun appearing in most of the main newspapers, always accompanied by a photograph, so no possibility of denial.

After the programme went out, one of the health care assistants at Sloane House wrote me a poem, which really moved me. It was very touching to know that I had made a bit of a difference and that my 'courage' had helped her to come out, even if it was initially only to me. I was beginning to experience a slow but liberating metamorphosis: feelings of shame and embarrassment were being replaced by an increasingly strong sense of defiance and pride. It was exhilarating to be spending so much time in the company of people, straight and gay, for whom my personal life choices and preferences were irrelevant. They were, quite rightly to my mind, more concerned with how we treat one another as fellow human beings.

For Elaine

I sat and watched in disbelief
The tears welled in my eyes
I felt your pain and lived your grief
At their ignorance and lies
The torture that your pride has suffered
In their careless hands
No thoughts of time and dedication
Just bigotry and plans
Discarded at a whim and rules
That mean not what they say
To rip apart your whole damn life
Because, like me, you're gay
No crime I say, it's legal here
To live the way you feel
Their prehistoric judgments
So absurd it's just not real
Your courage made me feel so proud
I think of you and smile

In times of my disheartened thoughts
You made my choice worthwhile
I am ecstatic in the way I feel toward your strength
I'll never find the words to tell you how at any length
So here they lie, my words of praise
Not for your eyes to see
But knowing on despondent days
Your strength will comfort me

30 June 1991

The day following the broadcast, I got a telephone call from Mum and Dad. We discussed their reaction to the programme. I was greatly relieved to learn that they had thought it balanced, fair, unsensationalist and that Robert and I had acquitted ourselves very well, unlike the moronic, reactionary old fogeys who were the flip side of the argument's coin. Robert was with me that day, as he had come from his home in Bristol to my flat in Beckenham so we could watch the programme together. We had no editorial control and therefore felt very nervous as to what would be shown. Having both been interviewed over a number of hours, it was very nerve-racking not knowing how it would have been compressed down and edited into a half hour transmission.

Funnily enough, Mum also mentioned that they had had an unexpected call from my former boyfriend Steve Moody from the post office: did I remember him? And that they hoped I hadn't minded, but they'd given him my number.

Literally minutes after I said goodbye to Mum, the phone rang again. I came to the phone to hear a familiar voice and the years just fell away: 'Laine, I'm so proud of you girl! I was just flicking through the channels, thinking about an early night when I heard your dulcet tones and thought "It can't be!" – I nearly choked on my cocoa!'

It was so lovely to hear Steve's voice again, and also a huge relief that he wasn't calling to berate me for having deceived him all those years ago when we were going out! After a brief catch up as to what had been happening in each of our lives (although he of course had a head start as to what my life's twists and turns had been), he dropped his little bombshell – 'Well, Laine, you'll never guess what...'

'What then? Tell me!' I said, half expecting him to say he was married and the father of a massive family of gorgeous children.

There was a dramatic pause, then he announced: 'I'm gay too!'

Many times since I have joked that it's hardly surprising that I never managed to get him to bed me. But if truth be known, we were always destined to be friends rather than lovers. He always says I duped him, but I think we were perhaps both guilty of that! We met up again soon after the call, enjoying a wonderful sunny afternoon at Mum and Dad's, along with my Uncle Tony and Aunty Dora. Reminiscing over barbecued goodies, cool drinks and excellent company, we agreed how incredibly lucky it was that Mum and Dad hadn't moved and that he'd kept my old phone number, otherwise we may never have caught up again. Our renewed friendship has since gone from strength to strength and I feel blessed to have him in my life.

Rank Outsiders

Robert and I were naturally on tenterhooks after the *Heart of the Matter* programme was broadcast to see how it would be received by the general public and members of the Armed Forces. In actual fact, it was quite useful for us, because it led to a fair bit of interest, not least because it wasn't a subject that many people had known about. Most of Joe Public had no idea that a ban even existed, let alone that innocent people serving to protect their Queen and country were being hounded out as criminals!

As Stonewall and Robert began to gather more stories throughout the early 1990s, the extent of the number of lives ruined was becoming clearer. We were certainly far from alone. Many hundreds or even thousands of excellent servicemen and women had been forced to leave the careers they loved and for which they had been eminently suited, all because of their sexual orientation.

Robert and I decided what was needed was a two-pronged approach. We would try to form a group of people who had been through the same experience, perhaps along with interested supporters such as family and friends or fair-minded individuals (straight, gay or indifferent), who were willing to stand up and be counted. We would do this not only to lobby for a lifting of the ban and to publicise this appalling injustice. Perhaps more importantly, we also wanted to create a support group.

The aim was to offer somewhere for those in the Forces to turn to for help and advice if they were afraid they might be under suspicion, or were even in the process of being investigated. We felt they might not realise they could have choices as far as legal advice went. Many of us didn't even think to ask for civilian lawyers or to refuse to answer such dreadful questions – we were all too used to a disciplined life of obeying orders. And of course, huge numbers of investigations would have taken place in the times when there was no internet on which to seek advice or information. The so-called pink press had small ad sections used by gay-friendly solicitors, but most LGBT service personnel wouldn't have dared risk keeping copies of such magazines and newspapers, for fear of incrimination and blackmail.

We came up with the name 'Rank Outsiders' whilst driving to visit another friend of mine, also called Steve, in Southsea. We were in the car belonging to my then girlfriend, Alison, all chattering at once and very excited about this new project. It worked on so many different levels. We also eventually designed what I thought was an excellent logo – a sergeant major type symbol, but with the three chevrons coloured navy, red and pale blue from top to bottom in reference to the colours representing the three services in chronological order of their founding – Navy, Army and RAF – and with the usual small crown above them replaced with a pink triangle edged in black. The pink triangle is traditionally used to symbolise homosexual men and has painful origins in the Holocaust: in the same way that Jews were forced to have yellow stars stitched to their tunics, gay men had pink triangles. The black edging round the triangle refers to the black triangles worn in the death camps by lesbians, trade unionists and troublemakers. I rather liked the notion that at one time or another I would say I fitted all three of those descriptors! In the 1980s, black triangles in jewellery were almost as good a way of dyke-spotting as the double-headed labrys or the pinkie ring.

Through my regular contact with Gay's the Word, I was by now making up for lost time in terms of reading as much as I could about lesbian and gay history – or should that be herstory? The debates about the watering down of feminism and oppression of women were fascinating. Little did I know they'd be raging as strongly as ever 30 years on. I was stunned at my ignorance, so lapped up all I could. I was reading voraciously and, through the friends I was making, seeing films depicting lesbians not as deviant perverts, sad lonely psychos or full of desperate self-loathing. Donna Deitch's incredibly uplifting *Desert Hearts* became a personal favourite. Being able to socialise in London at this time was just phenomenal – the British Film Institute, at the Southbank near Waterloo, even showed rarely-screened LGBT-themed films on the big screen. I was in heaven.

One of the first big events Robert and I attended was Pride in London, which was then known as Gay Pride. It was much more political then as we were just at the end of the Thatcher years, but Robert and I were very shocked at how we were treated by the so-called gay 'community'.

I'd spent most of the evening before creating a home-made banner. This was before the 'sergeant major' logo had been thought of, so it was a very simple design. I created large stencil letters in cardboard to draw around, spelling out 'Rank Outsiders' in uppercase in the centre of the banner (a white bed sheet, ironed, folded in half with stitching along the sides to allow two long broom handles to hold it aloft) with smaller text beneath: 'Ex Armed Forces lesbians and gays'. To cover the back, because the bright red marker pen filling in the black edged letters was visible from behind, I'd got an old Union Jack flag from a charity shop – big mistake! The lovely, right-on, left-leaning, liberal lezzies and gay boys seemed to think we were something akin to Mosley's black shirts! We got a lot of verbal abuse and were made to feel very uncomfortable – wow! Nobody wanted us! In later years, other Rank Outsiders members reported having been spat at by fellow Pride marchers.

We persisted though, and had a three or four-page feature in America's leading gay magazine *The Advocate* as a result. It had been written by Mark Simpson, now perhaps best known as the originator of the term and concept 'metrosexual', and once described as 'the skinhead Oscar Wilde'. We were being invited to discuss the matter more frequently and our membership steadily grew. We had our initial meetings in an upstairs room at the LLGC and began appointing roles such as chair, secretary, press liaison. Robert was the first chairperson, but expressed the wish early on not to remain so. He preferred to concentrate on the not insignificant task of creating a proper, written constitution. It was vitally important that we be seen as a serious outfit.

Outside the MOD – moved along by security!

Other TV appearances followed over the next few years. Early in 1994 I featured in a brief piece on BBC Breakfast News, along with Mike, one of our earliest secretaries. He chose to keep his face hidden, but with my new-found confidence, I was fully in shot. Out and proud. I had by then briefly returned to nursing, so was filmed wearing my royal blue sister's dress, my blue enamel Army-trained nurse's badge clearly visible – and then the tear-jerking shot: I undo my blue Petersham belt, having come home after a shift, lay it down very tidily on my bed, and they focus in closely on the QARANC buckle I'd trained for three years to earn the right to wear.

Robert and I also appeared in a daytime magazine programme fronted by Miriam Stoppard, called *People Today*. The feature on gays in the military was prefaced by a filmed comic sketch with Hugh Laurie as a high-ranking officer attempting to address the issue, which was very funny indeed. What wasn't quite as funny was the fact that my journey by train, from London to Manchester, was a total nightmare. A series of delays meant I literally only just made it in time, our slot having had to be rescheduled towards the end of the show. After the driver deposited me at the studios, the make-up team were faced with a very florid, stressed young woman, with a tendency to blush and blotch all too easily. I was amused to see the taped show later – I look very pale and rather like the proverbial stunned rabbit in the headlights; I'd literally been ushered on set with seconds to spare!

There were a few other members of Rank Outsiders participating in each of the four main channels' news programmes. One of my appearances was on ITV's *Whale On* with James Whale (this was not only about the military but included members of LAGPA – the Lesbian and Gay Police Association). As someone who is normally very self-critical, *Whale On* was the single show that I was most content with. It felt the most real I'd ever been. True to myself, I suppose might be a way to explain it. I wasn't classically butch in my appearance, but I have always felt most comfortable in trousers. I was in jeans, men's shirt and jacket, brown leather ankle boots, buckled and yes, of course flat heeled – for this by now bona fide, openly dyke 34-year-old woman, comfortable shoes were de rigueur. I'd worn stilettos for years as part of my lengthy phase of trying to fit in. My only concession to accepted standards of femininity was a modicum of make-up – a thin line of black kohl beneath lower eyelids, black mascara, clear lip gloss. I was wearing contact lenses then and my eyes are quite small, hence my letting the make-up ladies attempt to create the illusion that they were larger and my lips fuller (they're far too thin for my liking!).

Interestingly enough, Gaytime TV and flagship gay programmes such as *Out on Tuesday* rarely seemed interested. Also, although Stonewall has often been lauded for its involvement in the work to get the ban lifted and quotes the 'gays in the military' campaign as being one of its most successful, some of its members at the time were initially very reluctant to get involved. I think the main things that concerned them were similar to what Robert and I encountered at that first Pride march – people simply had issues with anything to do with the military, full stop. If they were pacifists, they couldn't see beyond that. When Stonewall did come on board, under the directorship (1992–2002) of Angela Mason CBE, I remember Anya Palmer, one of the team, admitting that she couldn't understand why anyone, regardless of their sexuality, would *ever* want to join the military. But she would absolutely defend their right to do so and would battle to stop them being excluded because of their sexuality rather than their capability (or otherwise) of doing the job. It was over a century ago that Evelyn Beatrice Hall, in her biography of Voltaire, wrote, 'I disapprove of what you say, but I will defend to the death your right to say it.' It is still relevant today.

I was reminded, after speaking with my friend Ed Hall, author of *We Can't Even March Straight*, that he also encountered a fair bit of resistance when he first set about trying to get his Armed Forces Legal Challenge Group started. It seems hard to believe that it was felt that no lawyers or solicitors anywhere in the UK would even consider trying to challenge the ban. Stonewall did eventually come on board, as did Tyndallwoods Solicitors in Birmingham. Ed had asked everyone who might be interested in cases to attend a meeting and Tyndallwoods came along. It's incredible when one looks back, to remember the difficulties that were faced little over 20 years ago.

How Ed came to start the group is in itself worth telling here. It strikes me as reminiscent of the ripple in the pond or domino effect.

Ed had written a piece in the *Independent* in August 1993, detailing the experiences of RAF Sergeant Simon Ingram. Simon had served six and a half years as an air electronics operator, serving in the first Gulf War and had been twice recommended for a commission. Then he was reported to the RAF police by someone he'd thought was a friend, who had even met his civilian boyfriend.

On the back of this piece, Ed was then commissioned to write a book. Ed had served as a Royal Navy officer for two years before acknowledging his homosexuality and resigning his commission. He wrote the book as part of the campaign to drive the British government into lifting the ban. As he was finishing it, in August 1994, the *Guardian* published a big article about both Ed and the book. He also appeared on *Newsnight* on BBC2 that same day, alongside the chair of the Armed Forces Select Committee. This is the committee to which Robert Ely had testified three years earlier, bravely drawing attention to the ban for the first time in any meaningful way.

The legal case began because of the reaction to Ed's book and his having been asked about the campaign because of the 'don't ask, don't tell' policy across the pond in the US. Under Bill Clinton's presidency, this controversial Department of Defense Directive, introduced on 28 February 1994, prohibited military personnel from discriminating against or harassing *closeted* homosexual or bisexual service members or applicants, whilst barring openly gay, lesbian or bisexual persons from military service. It was to remain in effect until 20 September 2011. Post 1993, more than 13,000 US troops were discharged for being openly gay. The numbers decreased after the 9/11 attacks of 2001, but more than 600 servicemen and women were discharged every year until 2009.

At Rank Outsiders, reactions to the idea of openly supporting and promoting a legal challenge were split – but eventually we decided it was too risky. We were trying very hard to set up meaningful channels of communication with the MOD, so it was felt that if we were seen as the driving force/public face behind mounting a legal challenge, it might jeopardise any inroads we were close to making. As we wanted very much to be able to offer real and effective support to any serving LGBT personnel, it was reluctantly decided not to publicly back or endorse any challenge. Ed felt this was a mistake and that Rank Outsiders could still do both things. However he was voted down in a committee meeting, so decided to set up a group independently, which became known as the Armed Forces Legal Challenge Group. Thankfully, he remained an active member of RO as well.

Rank Outsiders had continued to expand, with membership eventually numbering in the hundreds. Word of mouth, articles in the mainstream and pink press, home-made flyers left throughout gay clubs, pubs and venues were beginning to get us known. We attempted to persuade the powers that be at the MOD that we would simply like to meet with them to discuss things. It was virtually impossible for us to make inroads at first. Apparently, the thought within Whitehall's hallowed halls was that we were attention-seeking individuals who were something akin to groups such as Outrage!, the Lesbian Avengers or Act Up, out to make trouble.

These organisations each battled for LGBT rights for many years. Outrage! was founded on 10 May 1990 after the murder of gay actor Michael Boothe. Veteran campaigner Peter Tatchell, who had been active in the Gay Liberation Front, was at the first meeting. Many of their campaigns were deliberately provocative and of course fantastically successful, especially in terms of gaining publicity. The kiss-in at Piccadilly Circus in September 1990 was a highlight. Their intended outing campaign, revealing famous, rich, powerful closeted LGBT people, was often the cause of very heated debates in late night TV programmes and in the LGBT press.

The Lesbian Avengers began in New York in 1992, as a direct-action group focused on issues vital to lesbian survival and visibility. A British chapter was formed in 1994 from members of Outrage!, and one of the group's earliest and most high-profile actions came when Sandi Toksvig was dropped by Save the Children charity after she came out. Protests organised by the Lesbian Avengers led to the charity apologising.

Act Up, the AIDS Coalition to Unleash Power, was formed in March 1987 in New York. Larry Kramer, playwright, author, public health advocate and LGBT rights activist founded it. This became an influential international direct-action advocacy group, working to impact the lives of people with AIDS.

Rank Outsiders, by contrast, had deliberately decided very early on that, much as it might be amusing to raid the BBC and sit on Nicholas Witchell (maybe Anna Ford would have been preferable), stage kiss-ins, abseil into the House of Lords and wake up the crusty old farts, we were going to take a calm, professional and orderly approach. We were not going to ally ourselves with any political group – we were trying very hard to prove the point that the MOD's actions and discriminatory behaviour was costing them dear. They were spending a fortune to train us to their rigorous standards only to eject us, despite consistently excellent reports about our work and conduct! None of what they were doing had any basis in fact and the tired arguments about how the presence of gay soldiers would 'undermine unit cohesion' were increasingly being shown to be facile and unsupported by hard evidence. The old guard knew they were beginning to look and sound increasingly desperate and some of the programmes of that time make painfully amusing viewing as they squirm whilst trying to defend the indefensible. I do think it would have been hilarious if we had learned the Monty Python 'camp soldiers doing drill' routine though, and performed it in front of the MOD, dressed in camouflage fatigues and pink tutus – 'Ooh, get her!'

Our numbers continued to grow, despite there being no social media to alert potential members to our existence, and we decided to develop our own monthly magazine, *Breaking Ranks*. Sadly, I don't remember exactly when we started producing it, but I think it was fairly early in our existence, so probably around 1992. (We have lost touch with our member who was acting as an archivist, but hopefully we may yet manage to track her down.) The MOD were still refusing to meet us and would not countenance any request to allow us to place adverts in any military publications, so we thought we would create our own tool of communication. It included articles, information, helpline contact details, AGM reports, social bulletins and the like. It was sent out monthly to any paying member.

It was thanks to Stonewall that a really significant milestone was achieved. They helped fund a telephone helpline to be run from their offices in Greycoat Place, Victoria. As it was to be manned by volunteers, we could initially only offer the helpline on Wednesday evenings, but plans were to expand it when possible. This was a significant step forward in terms of being able to offer real, tangible support to anyone either being investigated, under suspicion or simply wanting to know what their position was as a closeted member of HM Forces.

It was instantly clear that some people were naturally very suspicious as to whether or not it was genuine. There was a real fear that the MOD was prepared to go to extraordinarily devious lengths to entrap homosexual 'offenders'. It was not beyond the realms of possibility that the whole thing was fake! Even as I write that, it just seems utterly incomprehensible. But the ridiculous sense of paranoia I am describing was completely real. Considering the nature of what were once deemed to be 'offences', supposedly capable of 'undermining unit morale and cohesion' – it seems utterly ridiculous now. Yet lives were being ruined by this policy right up to the year 2000. Trying to discover definitive numbers can be difficult – the Royal Navy often categorised discharges for homosexuality as 'medical'. And officers like me, who chose to resign their commission rather than face a court martial or being dishonourably discharged, wouldn't show up on an official count as being LGBT.

I personally do believe that my phone line was tapped and I know many others who are equally certain that they too were under surveillance in the early '90s. Whenever I made calls from home, there were always discernible clicks and hisses that BT (British Telecom) had investigated many times. I was always assured that their checks revealed no technical faults with the line. As I knew I had nothing to say that could ever be of the slightest concern to anyone, nor that I could ever pose a security threat to my homeland, I would occasionally take infantile delight in talking absolutely filthy, inane, crude gibberish with whichever Rank Outsider member was at the other end of the line. Sometimes I'd do impersonations. Because many of us were experiencing the same thing, we felt it was only fair to offer a bit of light relief to the poor minions listening in.

Some of our members, or people who called the helpline but were too afraid to join, would recount stories of their personal mail having shown signs of tampering, or feeling they were being followed or watched when they were off duty and went off base. I am sure that these practices will eventually come to light under the Data Protection provisions, vindicating what could have been viewed by the tabloids as a load of silly queens and dykes' paranoia. How the UK government might choose to justify spending taxpayers' money in this way could prove very interesting. It seemed very wrong to be closing public libraries and community projects whilst wasting valuable resources on such pointless activities.

Due to the exposure we were beginning to get across mainstream media, we were finally managing to make contact with people who might be able to help us. We met with a number of MPs, including Labour's Chris Smith, who, in 1984, had been the first MP to come out as gay. He became the Secretary of State for Culture, Media and Sport in 1997, in Tony Blair's cabinet.

The real impetus for change and a significant increase in publicity came after Ed's Armed Forces Legal Challenge Group finally came into being. The main aim was to challenge the ban itself, with a view to forcing it to be lifted. The UK's membership of the European Union afforded us certain protections as EU citizens, regardless of where we were employed. The oft-derided European Court of Human Rights was likely to be the only organisation with the power or authority to challenge the UK government's treatment of many of its own citizens. Forces personnel were defending their country and its people, yet our own rights and freedoms were ignored and debased. A secondary aim was to gain some form of compensation to make up for the very real financial impact we had all experienced, simply because we were not being allowed the fundamental human right to a private life. Although there were eventually somewhere in the region of 70 to 80 challengers on Tyndallwoods' books, there had to be a focal point. The 'Armed Forces Four' became an oft-seen item in newspapers, radio and TV shows. Duncan Lustig-Prean (Royal Navy lieutenant commander), John Beckett (Naval rating), Graeme Grady (RAF administrator) and Jeanette Smith (RAF nurse) became the faces of the challenge. There were a few separate cases under different solicitors, but the vast majority were those of us with Tyndallwoods.

I had very much hoped my case would have been included, especially as I had served in both the ranks and as a commissioned officer. Proportionally, it seemed that far more women than men were discharged and, I believe, more Army personnel than from the two other services. It seemed odd to me not to have an Army case to balance it out. But it wasn't to be. I suspect the fact that I had been accused, albeit falsely, of forcing unwanted attention upon fellow officers made it wiser to pick cases that would be less likely to draw the scorn and derision of such tabloids as might be considered to espouse homophobic views.

The legal battle that followed was even longer and more stressful than I think any of us could ever have envisaged. Throughout 14 very long and testing years, from 1995 to 2009, the MOD, via their legal representative, the Treasury Solicitor, was completely unreasonable and obstructive at every turn. They used delay tactics and absolutely refused point blank to acknowledge any wrongdoing on their part. Every time we got close to a point where it might be possible to have our day in court something happened to delay matters. I once got to the Industrial Tribunal in Croydon, but yet again, never got called to the stand as a witness. This was a matter of enormous annoyance to me. Although I was nervous about the prospect of being grilled by the MOD's people, I wanted to show them that I was an intelligent, articulate, reasonable person and to prove that their policy was farcical and blatantly unjust – they were throwing people out for what, exactly?

I was, and am still, enraged at the utterly disgusting and unfair way in which the MOD acted during those incredibly stressful years. Their tactics were nothing short of underhand and downright deceitful. Those of us who took them all the way to the European Court of Human Rights in Strasbourg were merely trying to use whatever recourse possible to recompense us for very real losses. We knew there was nothing to be done as far as the emotional turmoil was concerned. But we did feel, given the acknowledgement that, like it or not, our human rights really had been breached, there should have been some 'payback'. Most of us had faced enormous financial difficulties in the years after dismissal. We were given neither resettlement advice nor assistance. Job interviews were made much more difficult, because how could we explain 'services no longer required' without having to 'out' ourselves in an era when Section 28 of the Local Government Act 1988 prevailed?

Tyndallwoods asked us to work out what our pecuniary losses were. A legitimate template tool was used. Given the years of loss of salary, pension rights, travel, health, dental benefits, free sport facilities, accommodation, food and uniform, training – well, the sums were pretty hefty. Many ran into six figures. The MOD eventually made their individual calculations using the most blatantly iniquitous formula ever. But prior to this, they just made blanket offers, gradually raising the sums as the months became years and the death knell for the ban rang ever louder. We were first offered £5,000, then £10,000, then £12,500, then £19,000, then £30,000.

When the European Court ruling was imminent, they personalised the frankly insulting and derisory offers by referring to 'median' lengths of service, but these did not allow for differing, individual circumstances. For example, most QA officers were direct entrant, NHS trained nurses on Short Service Commissions, most commonly of only two years. The majority left after that, either to return to the NHS, having gained valuable experience, or because they had to leave after having got married. Pregnancy and marriage then required women to leave. So how did that apply to my very different circumstances? I was incandescent with rage and wrote many letters to my MP Joan Ruddock, Geoff Hoon, the then Defence Secretary, Prime Ministers John Major and Tony Blair and of course Tyndallwoods Solicitors themselves.

They were in many ways very brave to take on what was largely felt to be an unwinnable case. But as the years rolled slowly by, they did seem to lose momentum. The first three solicitors, all women, were fired up and enthusiastic. There was rarely a week that went by without another copy of a letter they'd sent to the MOD's Treasury Solicitor falling on the door mat. My lever arch files got filled very quickly. Sadly for us, each of these feisty women moved on. The first, Madeleine Rees, went on to work for the Office of the High Commission for Human Rights, becoming the gender expert and head of office in Bosnia and Herzegovina. Her story was portrayed by Vanessa Redgrave in the film *The Whistleblower*. She is, at the time of writing, the current Secretary General of the Women's International League for Peace and Freedom.

Next came Jean Gould. She was also very active and kept us well-informed as to what she was doing on our behalf. She helped found Public Law Solicitors, a firm specialising in public law, human rights and community care law. After she left towards the end of 2000, Helen Goldie took over. Luckily for us, she was very experienced in employment law and seemed to be firing on all cylinders. I was delighted, as the momentum seemed to be picking up and I had the feeling she was determined and absolutely prepared to challenge the Treasury Solicitor very strongly. Sadly for us, she too left just a few months later.

Every time it looked as if we might have our day in court, something would occur to thwart us. It was incredibly frustrating, especially as it felt as if we were forever awaiting the outcome of other significant, but often unrelated, cases. This was because the decisions might have helped us in our own battle. There was Advocate General for Scotland v MacDonald (2003); Pearce v Mayfield School (2003), also Lisa Grant v South West Trains (1998). These cases each essentially challenged homophobic behaviour, being UK labour law cases concerning sexuality and sex discrimination. If the plaintiffs had won, this could have led to some enforced changes in various laws that might set a precedent to treat LGBT citizens fairly and equally to their heterosexual counterparts.

Mr MacDonald was a pilot who had been sacked from the RAF for being gay – the Sex Discrimination Act of 1975 did not cover sexuality discrimination and was meant only to cover gender, not sexuality. Shirley Pearce was a lesbian teacher whose employers had made no effort whatsoever to protect her from homophobic bullying and harassment by pupils. Lisa Grant took South West Trains to court because she was not allowed to confer her travel benefits to her same sex partner, yet unmarried heterosexual employees' partners were entitled to qualify for travel passes worth £1,000. She lost because male and female employees would be affected identically by the denial of benefits so there was no discrimination on the basis of sex. There was no 'sexual orientation' discrimination because the EC Treaty only referred to sex discrimination at that time.

For those who don't know, you have to exhaust every legal avenue in the land before being able to take a case to Europe. Eventually, the cases of MacDonald and Pearce reached the Law Lords. This is as far as one can go in the UK. If the case is not satisfactorily resolved at this stage, the last option then becomes to submit a case to the ECHR in Strasbourg. Roddy MacDonald's case was essentially the same as ours, so the outcome was vital as it would determine our path to

Strasbourg. His case was finally decided on 19 June 2003, along with that of Ms Pearce. It seems incredible now, but the reason they lost their appeal was because discrimination was only then illegal in terms of sex, but *not* sexual orientation. In other words, as Lord Nicholls of Birkenhead stated:

> Much of the argument in these two appeals was directed at identifying the appropriate persons with whom the appellants are to be compared when making the 'less favourable treatment' comparison. The statute… envisages a simple comparison of how the claimant was treated and how a person of the opposite sex would have been treated in the same circumstances. Had… he been a woman, he would not have been dismissed. But the opposing arguments focused on the need for a 'like with like' comparison… To compare him with a heterosexual woman is not to compare like with like. The appropriate comparator is a lesbian. She too would have been dismissed under the policy then prevailing in the Armed Forces. So Mr MacDonald did not receive less favourable treatment on the ground of his sex. Similar arguments were advanced in the converse case of Ms Pearce.

Cases like these were vitally important in leading to amendments in anti-discrimination laws, finally including sexual orientation in the Equality Act 2010. The 'Armed Forces Four' got their court ruling in June 1995. Although Lord Justice Brown and Mr Justice Clegg of the High Court upheld the legality of the MOD position and rejected the applicability of European Community (EU) law, the former judge was notable in expressing his sympathy for the plaintiffs. The ban was again upheld by the Appeal Court in November 1995, but very significantly, one of the three judges found in our favour. It was becoming increasingly clear that the winds of change were finally blowing in the right direction.

Despite some high-profile naysayers, such as the then Minister of State for the Armed Forces, Nicholas Soames, insisting that speculation that the MOD might be reviewing its ban on homosexuals was 'wholly inaccurate', such opinions were beginning to seem out of place with the wider world. In 1995, apart from Luxembourg and Turkey, no other NATO country imposed an absolute ban on homosexuals in their armed forces. The USA and

Germany had partial bans. Commonwealth nations such as Australia and New Zealand, where their armed forces had similar traditions and legal base to Britain, had altered policy in 1991. Anyone applying to join the Australian Defence Force (ADF) was no longer required to declare their sexual orientation and the admission of homosexual activity by service personnel no longer, by itself, constituted grounds for discharge. New Zealand followed the changes in Australian policy and declared homosexuality to no longer be a bar to military service. The UK was beginning to seem very out of step.

Where Are All the Women?

As time went on and the RO membership numbers continued to swell, one interesting phenomenon occurred. By around 1998, the ratio of male and female members was completely disproportionate to the numbers being made to leave the Forces. Given the much smaller number of serving women than men, the number of lesbians being ejected seemed proportionally much higher than that of gay men. I believe that in 1990, women only accounted for 5.7 per cent of UK Regular Forces.

I have endeavoured to find figures that accurately break down the number of servicemen and servicewomen discharged for homosexuality, but with the MOD having been reluctant to reveal numbers in the past, I have failed dismally. The Armed Forces Bill of 8 December 1995 states:

> Some 260 Service personnel were discharged for being homosexual between 1991, when homosexual activity in the armed forces was decriminalized in practice, and 1994. Stonewall, a gay rights pressure group, claims that another 240 found the pressures of being homosexual in organizations in which gays were prescribed unbearable and also left the forces between 1991 and 1995.

However, our membership had hardly any female members and we endeavoured to find out why. At the most, we ran into a few dozen. Those of us who were regular attendees at meetings were sometimes one of only between two and four women. I think the reason we were thwarted in the aim to get more female members was because many of the male members really weren't that interested. It may well be quite a contentious assertion to make, but I'm going to put my neck on the line and stick with it. That's not to say that *all* the men felt that way. I was always very impressed with one of our chairs, Patrick Lyster-Todd, who seemed genuinely concerned about striking a fair balance and treating all members respectfully. And some of our most loyal members, such us Roger Garford, really did try to make sure we were listened to. But it felt very male-dominated and, oddly enough, very Royal Navy-dominated too. The Senior Service often seemed to hold sway. I am not saying this in a negative way, just making an observation.

One thing that I am certain did put women off attending some of our by now regular meetings was the choice of location. The gay scene then was very divisive, with very few pubs or bars having an equal division of male and female customers. There seemed always to be a tendency either towards primarily gay men with a few female guests or lesbian bars with a few gay men as guests. Nothing much in between, sadly. Some of the more 'balanced' places such as the Angel bar in Islington, rarely, if ever, got voted as the choice of venue. Unfortunately, the LLGC had become less of an option when their management changed and the cost of hiring a room became too much. Also, although many of our members were based in and around London, we were aware of the need to try to set up local support groups, even if there might only be one or two members in the vicinity of some of the smaller, more rural towns.

We once held a fancy dress fundraiser event at the Railway pub in Aldershot. That felt especially amazing. Not only to be openly gay in the town in which I'd spent two and a half of the happiest, yet most closeted, years of my life, but to be in a gay pub that had always reputedly been best known as a knocking shop!

Occasional, cursory efforts were made to find somewhere that might have been less intimidating to women, but for the most part, many of our meeting places tended to be quite rough. I forget the name of some of the pubs round King's Cross, but they weren't great. I don't know if women are so anxious about walking into a bar or pub alone these days, but back then it was quite an ordeal. If the pub was packed to the rafters with gay guys from the S&M or 'bear' crowds, it could certainly be pretty off-putting to many women. Some of the bars had back rooms and basements where the guys would go after the meetings for whatever sexual adventures went on there. It was something about which I never felt judgemental – each to his own, as long as it's mutually consensual. But I never really understood the drive for sex with strangers.

I suppose one thing that deserves a mention is the fact that, for many of our male members, the freedom to be openly gay, out and proud probably led to some wild socialising and sexual exploration once the business side of the meetings were concluded.

I did once consider putting myself forward to be the chairperson, but fate had offered me the chance to work in my favourite country, France, so my time with the organisation wasn't that long. My main contribution, other than getting it off the ground and acquitting myself well televisually, had been to attend meetings regularly and to try to influence matters as best I could. It honestly wasn't always easy when the men tended to dominate so much. There were some very passionate and intense members, so our committee meetings were often heated and lengthy. I had been secretary for a while, but the move to France, early in 1992, had meant my contributions temporarily ceased. When I returned to the UK, 18 months later, in September 1993, I re-joined and even managed to fundraise nearly £400 by doing a 'sponsored walk' in an attempt to conquer the southern half of the Pennine Way with Steve. Mum was amazing, working her socks off to get her colleagues and neighbours to contribute.

But the second time around, something happened to make me eventually distance myself from the group even further.

One of our earliest, most reliable members, Chloë, and I had been considering forming a breakaway, women-only group, because the men were getting on our nerves a bit. Most of them were great, but we still felt we were sometimes being sidelined. This was probably around 1997/8.

With an increasing number of new people joining, there came a shift in the dynamic of what had once felt like quite a tight-knit and supportive group. One new member, Bill, seemed to be friendly enough. He eventually launched his campaign to become chair and after a particularly tense and fractious meeting, he was elected. He was, in my opinion, not very articulate and I therefore offered to 'proofread' any written work he might wish to send out in his position as chair. His was, after all, the new face of Rank Outsiders, so it was important that we maintain the professional and competent image we had worked so hard to attain. People like Simon Langley, who had been our press liaison person, and our earlier chairs, Patrick and Duncan, had been excellent communicators. Bill and I could not work well together, sadly.

I had eventually reluctantly accepted a nomination as a vice chair/secretary under our new, dreadful moniker, AFLAGA (Armed Forces Lesbian and Gay Association). We each had different responsibilities – mine was to head a sub-committee responsible for looking at memberships, welfare and support; another member, Charles, had policy and development. Chloë became treasurer. Other committee positions included relief treasurer, support coordinator, memberships secretary, director of policy development and MOD liaison officer, press officer (co-opted) and web administrator (co-opted).

An incredibly loyal friend and member, Roger, left the group after the meeting. He had done an enormous amount of work towards trying to get charitable status. He was very hurt and angry at the way things were going. I felt really unhappy when he left and was uncomfortable about being part of a committee where longstanding members who were friends had felt let down and sidelined.

That whole period was, for me at least, pretty awful. As we approached and then passed what should have been the most incredible vindication of our existence, the removal of the ban, instead we seemed to be falling apart. It was as if we no longer had a purpose. Once the ban was lifted, we would no longer be 'outsiders'. Yet, for many of us, we couldn't return to being 'insiders' either. It was a deeply depressing sort of no-man's land. Charles and I exchanged a couple of tense emails when he said that he didn't want to include reference to Rank Outsiders in his tentative dealings with the MOD, because we were perceived as 'the past' and had a reputation, albeit unjustified, as having been trouble. I knew he was potentially a really important member – as a serving officer, his contacts within the MOD could really help us. But what I have since discovered, as we have recently been in contact again, after nearly 20 years, is that we were both unaware of what was going on behind the scenes in one another's lives. It felt to me as if he, and many others whose careers would now be 'safe' after the ban had gone, were destined to reap the rewards of our hard work. At that time, it seemed as if they were free to go off into a rainbow sunset without looking back at us poor saps left behind. I'm delighted to report that as the years have flown by, those very real, negative emotions have been softened, nay obliterated. But they were very painful and debilitating at the time I experienced them.

Another important issue regarding the treatment of women relates to a Wren (WRNS – Women's Royal Naval Service) who got in touch with us. Michelle had been in a relationship with an officer and following her investigation, a number of newspapers (I use the word loosely!) somehow got wind of her story. She told me how she felt she was harassed and harangued in the most appalling manner by these filthy, sensationalist, red-top rags. One ran a two-page spread about her situation and even asked their readers to vote on whether or not she should have been sacked. Around 67 per cent of those who decided to respond to the poll felt it was right for her to be fired.

She had called our helpline and it was thought it might be good for her to talk to a female member. I was of course horrified at her account of what had happened to her. Wasn't it enough to have suffered the indignity of an investigation, break up of a serious relationship and loss of a career? Apparently not – that a national newspaper felt it had the right to dissect and analyse a vulnerable young woman's sexuality in such a public, demeaning and insulting way was brutally cruel and unforgivable.

But her situation highlighted the tragedy of the MOD's continued refusal to deal directly with us. I was not a trained counsellor and was still deeply damaged by my own experience. I wanted to help her, yet wasn't really comfortable about how I could, without risking making things worse for her, due to not having the expertise nor, to be brutally honest, the desire to become too personally involved. I believed she desperately needed professional help, perhaps counselling, but it felt like it was almost 'expected' by some of our male members that I was in some way responsible for looking after her. Perhaps it was also the fact that I was a nurse, part of a caring profession, that led to this assumption that I somehow had a duty of care to this very fragile 21-year-old woman.

We met once, after having talked at length over a number of phone calls from my home in Beckenham. But I had to gently distance myself from what could have become a difficult situation. I felt as if she was at risk of becoming emotionally dependent upon me, perhaps viewing me as a sort of protective guide.

It was the first time that Rank Outsiders' role as a support group was called into question for me. It hit home very hard that the vast majority of our members were 'damaged' souls – deeply traumatised from our harrowing experiences at the hands of the military, yet discharged with absolutely no pastoral care, psychological or emotional support, let alone any practical or financial help to soften the blow of an unwanted return to civilian life.

Despite the issues I had with the organisation, there were lots of aspects of it that I really liked. RO events were pretty successful, like our Annual General Meetings which were most commonly held in Blackpool. Although they were nearly always sometime in March, when the wind blowing in from the Irish Sea is at its most bitter, we always had a great time. They would take place over a weekend, with most of us staying in one B&B, such as Raffles or the Tremadoc, where the meeting would be held. This would be the 'business' side of things – discussing strategies, membership, appointing to roles, the legal challenge, manning the helpline, fundraising, publicity, etc. Then we would have the rest of the time free to have fun on the scene; dancing and boozing the night away at Basil's, the Flying Handbag, Funny Girls (before it got completely overrun with hen parties) and ending up at Flamingo nightclub until the wee small hours. The inevitable grisly hangovers were beaten with a huge cooked breakfast followed by stomach-churning rides at the Pleasure Beach – marvellous!

There was even a predominantly lesbian bar in Blackpool, I think called Lucy's. The RO boys once came along to keep me company and even acted as matchmakers, approaching a woman I'd told them I fancied, while I had popped to the loo. I came back to our table to find my object of lust and the friend she was with sitting with us! Although at the time I could have happily killed Mike, our secretary (for 'twas he who had approached her) it ended well because the evening finished with an exchange of phone numbers after a very lovely goodnight snog. We did get in touch afterwards and actually dated for a while, but it wasn't easy because she lived in the Midlands where she worked as an Army physical training instructor! You see, the cliché is true – all PTIs *are* lesbian!

We also organised some annual dinners, where we would get together at a hotel purely to have fun; no business activities at all, just fine food and drink, a few speeches from honoured guests, then dancing the night away and catching up with old and new friends.

One of our earliest dinners, probably in around 1995, saw Ian McKellen as our guest of honour. He gave a marvellous speech, looking very dandy in a pair of black leather trousers. He also presented our newly-created 'Alan Turing Award' to its first recipient, a woman who had been an early member and had carried out work for the group over a long period of time. This was given in recognition of anyone who was felt to have been particularly helpful to the group's aims in some way. The award had been made possible when one of our members kindly left us a legacy after his untimely death.

Her story was yet another utterly reprehensible example of how badly so many people were treated in the Forces. She was a Wren and had been regularly forced into sexual relations with a male on-board ship who was effectively blackmailing her because of her sexuality. Eventually, pretty much at breaking point, she reported what was going on. After initially looking as if there would finally be a proper investigation into this violent abuse of rank, when her attacker told the investigators about her sexuality, it was as if any mention of rape, assault or coercion had never been made and was certainly no longer the key focus of their attention. There was a switch to interrogating a vulnerable woman in a bid to force her to admit to being a lesbian. Eventually, she was forced to leave, Services No Longer Required. As far as I recall, nothing was ever done about her attacker.

Other speakers included the then leader of the Liberal Democrats, the late Charles Kennedy MP, and we received messages of support from various cross-party MPs, such as Edwina Currie.

Things were looking up. In 1996 Robert and I were asked to present the Stonewall Awards to two incredibly brave activists, Simon Nkoli, recognised as the founding father of South Africa's black gay movement, and a young lesbian whose name escapes me. It may have been Mfumi, but sadly, I've been unable to find out – Stonewall's website timeline only lists awards given from 2006. Their annual fundraiser events held at the Royal Albert Hall were always a highlight of the LGBT social calendar. These were fantastic, star-studded shows so we were thrilled. We didn't have to say anything, just stand on stage holding the awards then present them after they'd said their bit. The rehearsal was directed by none other than our old friend Sir Ian (he'd been knighted by then). To know that a bunch of my fabulous friends were amongst more than 5,000 people who applauded and whooped like crazy when our names were announced as the co-founders of Rank Outsiders, was an incredible sensation – I loved it and felt absolutely elated. A year or two later, I think in 1997, RO was jointly awarded (with the Lesbian and Gay Police Association) the Stonewall Award, so we had to all troop on stage to actually receive the award rather than present it. Another great moment and one that made us feel that some of the pain we had been through was beginning to almost be worth it. We were making progress, albeit ever so slowly.

Non, Rien de Rien...

At this stage in my life, aged 58, with the wisdom that comes with age enabling me to view things very differently, it could be comparatively easy to paint a contented, sweet-natured, saintly, positively angelic self-portrait. How blessed with forgiveness and understanding, what an inspiration! Perspectives shift and change. Things that once seemed so important are now shown to be meaningless and completely trivial. But, if one thing has been a constant, fixed, immutable element through my life thus far it is honesty – so, could it really be true to say that I have no regrets?

Well, by and large, yes it would! I cannot pretend that the 14 long years of legal battle were not extraordinarily frustrating, nor that I wasn't initially horribly embittered and angry. This was especially true in terms of people whom I resented with a deeply-felt passion and intensity for a number of years. I was beyond enraged that many other high-ranking lesbians were continuing their careers untouched, enjoying all the blessings and perks that a life in the military could bring. A former fellow officer, who'd been on student officer basic training with Gail and me, told me how lovely it had been for her to see one of the corps' highest-ranking officers attend a regimental/retirement dinner accompanied by her female partner, after the ban had been lifted.

In addition, having what had seemed like a long and secure future suddenly snatched away was such a massive thing to deal with, on so many levels.

However, I find it impossible to regret everything that happened, as traumatic as it was at the time. If nothing else, it made me really closely examine my feelings. I finally began to accept who I am and what makes me, me.

I have often been asked if I would have liked to re-join the Army after the lifting of the ban. Sadly, this hypothesis was unrealisable, as I was 39 years old in January 2000. The age range for acceptance into the corps was between 18 and 38. I can't deny it did sometimes feel as if fate was always destined to be unkind. But, truthfully, I am not 100 per cent certain that I would have done so even if it had been possible. The corps was small enough for the grapevine to have been very effective at ensuring personnel at any posting would likely have known about the case. Although I knew I had done absolutely nothing of which to be ashamed, people were bound to gossip and surmise. Certain ignorant homophobes would be likely to ensure my life was made a misery.

Another worry was the fact that, despite the initial euphoria we felt when justice seemed to have been done, there was a distinct possibility that rank and file forces personnel *might* behave as the naysayers had forewarned. What if they did take umbrage at being forced to accept openly gay soldiers, sailors and airmen and women into their sphere of operation? Despite the rational evidence to the contrary, I think many of us were silently feeling the odd twinge of doubt – what if the blithering old fogeys had been right all along? What if vast numbers of heterosexual personnel refused to welcome this long overdue change?

Well, we needn't have worried. Whilst it is true to say that not all LGBT personnel felt safe or comfortable enough to declare their orientation immediately in the aftermath, it was a huge relief to learn that, in the vast majority of cases, coming out was pretty much a non-issue. And I know of at least one person who, having been thrown out shortly before the ban, was able to go back and continues to serve, very successfully, as a full colonel at the time of writing. Not bad for someone who was briefly a member of Rank Outsiders!

Despite its longstanding, entrenched declarations that homosexuality was incompatible with Forces life, the MOD responded appropriately and immediately to the ruling of the

European Court of Human Rights towards the end of 1999. Simon Langley, one of our longstanding members, had resigned from the Royal Navy as a lieutenant QHI (qualified helicopter instructor). From attending his first meeting at Stonewall's offices in Greycoat Place, Victoria, in 1993, he ran our media and communications for many years. Towards the end of the campaign, he became vice chairman and was the last member to receive our Peter Clarke Award, given in recognition of his service to the group. Peter had been a member and, after his untimely death in around 1994/5, his family gave us a cash bequest. It was used to help fund many of our expenses, including the trophy. Simon recalls being invited to the MOD, with our final chairman, to meet with the Deputy Chief of the Defence Staff and discuss proposals of how to proceed in the event that the ban be lifted. They wanted to consider how a new policy on behaviour might be implemented.

Having given many interviews on behalf of RO through the years, encountering many openly hostile supporters of the ban, this was an incredibly important and significant moment for Simon and all of us. For such a long time, we had been 'out in the cold', because we had dared to expose this little-known or discussed ban. Simon recalls how shocked the media and general public were to discover that such a ban even existed, let alone that it was backed in law. He recently reminded me of the outraged furore in 1994 when Rank Outsiders blew the whistle on Royal Military Police records that were being kept on those unfortunate enough to have been investigated. People were being recorded as sex offenders even though they (the RMP/MOD) knew this was patently not the case. He told me about one case he knew of where a member had applied for a job as a rape crisis counsellor only to find himself nearly in a great deal of trouble for supposedly concealing the 'fact' that he was a convicted sex offender, which, of course, he wasn't!

There was also a great deal of commotion in the Commons during the debate on the 1994 Criminal Justice and Public Order Act, because we had brought to light the fact that some doctors and padres were breaching rules of confidentiality and reporting service personnel to the Military Police. If someone went to a padre to confide their feelings, believing that the usual confession box rules of non-disclosure would apply, they would soon discover how mistaken they were. Any mention of 'unnatural' acts, thoughts or feelings would land you in big trouble and lead to the inevitable knock upon the billet or mess door. It was also the same with doctors. Medical officers could not be relied upon to observe the usual rules of confidentiality if what one confided was about one's sexuality.

This 1994 Act of Parliament, brought by the MP Michael Howard, helped bring the repeal a step closer because it decriminalised homosexuality within the Armed Forces, finally bringing them into line with the rest of British society – a mere 27 years after Lord Wolfenden's ground-breaking report led to a partial decriminalisation of homosexual acts in 1967. It still meant homosexuality remained 'incompatible' with Forces' life, but it was an important nail in the coffin of the ban.

My friends Duncan Lustig-Prean, Ed Hall and Tremaine Cornish (a Vice Chair of RO) were recently remembering the tumultuous times we endured as members of RO. They reminded me of things I had either forgotten (menopause has a LOT to answer for!) or not known about at the time. On the 19th anniversary of the lifting of the ban, 12 January 2019, Duncan listed (on social media) what he felt were the key turning points in the battle. I have his permission to reproduce them here:

1. On the first day of the Armed Forces Four's High Court hearing, the QC for the crown turned to our QC and said 'You do realise that I am defending the indefensible?'
2. The report of the HPAT (Homosexual Policy Advisory Team), published a few months after the first hearing, ruled out the 'Don't ask, don't tell' compromise, thus effectively forcing the government into a corner – all-out win or all-out lose.
3. The masterstroke of having a Conservative MP and former Cabinet Minister, Edwina Currie, moving the amendment in 1995, rather than someone from the Lib Dems or Labour.
4. The behind-the-scenes willingness of the MOD to cooperate on casework and to involve RO team members in rewriting the rules up to six years before the ban was finally repealed.

5. Geoff Hoon, the Secretary of State for Defence, on the night of the victory in the ECHR, assuring Duncan that, after a suitable pause for the media and senior military to catch up, the ban would be lifted in January 2000.

6. After rushing to Day One of the Labour Party Conference to steal their headlines and have a victory lap, Duncan was dancing with Mo Mowlam when Peter Mandelson tapped him on the shoulder, not to cut in, but to say 'That was a flawless campaign'!

As Duncan rightly says, not bad for a small organisation with little money, fighting the State!

Another key moment was when the *Daily Mail* started asking why money was being wasted in pursuing homosexuals in this way. We knew we were winning, the barriers were falling.

Official guidelines were quickly drawn up and distributed to all commanding officers throughout the three services. At last, with clear instructions, to be followed to the letter, it had happened. What we had been asking for for years, when we first attempted to engage with them and lobby for change, was now to become enshrined in service law. Rather than having orientation-specific offences, there were rules pertaining simply to *any* type of sexual misdemeanour, regardless of the perpetrator/victim/accuser's declared sexual preferences. Hallelujah! A rational response at last! We had never tried to espouse special, separate or preferential treatment. We knew that sadly, as in any large, hierarchical organisation or institution, there would always be occasional cases of bullying, harassment or intimidation necessitating investigation. But this was the first time that a truly equal approach was to be adopted to all cases where such a potential offence might have occurred. The alleged offences were to be investigated, not the sexual orientation of those involved.

Unbeknownst to so many at the time, we had finally begun to come in from the cold – our knowledge, experience and expertise were being recognised. Our members were helping the MOD behind the scenes, in readiness for a post-ban era within our Armed Forces. History was being made.

I suppose it is logical that the military's response to an order, given on 12 January 2000, albeit one from those interfering busybodies in Strasbourg, was breathtakingly swift and undertaken to the letter. It may well have left certain 'old school' serving and retired field marshals, generals, First Sea Lords, Admirals of the Fleet, Air Chief Marshals and the like apoplectic with indignant outrage. However, many younger, more forward-thinking officers were ready to embrace the challenges it brought. These same officers, making their way up the chain of command as their careers progressed, are now able to be highly visible 'straight allies', truly inspirational to the men and women under their command.

This term stems from 1973, when PFLAG (Parents, Families and Friends of Lesbians and Gays) was founded in the United States. A straight ally is a heterosexual or cisgender (someone whose gender identity matches the sex that they were assigned at birth) person who supports equal civil rights, gender equality, LGBT social movements and challenges homophobia, biphobia and transphobia. They believe LGBT people face discrimination and they aim to use their position, in a society focused on heteronormativity, to fight these phobias. They are the absolute embodiment of the type of 'lead from the front' commanders needed in a modern, inclusive society.

Having met then Lieutenant General Sir James Everard KCB, CBE, Commander Field Army, at the 2014 Pride parade in London, I was close to tears when I witnessed him giving a stirring pre-march speech.

There were dozens of serving members of all three services, resplendent in their number two uniforms, readying themselves to lead the parade through the streets of our capital city. Each man or woman openly identifying themselves as L, G, B or T in the proudest and most public manner possible. The atmosphere was buzzing with excitement and I felt such a lump in my throat as silence fell and he began to speak. His complete commitment to ensuring equality means it is not just a buzzword in today's Army, but a reality and a fundamental principle upon which to run this service. He has served as a patron of the Army LGBT Forum since 2010. It is beyond belief that there has been such an incredible turnaround in such a comparatively short period of time. He is truly inspirational and I was humbled and honoured when he name-checked me in his speech, acknowledging the dreadful harm that had been done to so many excellent men and women, but thanking me and many others for having had the courage to stand up and be counted. To bring to people's attention the fact that such iniquity even existed. It was a day I shall never forget, the memory of which, in writing about it now, nearly makes me shed a tear.

In his blog of May 2015 he wrote:

The Army's LGBT conference at Sandhurst this week was by far our biggest yet with more than 230 people attending – representing members of the Army's LGBT community, their chain of command, friends and colleagues. As well as sharing best practice and resources, the conference was a real celebration of the modern, inclusive employer the Army has become... The LGBT community is a rich seam of diverse talent that brings broader perspectives, networks and experiences to our organisation. We need to think differently if we are to succeed, remembering that people perform better when they can be themselves. The forces of ignorance are receding. In the Army today, you can be yourself.

I am delighted to know that in March 2017 he became a general and NATO's Deputy Supreme Allied Commander Europe.

As the inevitable death knell for the ban approached, membership of the newly renamed Armed Forces Lesbian and Gay Association, pronounced A-flag-A – horribly clunky, unwieldy and uninspiring – naturally dwindled. Some of us had hoped that Rank Outsiders would somehow have been absorbed into the newly open Forces networks, but alas, it wasn't to be.

Many heated debates ensued about whether or not we needed to change our name, but I think those of us who'd been involved from the start, now more than 10 years on, had begun to weary of it all. What with the battle for proper compensation still lumbering slowly on, despite the ban having gone, it was becoming tiresome and frankly bloody irritating. We had worked so damned hard, yet what did we really have to celebrate? Most of us weren't going to benefit in any way. The Treasury Solicitor's derisory offers persisted, despite the joy that so many were expressing. As late as 27 November 2003 I was instructing Tyndallwoods to inform the MOD that I was not prepared to accept their new offer of £10,000 in full and final settlement of my claim. A year later, in December 2004, they increased their offer to me – £19,000 was also rejected.

Those coming after us would really benefit from the ban's demise. Some who'd managed to stay closeted before January 2000 would now be able to come out and continue their careers finally free to be their true authentic selves. People enlisting after the ban was lifted would eventually not even know that homosexuality had ever been forbidden.

AFLAGA was eventually disbanded in 2003. It had been succeeded by Proud2Serve, an in-house Forces website. This in itself seemed nothing short of miraculous to those of us who had never been deemed worthy of a meeting with the MOD. An internal website, with no fear of logging on leading to a knock at your door and an end to your career? Unimaginable! This seemed incredible to me, but I cannot deny feeling quite embittered at the time. It felt as if, having done all the ground work to make this historic change possible, a number of years sooner than would have been the case without our intervention, we were now, once again, surplus to requirement. It was perhaps naïve, but I had hoped there might have been some sort of way in which we could have played a part in the newly out regime. But it wasn't to be. Many of us fell into the 'too old to re-join' category or had forged new lives, careers and relationships in civvy street. Lives that were perhaps no longer compatible with the rigours and peculiarities of service life. It honestly felt like we were being cast aside for a second time – SNLR yet again!

I also believe the resentment would have been much less intense and would have diminished much sooner had the UK government 'played fair' with us and instructed the Treasury Solicitor to deal with our pecuniary losses in a truly respectful and reasonable manner. Such a response may have softened the blow. But the fact is this – we were treated appallingly, and it became increasingly galling to see media reports of wildly inappropriate 'compensation culture', with payments being made to all manner of criminals, paedophiles, perverts and the like – people who in my opinion, were completely undeserving, or worse still, were deliberately and successfully jumping on bandwagons. I don't know what incenses me more, the claimants or the legal eagles who encourage this blatantly opportunistic avarice – deliberately undermining the original, wholly laudable and honourable intent of the 1948 Universal Declaration of Human Rights, a historic piece of legislation designed to enshrine equality for all human beings, aimed at preventing a repeat of the Holocaust. Actually, I *do* know – it's the lawyers who use their undoubted skill, knowledge and intelligence to interpret perhaps too-easily-interpreted or poorly-structured laws to their advantage. It is my belief that their actions are completely unethical and they make a mockery of their noble profession. Of course it is naïve of me, but I honestly believe the legal profession should be wholly and exclusively about truth and justice. Righting wrongs, not creating cynical money-making opportunities for opportunistic freeloaders. Perhaps a law should be drafted to prevent such actions?

The legal case with the MOD reopened a lot of old wounds and it was a difficult period to get through. My depression about the outcome was mirrored by what was happening at home with my parents. Now in their sixties, they were facing their own problems.

Curveballs

Ian's death in 1993 had been like a stone falling in a pond: the ripples spread outwards and touched every aspect of our family. The way in which he had been treated, during his attempts to extricate himself from the bonds of dependency, definitely contributed to Mum's deepening sense of despair and depression. The light went out of her life after Ian died, and she stopped looking after her health.

Eventually, in 2004, she contracted smoking-induced lung cancer. Although she pulled through on this occasion, she never really embraced the chance to grab life by the balls and relish the incredible second chance she'd been given. After 14 hours on the operating table for a partial pneumonectomy, then a brutal course of chemotherapy, she stopped smoking. Just a few short months later, she started again.

Four and a half years after she'd been cured, a second, much worse smoking-related cancer occurred. This time in her oesophagus and just beneath it, with secondaries (metastatic spread) throughout both lungs. This time it was terminal. Although tears were shed and hands held tightly as the oncologist at Mount Vernon Hospital confirmed the suspected news, I sensed a strange feeling of relief. I felt she welcomed the idea that there would be an end. Friends, family and neighbours all seemed quietly impressed at her apparently sanguine acceptance of such a devastating diagnosis and prognosis. She almost seemed to savour being talked of in this way – enjoying being viewed as someone facing death with such composure, such grace.

She died on 30 June 2009, aged 67. It had been only eight weeks from diagnosis to death.

Lots of strange, deeply buried emotions about my mum surfaced at that time. I felt ashamed of resenting my dead brother – he'd obviously meant more to her than I ever could. The old insecurities I had quashed since childhood returned once more – angry, jealous, irrational! What was wrong with me? I intellectualised these feelings – introspective self-analysis was second nature to me – but it didn't matter how many times I tried to convince myself that it *wasn't* true that she hadn't loved me and Dad enough for her to fight to stay alive, that our existence on the same earth, our wanting her to be happy, our wishing always to try to please her could have been enough – the fact of the matter was that it *felt* as if I wasn't enough. That despite all I'd ever done to try to please her, to make her proud of me, none of it would *ever* matter.

I was my mum's first child. We had been like sisters until I had written her that 'life story' epistle from Hannover. Outwardly she was amazing – proudly telling all and sundry about Rank Outsiders, recording every TV programme onto VHS tapes, cutting interviews out of newspapers and magazines. Getting all her work mates to sponsor me when I walked the southern half of the Pennine Way with Steve, fundraising for the group. She would have torn a strip off anyone daring to have a dig at me. That had always been her way and nothing would change that. She'd stormed up the road to number 29 when, aged around four or five, I'd come in looking very sorry for myself.

'What's the matter, love?'

'Mr Foster always gives sweeties to everyone else, but he doesn't let me have any!'

She had hurtled past me, undoing her apron and throwing it to the hall floor as she dashed out through the front door, face like thunder. Nain took me by the hand into the back garden, but some years later Mum told me what had happened. 'That silly old sod was always looking down his nose at me! Thought he had the right to pass judgement on a 19-year-old having a kiddie "out of wedlock"! Well, I told him he could think what the hell he liked about me, but that he had no right to take it out on you – you were just an innocent little girl who'd done him no harm! You didn't ask to be born, but born you were and he could stick that in his pipe and smoke it!'

God, how I *loved* that side of Mum! She made me feel so safe and protected at moments like that. Mr Foster must have got the message too, for he never excluded me again and was always charm itself from then on. He was one of my biggest fans when I got into the Army, asking Mum to pass on a message of congratulations when he heard the news from Nain.

My deeply entrenched insecurity regarding Mum and Dad's 'preference' for Ian dated back to my childhood. They had never done anything to encourage this misplaced belief – we were treated equally, shown the same degree of love and affection. No, this was my problem, born of an early tendency to overanalyse everything. I think it mainly stemmed from knowing that Ian was my half-brother; it seemed logical that Mum and Dad had fallen in love, 'made' Ian together, committed to one another through marriage. Dad had even adopted me! Whereas my genetic father was unknown to me, having supposedly skedaddled as soon as he'd had his wicked way with Mum. To this day, I have no idea who he is.

At the time of completing the first draft of this tale, in 2017, I had been unemployed for three years. I was finding it nigh on impossible to change career at the ripe old age of 57. At the time when I had envisaged ending my Army career, in receipt of a very healthy tax-free gratuity (having completed a total of 33 years' service) and an extremely generous pension, I was instead facing poverty and possible homelessness. Why? Because life, being the fickle little bastard that it can be, threw yet another lousy curveball at my dad (and thus by association, me) in September 2014.

After Mum died he was living alone for the first time in his life, at the age of 74. Outwardly, he was managing OK, but those of us closest to him could see subtle signs that all wasn't quite well. His clothes were beginning to look worn, they smelled of stale sweat and the house was getting grubby. The heavy drinking extended from his lifelong Friday nights and Sunday lunchtimes to every night, alone

– the litre bottle of either Teacher's whisky or Captain Morgan dark rum on the floor by his feet, ready for constant top ups, the chaser being a literal splash of coke. He also had a weakness for shedloads of cheese and biscuits every evening and breakfasts fried in a pan swimming in lard, which was gradually, silently, clogging up his arteries like sludge in a drainpipe.

I had been living in the Isle of Wight for nine years when Mum died, having moved here in May 2000. By 2012, three years later, I was completely burned out as far as my work was concerned. I was a senior staff nurse in palliative care, at the Earl Mountbatten Hospice. It was becoming increasingly difficult for me to carry on – whenever a patient would be admitted with the same symptoms Mum had suffered, it acted as a constant reminder of how she had struggled during the months leading up to her diagnosis, then death. Although my immediate boss and friend Karen had tried to support me, it was becoming clear that something had to give. I knew I was close to becoming a liability, as my emotions were sometimes impossible to hide, causing other members of staff to feel uncomfortable if I was snappy or easily upset. I was beginning to feel as if I was heading towards a breakdown. I felt truly fragile and as if I had no control. I'd been offered free counselling through the Isle of Wight NHS Trust's occupational health department. I'd also seen my GP and very reluctantly agreed to take antidepressants for the first time ever. Although these measures were helping, it was time for a rethink.

The straws that broke this camel's back came in quick succession. Not one but two patients, within only two nights, haemorrhaged when I was the nurse in charge. Although I dealt with both situations promptly, appropriately and efficiently I just broke down once I got home, having somehow driven back on autopilot, vision blurred through tear-filled eyes, reliving my poor Mum's death following a haemorrhage of her oesophageal tumour. A death that both Dad and I witnessed at first hand, in hated Northwick Park Hospital, and which most definitely left him emotionally damaged. It is certainly one of the key moments that pushed him towards his own pitiful fate, because he chose to try shortening his own life expectancy by massively upping his intake of poison – copious quantities of booze.

He had always said he hadn't wanted to 'make old bones', so he set to...

I was beginning to feel that living in the Isle of Wight was becoming untenable. Not only in terms of the job, but also because a long-term relationship had ended in 2010. Although we had managed to remain great friends, I was beginning to feel it was time for a bit of a change, a new start. As Uncle Tony (Dad's closest brother) and Aunty Dora had been visiting Dad fairly regularly, I was aware that they too had seen the way in which Dad had been letting things slide, in terms of neglecting both the house and himself. Dora would often take it upon herself to spring clean every time, but it clearly wasn't a realistic long-term solution.

I plucked up courage and asked Dad how he felt about the possibility of my coming back home to Harrow, to live with him for a while. I'm sure we must both have had our reservations – he had managed alone for nearly two and a half years and much as I loved him dearly, I knew that as I was a 52-year-old, very independent woman, it could easily have been doomed to failure.

So, I resigned from the NHS after more than 12 years and left Earl Mountbatten Hospice after nearly nine years there. Although I was very sad to go, I knew deep down that it was absolutely the right decision.

After returning home, I quickly secured two very well-paid jobs that utilised my nursing skills but without any 'hands on' requirements, first as a nurse tele-interviewer then as a medical case manager. But it was a case of third time lucky when I finally ended up joining the bank of a private hospital not too far from home. I was incredibly lucky because the outpatients' department had plenty of shifts available. It was immensely busy, with dozens of different consultants' clinics taking place from 8am to 10pm nearly every day! The rooms had to be turned around really fast between different clinics. In this atmosphere some of the doctors could be incredibly rude and impatient at times, but the nurses and health care assistants were lovely – a really excellent, close-knit team who quickly showed me the ropes. I was soon getting three long days (12-hour shifts) most weeks, allowing me plenty of time to go out and play.

Although I missed aspects of the Isle of Wight, the return to my family home came at exactly the right time for me. I began to re-establish old friendships and was able to pop into the heart of London whenever I wanted. A slew of shows, film festivals, exhibitions, walking tours and social events followed. Everything was going well. Even the work was fitting my needs very well – I was by now confident enough to stand up to any imbecilic dinosaurs who should have been put out to grass centuries earlier, so for the most part it was money for old rope. I also enjoyed the mix of mainly admin or chaperoning with some clinical work, such as taking down or changing dressings, suture removal, assisting orthopaedic surgeons with pin removals or plaster of Paris applications, fitting pneumatic walkers, etc. It was good to learn new skills yet not have the stresses and strains of working in a ward. I seemed to be well-liked and soon felt as if I was a valued and reliable member of the team.

Dad and I, although having very differing lifestyles, got along pretty well. We ended up dividing the house so that downstairs was more his domain and upstairs mine. Since before Mum died, Dad had made the tiny box room his place to sleep. It was great that he offered to let me have the two double bedrooms as my own – it meant I had one as a sort of living room, the other to sleep in. When friends or family came to visit we had enough room because my double futon replaced the bashed up old settee in the front room. We even began to think about what decorating and home improvements we might carry out. Things were beginning to look good for the future of number 19...

But Dad's alcohol consumption levels just continued to increase. I would sometimes cautiously venture a comment, but was always wary as he had previously reacted very badly when I'd dared to express a slight concern that he might want to slow it down a bit. I had been very shocked at the level of what seemed to me to be a disproportionately hypersensitive reaction! So since then I had tended to keep schtum.

He'd often told me he wanted to 'go' like a pal from his regular drinking den, the Memorial Club in Harrow Weald. Said pal had spent a very convivial evening getting tanked up at the bar, staggering home and dying of a massive heart attack in his armchair. Clearly Dad was doing his best to emulate his friend's departure.

Just two or three weeks before he was due to go on holiday to Spain with my aunty Dora, I had come in very late from work. Dad was in his usual spot, sitting opposite the blaring telly, recliner armchair (a present from me) liberally sprinkled with biscuit crumbs and grease marks from bits of dropped cheese. He looked up at me, eyes rheumy and red-rimmed from the copious quantity of booze he'd imbibed in just one evening. The bottle, started late the night before, had about an inch of rum left. As he tried to focus on me I felt the strangest mix of pity, compassion and disappointment. I could easily rationalise the reasons – he'd lost his only son at 27, his wife at 67 and what was there left to live for? His middle-aged, adopted, lesbian daughter? I had never really doubted his love for me, even though he very rarely gave voice to the sentiment – he was of the generation where men being manly men meant no 'sissy' emotion should be shown. Even as Mum lay dying, with my urgent encouragement whispered in his ear – 'Dad, if you want to tell her anything, I'd say it now' – he just couldn't bring himself to say, 'I love you'. She had to settle for, 'We had some good times, didn't we, Annie?', his softly-spoken voice cracking from the strain of trying not to cry.

So, feeling knackered and fractious following an exceptionally busy day at work, I really wasn't in the mood, but Dad beckoned me over – 'Come an' 'ave a nightcap, love!' As I was due back on another 12-hour shift early the next morning I said I was too tired and just wanted to go up to bed, but he was in a jovial and insistent mood. I declined a drink as I'd be driving in less than seven hours' time, but sat across from him. Nervously, as it was early in the week, I ventured, 'So, what's the occasion then, Dad?' He looked very puzzled, so I continued, 'You're knocking them back a bit – you only opened that yesterday.'

Luckily, rather than take umbrage and become defensive, he actually looked as if he was thinking about my remarks – an almost lucid conversation ensued and yet again, for the umpteenth time, came the references to his happily demised pal and 'not wanting to make old bones'. He referred to the fact that there'd be nothing worse than ending up like his poor old mum or Aunty Ruby, both of whom had got dementia and had to spend the last months of their lives in nursing homes. I'd visited them with him on many occasions and saw how distraught he was at their situation – real 'God's waiting room' stuff, sat in those hideous high-backed, winged armchairs, placed in circles around the edge of a room, staring at one another and constantly awaiting the ministrations of hassled carers. 'I'd *hate* that,' he said, 'I'd rather kill myself than end up somewhere like they were!'

It was gone midnight by now, so wearily I took a breath then began. 'Look Dad, in an ideal world it'd be fantastic if we could all *choose* how to shuffle off this mortal coil, but none of us knows for sure how or when the time will come. Imagine if we could tick a box – "Die in sleep", "Crash car at high speed", "Heart attack whilst making love to sexiest woman alive" (we both smiled at that option!)... but all I do know is that we *can* choose to try to influence the likely outcome. You keep telling me you don't want to make old bones – fine, that's your preference. But Dad, what if, in your efforts to end your life sooner, you end up unintentionally fucking it up?' He was listening intently, much to my surprise. I was on a roll, so I went on: 'You might get lucky, but you're taking a punt – you might end up with a heart attack that doesn't kill you, just leaves you incapacitated or needing surgery and medication for the rest of your life. Or worse still, a stroke that leaves you unable to speak, stuck in a home like Nanny and Ruby. God forbid that it should happen Dad, but if you carry on like this, you're asking for trouble.'

He was still listening... blimey, was I about to have a breakthrough? Make him think about taking better care of himself? I carried on: 'I love you and I hope you know that I'd do whatever I could to help you, to try to sort things out for you, but I can't guarantee I'd be able to do it for however long you had to live like that. If you're really unlucky, you could live for years like that!'

We sat in silence; it had suddenly got a bit heavy and doomy. He pondered briefly, then refilled his glass right to the top with the last of the rum, raised it as if to make a toast – 'Cheers then!' with his usual grin. I smiled back, looked heavenward and said, 'I'm off to bed, Dad!'

A couple of weeks later, sitting in the morning sunshine of Spain, Dora, Les (her eldest son) and his wife Nikki were all shocked when, at breakfast, Dad took a pint glass and filled it right to the top, half and half with brandy and port. They were all able to hold their own, booze-wise – many of the Chambers clan are fairly hard-living, party-loving characters – but Dad seemed to be on a complete self-destruct mission after Mum's death. He of course denied it, but I will always beg to differ. The very next day, he suffered a very severe Total Anterior Compartment Infarction (TACI) stroke.

The stroke left him, despite months of intensive rehabilitation efforts at the specialist stroke unit at Northwick Park, paralysed down his left side, unable to stand or walk and requiring two people to transfer him at all times. He had to spend his days stuck in a wheelchair because his coordination wasn't adequate for him to safely manage a motorised chair. He suffered from urinary incontinence and soon began to show signs of incipient vascular dementia. The sole redeeming feature was the fact that his dominant right hand was unaffected, so he could at least use the call bell, hold a telephone to his ear, operate the TV remote and, most importantly, hold a cut-glass whisky tumbler in his hand. His speech improved sufficiently that he was, for the most part, able to make himself understood. This was of course the most important thing. He was always pretty softly spoken, so didn't sound very different, apart from when he was tired. Then he often repeated the last word of a sentence over and over – almost like a stutter.

Without going into too many details of what has happened since – that could be another book all by itself – suffice to say there's not what I would call a particularly happy ending. When Northwick Park Hospital was ready to discharge Dad, he of course wanted to be cared for at home. A full package of care was set up and I let work know I was going to be at home initially, until we saw how it would work out.

Despite there being two carers visiting four times a day, it didn't work out. Number 19 had to be sold in order to fund Dad's not inconsiderable nursing home fees. We eventually decided, much to my surprise when Dad agreed, to leave Harrow and move to the Isle of Wight. The choices of care home were much more suitable, in nicer settings and cheaper.

Dad was very well cared for in a lovely nursing home just ten minutes' drive from me. We bought a house, partly as an investment, partly to give me somewhere to live. When the balance of the money ran out, three and a half years later, we had to sell the house. By then I was lucky enough to have finally landed a job. Having decided to permanently leave the nursing register, it had been really tough to find work. But I was able to move into rented accommodation as the house sale proceeded.

Despite Dad's not inconsiderable health issues, he never qualified for anything other than Attendance Allowance, which sadly didn't make much of a dent in his fees.

His health gradually deteriorated and he died exactly nine years to the day after Mum's funeral. I cannot lie – it was a blessed relief.

I know that our woes and miseries are no more or less than those of millions of people the world over. I don't tell my stories to engender sympathy, I am merely doing what I have always done – telling it like it is.

Unlike my dear old Dad, I would very much like to make old bones, which is probably why, despite a pretty relentless series of difficult events occurring throughout my life thus far, I am blindly determined to remain cheerful and optimistic until the hopefully not-so-bitter end!

Epilogue

Although the European Court of Human Rights had forced the UK government to lift the ban, which was the most important thing, it rarely intervenes in matters of financial compensation. It is primarily concerned with making member states rectify any legal wrongs. Once the ban had been repealed, Strasbourg's work was done. Sadly, this allowed our government to continue to refuse to play ball in respect of making fair and reasonable offers of compensation.

So after the edict had been passed in Strasbourg, thus rendering our cases closed, five of us got together and hired a barrister, Tim Eicke, and met in London. Of around 80–90 plaintiffs, we were the last diehards who just could neither believe nor accept how badly we'd been treated by our own country. Although not one of us was really in a stable financial position, and could hardly afford to pay his fees, we all felt so strongly that true justice had *still* not been done. What we had been hoping for was that there might be some way in which the ECHR could force the MOD to honour the way in which we had calculated our pecuniary losses. They had been worked out according to guidance and advice furnished by yet another expensive (but reputedly expert in his field) barrister engaged on our behalf by Tyndallwoods – we were not plucking figures from the air! All the other remaining clients had thrown in the towel and accepted the derisory offers as they had been advised that we had, at long last, after 13 years, finally exhausted all legal remedies. In other words, we supposedly had no choice. It had come down to a 'take it or leave it' situation. Having gradually increased their offer from £10,000 to

£19,000 by the summer of 2004, it was clear they were trying to wear us down into submission. It worked with many claimants who had simply lost the will and energy to keep on fighting.

I therefore eventually accepted their final offer to me, made late in 2008, under extreme duress. It was utterly sickening to read quotes from MOD spokespeople in the press, such as:

> It is the right of each and every member of the Armed Forces to work in an environment free from harassment, intimidation and bullying. Over the past few years the MOD has made strenuous efforts to reach amicable settlements in relation to those legal claims which remained outstanding, and we are pleased that compensation has now been awarded in all these cases.

Strenuous efforts? What a bloody cheek!

Of course they were pleased – they'd worn us down, dragged it on for *eight years* after the ban had been lifted, got away with cheating us out of what we'd lost through their illegal denial of a right to a private life under articles 8 and 13 of the Declaration of Human Rights. I therefore wrote an explanatory letter for Tyndallwoods to pass on to the Treasury Solicitor on my behalf. It made it crystal clear that I felt their offer was totally derisory and insulting and that I felt their actions to be utterly disgraceful and dishonourable. My actual pecuniary losses had been calculated openly, honestly and fairly. Had I wished to, I could have pushed them to agree that, given my intended career trajectory, I would have applied for and gained a Regular Commission after completing my eight-year Short Service Commission. It was an acknowledged fact that I would have been promoted to the rank of captain on 23 July 1985, only six months after I had been forced to resign my commission. Had I then become a midwife, as planned, I would certainly have at least attained the rank of major. Colleagues with whom I had trained as a student nurse had all followed the same trajectory without difficulty, so it was fair to assume I would have done the same. In an effort to show a willingness to cooperate and be reasonable, I did not try to claim any loss of earnings at any rank other than that of captain. The difficulty was that I could in no way *prove* my intentions career-wise. Nor could the MOD *disprove* them, so once again we were at stalemate. Ultimately, despite my best efforts to try to show a willingness to not be greedy and to accept a fair offer (had one ever been made!), the MOD point blank refused to play ball.

I had submitted a detailed 'Schedule of Damages', claiming £423,000. It was a figure arrived at fairly, with full supporting evidence. Luckily, due to my ongoing predilection for keeping things, I had every payslip from every job I'd ever done, so was able to clearly prove what I had earned since being forced to leave. I eventually felt as if I had no choice but to accept their final offer of £63,000, but Tyndallwoods' fees were not paid by the MOD so were effectively 'deducted at source', leaving me with £45,000. The 'shortfall' was a mere £378,000, so why should I feel hard done by? Over many years, I had accumulated massive personal debts of around £45,000. This had been through constantly taking out loans, for example to pay a deposit to get a mortgage on a flat, eventually managing to get myself into increasingly messy 'borrow from "Peter" to repay "Paul"' cycles. By the time I'd cleared those debts, there wasn't much left to shout about. The most expensive thing I bought with my 'winnings' (I think 'losings' would be more apt) was an Apple MacBook. Having hoped I might at least have enough to buy a small flat or invest in a pension, as I wouldn't get an Army pension, it didn't fill me with joy. Fourteen years of stress and anxiety had come to not very much...

I spent many years struggling to come to terms with the appalling treatment that had been meted out to me, despite having been prepared to die for my country. I cannot deny the massive, negative impact it had upon me – I was angry and embittered. The worst thing for me, from beginning to end, was the sense of complete impotence. Knowing I would never be able to have any real influence upon the outcome of this battle. I had always wanted merely to talk to someone, anyone with the power to influence the outcome. I honestly felt that if 'they' could see the issue in a human context – meet with real human beings, people who had been prepared to put everything on the line in an attempt to protect our democratic ideals, well surely then they would be reasonable?

I know how ridiculously naïve that seems, but having written dozens of letters, trying to personalise and humanise a story that the Treasury Solicitor seemed only to see in terms of the financial implications, I still wanted to trust that someone, somewhere would be honourable and believe in justice.

Rumours flew around for a number of years that the Treasury Solicitor did in fact have a large sum set aside to cover the costs of our claims. They were readying themselves for the European Court of Human Rights to force them to pay up. They had already coerced a fair number of Tyndallwoods' clients to accept offers made at various stages throughout the 14-year process. Some accepted because the time it was taking had simply worn them down. Or their financial situations were already so precarious that even a paltry sum like the initial blanket amount of £10,000 that was offered to all of us, regardless of our own individual circumstances, seemed better than nothing.

All of this makes my blood boil, but the most galling thought of all is this – the Treasury Solicitor's glee at having 'saved' so many millions of pounds. Money 'saved' to which I, as a UK tax payer, since I first started work at the age of 18, contributed. It enrages me even now.

The last few years have been very strange, because they've seen a mix of deep personal tragedy and difficulty juxtaposed with wonderfully optimistic occasions. I decided to voluntarily come off the nursing register in 2016 because I'd reached a complete feeling of burn out, after Mum's two cancers and death, my Uncles Tony and Bill dying within months of one another from lung cancer, then the fallout after Dad's stroke. I simply couldn't face the thought of nursing again.

But in 2014, I attended the inaugural LGBT Veterans Ball at the Union Jack Club in London. It was a wonderful occasion, with inspirational speeches from my old pal Ed Hall; Stonewall's Mandy McBain MBE (formerly the Royal Navy's highest-ranking openly lesbian officer) and Councillor Anwen Muston, a transwoman formerly having served in the 1st Battalion of The Staffordshire Regiment. Live music was provided by an RAF band and it felt wonderful to see people in uniform or in their best evening gowns and dress suits looking fabulously happy and relaxed. Alastair 'Smudger' Smith of the Princess of Wales Regiment had organised it, and he later became the first serviceman to be permitted to marry his same sex partner, Aaron, at his overseas base in Cyprus.

Veterans Ball 2014

The following year's ball saw me being invited to speak, along with Jacqui Gavin and Kirsty Fletcher. I asked the woman next to me who she was and what her connection was to the event. She said she was Linda Riley and very modestly alluded to her incredibly influential work for the LGBT community. I felt a bit daft not knowing who she was, but have since learned of the numerous diversity initiatives she has created. She is now probably best known for publishing the lesbian/bisexual lifestyle magazine *DIVA*. The other guests included the actress Sophie Ward and her wife, Rena Brannan.

After I made my speech, I was thrilled and humbled to get a

standing ovation from the 150 attendees, and was bewildered but delighted when I was asked to autograph a programme! People were immensely kind and complimentary about what Rank Outsiders had done to help expose the cruelty and illogical continued application of the ban to a hitherto unaware public. It felt quite weird, because whilst the joy and openness of these events was inspirational, vindicating and very uplifting, I cannot deny it was very slightly tinged with sadness. I couldn't help but feel a bit jealous of the freedoms these beautiful young people had, not only to serve their country, but to do so protected in law rather than persecuted by it, as we had been. I know Robert Ely, our co-founder, felt the same tangible wave of sorrow over the lost opportunities of combining a rewarding and successful career with the possibility of being able to openly love someone too.

Ultimately, despite any sense of loss and envy, seeing dozens of openly LGBT personnel made me feel that what we had suffered had almost been worthwhile. We had most definitely caused the ban to be lifted sooner than would have been the case had Rank Outsiders not existed.

Later in 2015 I was invited to attend a reception at the Ministry of Defence, by the Second Sea Lord no less, to celebrate – yes, celebrate – the 15th anniversary of the lifting of the ban. It was billed as a 'diversity reception' with a wide-ranging guest list of 120 people. There were serving LGBT members from all three services; veterans like myself and a number of former RO members such as Robert Ely, Duncan Lustig-Prean, Simon Langley, Ed Hall and my friend Mike; Ruth Hunt, the Chief Executive of Stonewall; MPs, high ranking officers from across the services and a number of civilian guests such as Lisa Power and Michael Cashman. There were TV cameras too and Mike was asked to give a brief interview about his experiences of being imprisoned during his investigation whilst in the RAF. Afterwards, he was asked to chat with Robert and me so some background footage could be added to the news article on British Forces Broadcasting Services TV later. What a difference from 1994 when he'd appeared, along with yours truly, in a BBC Breakfast News item – his face hidden from view.

The guest speakers all lauded the incredible progress made by all three services since the ban was lifted in 2000. Given the media frenzy leading up to that historic moment, announced by the then Secretary of State for Defence, Geoff Hoon (who never did answer any of my letters, mind you!) it is deeply satisfying to know that the predicted collapse of civilised society as we know it – oh all right then, military cohesion and effectiveness – never materialised. And our Armed Forces, regardless of what one thinks about the reason or necessity for their existence, are still held in the highest regard.

Had I been asked just a few short years ago how I would feel about going into the very building whose incumbents once completely shunned me, refusing even to speak to us, despite many very polite requests, I would probably have told you that I would never expect to have a good enough reason to do so. Of course, I certainly never would have expected to have been in receipt of an invitation from the Second Sea Lord!

In 2016, I devised a questionnaire to send to any service personnel willing to participate. I hoped to include some of the results in this work, but I feel it might be more suited to an academic, analytical work. What struck me most was the fact that very few people had fallen foul of the widely-anticipated (mainly by the naysayers, that is) backlash from heterosexual military personnel. Even the one or two episodes described, from dozens of responses, had been dealt with by the senior officers to whom any issues had been reported. I had been hugely encouraged to learn of the existence of an independent Services Complaints Ombudsman for any situation unable to be resolved within the corps or unit. Luckily, the ombudsman told me that her services are rarely required, which is great to know.

The vast majority of respondents reported that their sexual orientation has posed no problem in respect of their working lives. Their partners can and do attend balls, social events, formal dinners and no fuss is made. They can live together in married quarters, march in uniform at Pride parades and operate recruitment stands at LGBT events. One tiny item reminds me of the progress made – I actually keep one in my bag because it makes me so happy – at last year's Pride festivals there were specially-made Army Pride camo sticks, making it possible to paint little 'Rambo-esque' camouflage stripes on one's face. But instead of the usual greens, blacks and browns, these were brightly coloured with rainbow stripes! But it was the wording, in tiny letters on the side that moved me beyond belief –

NORMAL CAMO IS FOR BLENDING IN
TODAY IS FOR STANDING OUT.
#THISISBELONGING

Find where you belong
Search Army Jobs

One questionnaire respondent, Sarah Cotman, a Princess Mary's RAF nurse, illustrates beautifully how much progress has been made:

I have marched in London Pride in uniform for the past seven years. It is always a very, very proud day, and every year I am really encouraged by the positivity of the newer 'younger' generation of service personnel that still feel this is one of the proudest days for them. It's really not to be taken for granted. Any day I wear No.1 uniform and parade is a good day for me, but to do it celebrating the fact that I am LGBT as well, knowing the service supports this, after everything that has gone before, makes me thankful for my generation, and proud I have played a part over the years to make it possible.

Every day I am amazed when I meet young, new entrants or people that haven't been in the service very long. Time and time again I hear they didn't know it was ever illegal to serve and be openly LGBT. Whilst I don't want them to forget the awful things that happened to you and RO... I think the perceived safety and that lack of awareness is a true indicator of how far, how quickly, we have moved on. And that should be celebrated again and again.

Knowing that people like Sarah and her wife, Lucy, enjoy such hard-won freedoms gives me great comfort. I feel I've done my bit, no matter how small.

Meeting people whose service lives are so different now is truly inspirational. I am delighted to be able to count as friends some of the amazing men and women who are prepared to put their lives on the line to protect their fellow countrymen and women.

One friend's experience almost entirely encapsulates the way in which our Armed Forces have metamorphosed. Sherry, who married her wife Mandy McBain in 2016, is serving in the RAF and is now on maternity leave, having given birth to their son. Three former transgressive impossibilities rolled into one – how fantastic that she will no longer lose her career for being lesbian, marrying 'wrongly' or getting pregnant!

On 19 July 2017, thanks to the wonderful Ann and Emma Miller-McCaffrey, I was invited to replace a delegate from the Foreign and Commonwealth Office and fill an hour-long slot as a speaker at the annual Army LGBT Forum's conference. I had met Ann and Emma through the veterans' bashes and had been honoured to be invited to attend their wedding in Liverpool in November 2016. Ann is in the RN Reserve and runs her own promotion company, Purple Tie Promotions, and her wife Emma is the community engagement manager for Diversity Role Models. She has done important work with Greater Manchester Police, increasing LGBT awareness and introducing better crime-recording methods in respect of hate crime and same-sex domestic abuse. They live in married quarters within the stunning setting of no less than the Royal Military Academy, Sandhurst, which is where the conference was held.

As is always my way (although this time it was at quite short notice), I wrote my speech on the train to Farnborough and finished it that evening at their place. Emma gave me a heartfelt introduction and I'm delighted to say it was very well received indeed. I was elated and felt so happy to see how far things had moved on since the ban had been repealed. Knowing that one of the lieutenant colonels sitting in the front row works in the Diversity and Inclusion Employment Branch of the Army is simply incredible, considering that less than 20 years ago such concepts simply did not exist within the British Military establishments.

When I left the stage, I returned to my seat in the second row, trembling but extraordinarily chuffed at the applause I'd had.

Lieutenant General Sanders CBE DSO, Commander Field Army, General Everard's successor, turned around in his seat in the front row, took hold of my hand, personally thanked me for what I'd done, and expressed his sorrow at how I had been treated.

Such warmth and, dare I say, respect, from these commanders sits in extremely stark contrast to the disgusting, hateful contempt and bigotry I faced back in the day. Whilst there were many shocking aspects to my case, one thing utterly confounded me. It was a letter in the files I'd obtained in 1998. Reading through the contents of two very full lever arch files containing all the paperwork related to my case was painful enough. The typed-out copies of Mr Lentman's laboriously hand-written interrogation records (he really did earn his money, didn't he?) re-opened wounds that had already taken way too long to heal. But this one letter left me fighting mad. It was a huge factor in my determined insistence in taking the battle right to the wire, even though I knew deep down that we were destined to fail. Reading it, my attempts to move on and rise above my tawdry circumstances, to adopt a mature, wise, forgiving approach to the enormous blow that I'd had dealt to me, well, they were instantaneously nullified. I was incandescent with rage at the unfairness of it all – I could not believe what I was reading. And the frustration at having no voice with which to respond! This has been a fundamental cause of the fury I've felt – feeling completely powerless to respond and let these people hear *my* side.

The exhibit was from one of the most senior officers of the British Army of the Rhine. At first, I couldn't comprehend what possible reason there could have been for him to have been made aware of my case, let alone to take the time to pass comment upon it. I had been an insignificant junior officer. After all, although the allegations levelled against me had been serious, they had never been converted to charges. Mel's eventual corroboration of my version of events proved that what had happened between us had been consensual and blown the blatant fabrication of indecent assault out of the water. But this high-ranking officer saw things differently. Having been presented with the very large report on Case No.43072/7, he made the following remarks:

OPINION OF ************
IN THE CASE OF CAPTAIN M BENN QARANC
AND
LIEUTENANT E M CHAMBERS QARANC

I have read the Special Investigation Branch, Royal Military Police report concerning the unnatural conduct between Captain Benn and Lieutenant Chambers which occurred at the British Military Hospital, Hannover, in the early hours of 13th June 1987. I have also had sight of the recommendations of the Commanding Officer, Commander Verden Garrison and Commander 1st Armoured Division, together with Captain Benn's and Lieutenant Chambers' representations concerning their commanding officer's report.

In the case of Lieutenant Chambers I find sufficient evidence to support a belief that she has homosexual proclivities and has on more than one occasion indulged in physical expressions of such homosexuality. In accordance with the policy contained in AGAI Vol 5 Instr No 3, I totally support the recommendation that the Army Board of the Defence Council should call upon her to resign her commission.

Concerning Captain Benn's involvement in this specific unnatural act, I believe that it was an aberration committed whilst her judgement was affected by alcohol. Additionally I cannot ignore the possibility of the effect of blandishments by Lieutenant Chambers who may well have sought to take advantage of Captain Benn's confused state. However, whilst I would be minded to view her involvement as being more sinned against than sinning I am disturbed by her duplicity when subsequently questioned concerning the incident and agree with the Commander 1st Armoured Division that by this duplicity, Captain Benn has demonstrated her unsuitability to hold the Queen's commission. I recommend that the Army Board of the Defence Council call upon her also, to resign her commission.

4 Nov 87

Once I'd checked the dictionary to establish the exact meaning of 'blandishments', I was beyond apoplectic with rage: 'something, as an action or speech, that tends to flatter, coax, entice, etc.'

Christ! Wouldn't that be marvellous? Silver-tongued Lainey tempts life-long straight women to a lecherous life of lesbianism simply because of her amazing way with a suggestive blandishment! Had he not read that Mel had said that my version of events was true?

That certainly didn't sound to me like someone in a confused state and I would argue, most vehemently, that I always felt as if I had been 'used'. And the use of the word unnatural is just so unbelievably offensive!

No matter what rubbish comes my way, my attitude has been pretty much in the 'what doesn't kill you makes you stronger' mould. I believe that day-to-day existence is sometimes frankly rather tedious and banal, lacking in interest and excitement. Again, this is not meant in a maungy, down in the mouth manner – I say it as an observation, not a criticism or complaint; I genuinely believe it's simply the truth! Contrary to how those words may read, written flatly and in only two dimensions, it doesn't indicate a doomy, pessimistic or self-pitying soul – I am inherently optimistic and very easily pleased by the simplest of things. Without wishing to come over as trite or glib, I do believe the two and a half years I spent living and working in Cold War Germany had a definite effect upon my outlook on life.

Although much of our off-duty time was spent in pursuit of fun and laughter – drinking and dancing in the NAAFI, Rugby Club or RintintInn Nightclub, eating out in the wonderful restaurants, visiting amazing cities and beautiful countryside – there were rare occasions when we would get into very deep and meaningful conversations about hypothetical post-invasion situations. When we really paused to think deeply about the reality of what those situations might entail, it was quite a tough thing for a bunch of youngsters in their early twenties to contemplate. We knew we'd sworn an oath, but the thought of having to honour it was a genuinely terrifying prospect.

Even since the crumbling of Eastern European Communism, the world is still in one hell of a mess and as a species, despite our undoubted intelligence and capacity for good, we seem pretty intent upon destroying one another. But amidst these unpalatable truths there are exquisitely sublime moments of sheer joy and perfection – tiny oases of pleasure and wonderment that are often fleeting and evasive, sometimes rare.

After one of my earliest, revelatory, 'deep and meaningful'

conversations with Helena, back in my little room in Tavistock Place, I decided to give the matter some thought... I took a sheet of A4 paper and carefully loaded it into the portable Smith Corona typewriter that Nain had given me some years before. A wonderful Christmas present for her first and favourite grandchild, her 'cariad', little Ellie who had learned to read long before going to infant school, who loved writing stories. I started to type a very simple list. I wanted to note down anything, anyone, anywhere that had ever made me happy. In my youth I had always tended to be a little sad and introspective, due to my dreadful shyness and insecurity. Clack clack clack – tap tap tap – clack clack clack – tap tap tap – then the bell and the swoosh as I pulled the carriage back to the next line, then the next. Deceptively simple things rushed into my mind – sunshine on my face, cheese, deep and meaningful talks with close friends, sunsets, soft bath towels... I was amazed and shocked to find myself very quickly at the bottom of the page, with still more 'delights' whizzing around in my head! It was such a revelation, a real epiphany! I had so many reasons to be cheerful, way more than Ian Dury's three minutes' worth! I folded that paper and kept it in my purse at all times, to be pulled out and re-read if ever I dared to feel sorry for my stupid self. It worked brilliantly and although I no longer need the list itself, the methodology continues to keep me going whenever I'm feeling a bit down or maudlin.

There is just one last story I think worth telling. One perfect illustration of why I believe it is so important to be true to oneself. Before I first moved to the Isle of Wight, I worked as an associate nurse at the Marie Curie Hospice in Caterham. One care assistant, Phil, was a really lovely young man – very popular and kind to the patients. We got on well and liked working together. Once, on nights, he made a negative comment about 'gays' that surprised and disappointed me. I decided to 'out' myself, saying something along the lines of, 'What? People like me, d'you mean?' A heartfelt and interesting conversation ensued, with Phil learning many things that he'd never even considered before that moment.

In 2014, I had hoped to go to a reunion of the hospice staff, but couldn't make it. Through the joys of social media, Phil and I were back in touch and I'd learned that after his marriage, not long after I'd left Caterham, he'd become a father, naturally immensely proud of his family. With his permission, here is some of what he wrote to me in a message when he knew I couldn't catch up in person:

> I wanted to remind you what a difference you made in my life. I was very young and sheltered… I had a very 'traditional' upbringing. I was extremely homophobic through ignorance when I met you… And you were the one who opened my eyes to the real world. I've never forgotten the impact you had on my view of the world, and I never will… I know you've been fighting your whole life against narrow-minded idiots… I became a better man BECAUSE OF YOU. And whatever else happens in your life, I never want you to forget that.

Of course, there is no chance of my ever forgetting it – having made a difference in this way, I know his own children will be taught a valuable lesson about not being so quick to judge others who aren't quite like us. His words touched me beyond belief; I felt truly moved when I read them for the first time.

My attempts to focus upon being positive and upbeat have led me to trying – admittedly not always succeeding, but for the most part doing all right – to live a life of mindfulness. Living in the moment, relishing anything and everything good that comes my way. One of my all-time favourite quotes comes from the incredible James Dean, my number one idol: 'Dream as if you'll live forever – live as if you'll die today.'

So that's what I do. No matter what misfortune comes my way, I refuse to allow myself to stay down for too long; life being, as the well-worn cliché rightly says, way too short. I relish those moments of sheer joy – they lift my spirits to a point where I almost feel as if I could levitate and float just an inch or two above the ground, unseen by those around me, but truly aware that one day I might fly high. So, I live for those fleeting moments, those delicious oases of unfettered, sublime happiness and delight. Until the next one comes along, this queer angel will be patiently waiting, now looking forward, not back.

Acknowledgements

When I first attempted to acknowledge the large number of people who in myriad different ways helped me bring this book to fruition, I mistakenly thought it would be a simple task.

It was genuinely humbling and uplifting to realise how lucky I have been. Support has come from so many different quarters. When I was at my lowest ebb, the realisation that I wasn't alone in wanting this story to be heard was what kept me going.

But listing names and explaining their part in the journey to publication posed a problem. Each time I thought I'd done it, I'd have a sudden jolt of guilt as I remembered another person I needed to include. In next to no time, the words were multiplying into a jumbled mass of obsequious gratitude that wouldn't have been out of place in a long night at the Oscars.

So, as I would hate to inadvertently omit anyone, I am going to be a coward and simply say that I could honestly never find adequate words to express my deepest thanks to everyone who has ever played a part in this story.

You know who you are – I love you dearly and am so blessed to have met so many wonderful people, many of whom have become close friends. And if you don't know who you are or what you mean to me, then I'll tell you when I see you!

And to those amazing people who had enough faith to pledge for their supporters' copies, then to wait such a long time to actually receive their book, how can I ever thank you? Your patience is legendary and I am genuinely so moved to know there were enough of you to make this happen.

I was lucky enough to have Katy Guest as my commissioning editor, so 'tis she you can blame if you're disappointed, as she felt this was worth publishing. Xander Cansell, Mark Ecob, the whole team at Unbound, 'Carmen Roxborough' and the legal, copyediting and proofreading team have my eternal gratitude for making my long-held dreams of becoming a published author a reality.

Finally, I especially want to thank serving and veteran members of our armed forces. I salute you.

Patrons

Roger Acres
Vikki Allen
Maureen Andrews
Matt Ashby-Cooper
Michelle Ayling
Jane Barmer
Louisa Bell
Richard Berney
Jessica Bish
Maggie Bolam
Emily Boulter
Anne Bramley
Gerry Bruce-Ahrens (ex QA)
Karen Burton
Dottie Calderwood
Tina Camp
Hazel Carey
Patricia Carpenter
Judith Casey
Kim Castle
Jenny Cattier
Derek Chapman
Glynis Chapman
Dee Chilton
Chris Clucas
Beri Cohn
Kevin Crimmons
Kaz Daniels
Michael Davies
Julie Davis
Cathie De Bruyn
John Devenney
Alison Devey
Jane Dommershuizen
Kelly England

Rebecca Evans
Terri Fletcher
Lesley Foss
Pat Gibson Mbe
John Giddings
Diana Greenway
Jackie Harte
Louise Hepburn
Jacqueline Hough
Carolyn Kammen
Adam Kastein
JP Kastein
Elena Kaufman
Sanyu Kawooya
Sarah Kearns
Ian Kenworthy
Linda Kerr
Stephanie Kershaw-Marsh
Patrick Kincaid
Angela Matthews
Jeanette Matthews
Carmen McTernan
Gerri Meredith
Nicole Moliner
Anne Morris
Margot Morris
James Muir
Carlo Navato
Dianne Nurse
Lou O'Connell MBE
Jackie O'Sullivan
Caroline Olive
Elizabeth Ottosson
Francis Owu
Justin Perkins

Tasha Peter
Brigid Plummer
Rachael Powers
Michaela Reay
Ali Reeves
Suzanne Reeves
Jo Renard
Alan Rolph
Suzy Romero
Alison Ross
Jo Sangster
Deirdre Schouten
Brian Semple
Debby Shaw
Ann Sills
Jane Slattery
Grant Smith

Cathy Soler
Kryan Soler
A Speirs
Jane Spencer
Suman Sund
Diane Swift
Joanne Thomas
Lani Tom
Katey Vaughton
Sarah Vernon
Sue Weall
Helen Whitwam
Susan Williams
Jan Wilson
Mary Wood
Amanda Woolley